River-class Frigates and the Battle of the Atlantic

A Technical and Social History

CW01035195

River-class Frigates and the Battle of the Atlantic

A Technical and Social History

Brian Lavery

First published in 2006 by the
National Maritime Museum
Greenwich
London
SE10 9NF

www.nmm.ac.uk/publishing

ISBN-13: 978 0948065 736
ISBN-10: 094 8065737

© National Maritime Museum
London, 2006
unless otherwise stated

All rights reserved. No part of this
publication may be reproduced,
stored in or introduced into a retrieval
system, or transmitted, in any form,
or by any means (electronic,
mechanical, photocopying, recording
or otherwise) without the prior written
permission of the publisher.
Any person who does any
unauthorised act in relation to this
publication may be liable to criminal
prosecution and civil claims for damages.

1

A CIP catalogue record for this book
is available from the British Library.

Design: www.poisedesign.co.uk
Printed and bound in Malta

Picture acknowledgements

Images from the collection of
the National Maritime Museum
are listed with their reproduction
and page numbers. They may be
ordered by writing to the Picture
Library, National Maritime
Museum, Greenwich, SE10 9NF,
calling 020 8312 6600 or e-mailing
picturelibrary@nmm.ac.uk quoting
the image reference number.
All images copyright © National
Maritime Museum, London

Pages:
P4076 19, F5140 24, F5139 27,
F5446 34, F5424 41, F5142 43,
F5146 48, F5144 (detail) 54, F5131
57, F5145 (detail) 59, F5148 71,
F5130 78, F5141 (detail) 83, F5149
(detail) 97, F5423 104, F5144 (detail)
119, F5460_2 126, F5149 (detail) 146,
F5148 (detail) 148, F5143 (detail) 151,
F5148 (detail) 156, F5150 157, F5149
(detail) 158, F5129 196, N23545 213,
F5151 216–17, F5147 218-19

Illustrations are also reproduced by
kind permission of the following:

Ian Buxton
page 210

Imperial War Museum, London
pages 137, 143, 165

National Archives, Kew
pages 75, 85, 90, 107, 113, 121,
172, 175, 182, 190

Ruth Murray
pages 201, 220-1, 222-3

Contents

Chapter 3: Weapons

Guns
4-inch Guns
The Gun Crew
Ammunition
Anti-Aircraft Guns
Other Weapons
The Guns in Action

Depth Charges
Principles
Charges and Patterns
Rails
Throwers
Release Mechanisms
Magazines
Depth-Charge Attack

Hedgehog
Description
Hedgehog in Action
The Londonderry Trials

Minesweeping Equipment
Contact Mines
Influence Mines
The End of the Minesweeping Role
The GNAT and the Foxer

Chapter 4: Sensors

Asdic
Principles
Features of Type 144
The Asdic Office
Searching
Identification of Echoes
Attack
Operating with Hedgehog

Chapter 8: Conclusion

Appendix

Notes

Index

Acknowledgements

I would like to thank Jock Gardner of the Naval Historical Branch, and D.K. Brown, formerly of the Royal Corps of Naval Constructors, for many helpful comments on the text. My thanks to Ian Buxton of the University of Newcastle for supplying information and pictures. I am grateful to many former colleagues at the National Maritime Museum, particularly the staff of the Ship Plans Department, including Bob Todd and Jeremy Michell. I would like to thank Nigel Rigby and Simon Stephens, and Rachel Giles and Abigail Ratcliffe of the Publishing Department as well as Sara Ayad and Ruth Murray for their help with photographs and maps. I would also like to acknowledge my late colleagues and friends David Lyon and David Syrett, whose frank comments on the study of warships and the Battle of the Atlantic are still missed.

Introduction

This book started off as an attempt to look at a single class of warship in some detail from as many angles as possible: design, building, armament, operation and so on. The River-class was attractive because it was one of the few types of ocean-going ship which was both designed and built during World War II. It was a much more mature design than the Flower-class corvettes which preceded it, and which have been covered in several works already. It was a British design – unlike its contemporary, the American-built Captain-class. This allowed me to use the Ship Plans and Ship Covers collections of the National Maritime Museum to the full. It entered service before the Loch-and Bay-class which followed it, so it had more impact on operations (though it was less effective than the Lochs in anti-submarine work). It was a true ocean-going ship, unlike the much smaller torpedo boats and gunboats of coastal forces. On the other hand, it was relatively simple compared with the much faster and more expensive sloops and destroyers, or the larger cruisers and battleships, which would need a much larger volume to do them justice. It was a surface ship from the traditional mainstream of the Navy, unlike the landing craft and aircraft carriers which interacted with the land and air, or submarines which, of course, operated underwater. It nevertheless used some of the most sophisticated technology of the day in its Asdic and radar. It was designed to be operated by amateur sailors, so I hope that an author who is neither a professional sailor nor a naval architect has been able to do them justice.

The River-class is an important group of ships. They were designed under great pressure in a rapidly changing situation, but proved highly successful at the role for which they were intended. They combined a blend of experience and innovation. They played a key role in the Battle of the Atlantic, one of the most important campaigns of all time. They were designed for a highly specialised task – to fight submarines in the Atlantic – but they had a surprising flexibility and became the ancestors of the modern frigate, which, paradoxically, has become a general-purpose ship. They are largely neglected by historians (though they appear in the fiction of Nicholas Monsarrat), but they can be counted among the classic warship designs of World War II.

B.L. 2006

Chapter 1: Origins

The Evolution of the Anti-Submarine Escort

Escort Design Before the War

The Royal Navy had been taken by surprise by the extent of the submarine menace in World War I. Senior officers such as Admiral 'Jacky' Fisher had been well aware of the potential of the new weapon, but had assumed that it would be used mainly against warships. This was partly confirmed in the first weeks of the war, when three old cruisers, the *Aboukir*, *Cressy* and *Hogue*, were sunk in a single day by *U-9*. But in 1915 and 1917, Britain was almost brought to its knees by German campaigns of unrestricted submarine warfare against merchant ships around the country, the result being a declaration of war by the United States in 1917. In response, the Royal Navy diverted destroyers and minesweepers, equipped trawlers for anti-submarine work, and produced several classes of small warships known as patrol boats and sloops. Many were designed to deceive the enemy, either by looking like merchant ships or submarines, or by being double-ended so that the submarine could not tell which way they were going. By 1917, the depth charge was proving effective as the main anti-submarine weapon. By the end of the war in 1918, the echo-sounding device known as Asdic (purportedly taken from the initials of the Allied Submarine Detection Investigation Committee) was being developed as a means of detecting a submarine underwater, and the Navy had great faith that this was the end of the submarine menace.

With dozens of ships left over after the war, it was 1927 before the Navy began to look again at what vessels were needed for anti-submarine work and minesweeping. As the First Lord of the Admiralty told Parliament that year,

> The time has come when the repairs of many of the existing Sloops and Minesweepers, which were built at high pressure during the war, would entail larger expense than is justified in view of the limited life that can be assigned to them, and it would therefore be uneconomical to delay their replacement.[1]

Two medium-sized ships, the *Bridgewater* and *Sandwich*, were ordered that year, to double as sloops and minesweepers. They were based on the dimensions and hull lines of the Flower-class sloops of 1915–18, though that class had no coherent deck layout: some were built to look like merchant ships of various kinds, often on the initiative of individual builders; some had one funnel, some had two, and there was considerable variation in armament. Like destroyers, the Bridgewater-class had a high forecastle so that the hull in the bow was two full decks above the waterline. The forecastle as such was quite short, as in a destroyer – though, unlike destroyers, the new ships did not need to carry torpedo tubes close to the waterline amidships. There was, however, a platform towards the stern which was joined to the forecastle by a deck with open sides below it. They had a low but roomy quarterdeck in the stern, intended mainly to operate minesweeping equipment, but equally suitable for dropping depth charges. There was no attempt to emulate wartime ships by making them double-ended, or to look like merchantmen. As well as minesweeping, they were to be used for peacetime duties on overseas stations such as Africa and China, and an imposing naval appearance was desirable.

According to the constructor Sir Rowland Baker, who came into the programme later, the lack of a true long forecastle was a mistake, giving low freeboard (that is, little height above the water, amidships), which had to be added to later[2]. The type began to develop slowly over the next decade, and four were ordered each year until the early 1930s. The Treaty of Washington of 1922 had imposed size limits on larger ships, but said nothing about sloops. Its successor, the Treaty of London of 1930, restricted them to 2000 tons, but the Admiralty was spreading its resources very thinly and saw no need to build them anything like as large as that.

The eight ships of the Grimsby-class paid slightly more attention to convoy escort, with increased gun armament and few depth charges. By 1933, the programme was divided into three types: sloop-minesweepers of the Halcyon-class of 850 tons; a convoy sloop, the *Bittern* (later *Enchantress*), of 1190 tons; and a coastal sloop, the *Kingfisher*, of 510 tons. The anti-submarine issue became increasingly important after the Nazis took power in Germany in 1933 and revived the U-boat arm in 1935, but priority was given to the larger ships, with orders for new aircraft carriers, battleships and cruisers. The Egret-class of 1937 was a further development of the *Bittern* and was followed by four ships of the Black Swan-class, begun in 1938–39. At 1250 tons they were about thirty per cent bigger than the Bridgewater-class which had begun the series. They were nearly 300ft (91m) long, with an effective armament of six 4-in. guns and forty depth charges in the first instance. Like all the sloops of the period, they were powered by steam turbines and they had a speed of almost 20 knots. They represented a hull form that was adequate for convoy escort, and a type which was capable of further development.

Destroyers could be used for escort duties. They were small and manoeuvrable enough for anti-submarine work, and were cheap and plentiful in comparison with battleships and cruisers. They were fitted with Asdics, and their low sterns were suitable for dropping depth charges. But despite their glamorous image with the public, destroyers were not ideal for this work. The newest and best ones were usually taken up for their designed role with the main fleet, and often only the older ones were left for convoy work. The last classes of World War I, the *V*s and *W*s, were available in 1940, but they had been designed for service in the North Sea, not the Atlantic. Like all destroyers, they had short forecastles so that their torpedo tubes could be accommodated amidships. In heavy seas the waves would break over the midships, cutting off one part of the ship from another. They were designed for high speed in good and moderate weather, but this was bought at a price: they needed much larger power plants than corvettes or other escorts, ranging from 27,000 shaft horsepower in the case of the *V and W-classes*, to 48,000 in the latest *L-* and *M-classes*, compared with 2750 horsepower for a corvette. They needed expensive turbine engines, using scarce skills in their production. Their speed of up to 36 knots (more than twice a corvette) could be useful in coming to the relief of a beleaguered convoy, as *Larne* and *Lance* did with the Gibraltar convoy OG 71 in August 1941, but in general they were faster than was needed for close escort with merchant ships that rarely exceeded 15 knots, and against U-boats that did not exceed 18 knots on the surface.

One solution was to design ships that were slightly below the normal specification of destroyers. The ships of the Hunt-class were intended to do all the duties of destroyers, except work with the main fleet. They were 50ft (15m) shorter than destroyers, and, as originally planned, they had no torpedo armament. Their guns were 4-in. compared with 4.7-in. Their planned speed was 32 knots – four fewer than a destroyer. There was a major error during the design process of the new class. Although they were designed side by side with the *Black Swans*, no one noticed that the latter ships needed a beam, or width, of 37ft (11m), compared with 29ft (9m) in the *Hunts*. After the first ship was launched, it was found that the stability of the *Hunts* had been miscalculated, and drastic amendments were needed to the armament, while the speed was considerably reduced. Sir Stanley Goodall, who had been Director of Naval Construction since 1936, offered his resignation but it was not accepted. Use of the Denny-Brown fin stabilizer did not solve the problem, for it merely created a jerky, unpleasant motion. Later ships had increased beam, but the speed was further reduced to 26 knots.

Eighty-six Hunt-class ships were eventually built in four different versions, but the type was expensive – £360,000 at wartime prices – and unsuitable for mass production. In 1942, in the middle of the war, Churchill asked if larger numbers could be produced, but he was told that, in effect, the class fell between two stools. Corvettes were already being built in large numbers, and the latest ones had the range to cross the Atlantic, which the *Hunts* did not. In the destroyer role they were too slow to accompany the great fleet of carriers and battleships which was being planned to fight in the Pacific.[3] However, the design was taken up by the United States Navy and became its main escort type.

The Flower-class Corvettes and their Problems

According to Director of Naval Construction Sir Stanley Goodall, the Flower-class corvettes originated in a conversation he had with Admiral Sir Roger Backhouse, the First Sea Lord, when

> … war clouds were gathering thick and fast and it was evident that the storm would break. He sent for me and said he was concerned about ships for anti-submarine duties. We must have great numbers. Of the types then in service, trawlers were too slow, and escorts expensive to build in money and time. He wanted some sort of ship that was faster than the trawler, could be built rapidly, and would not need a big complement such as our escorts required.
>
> About this time Mr William Reed of Smith's dock came to see me. He enlarged upon the properties of the whale-catchers of the Southern Pride-class built to the British Corporation's classification. It seemed to me that ships with the characteristics of *Southern Pride* would meet the requirements outlined by Sir Roger Backhouse.[4]

Modern research suggests that Goodall had somewhat exaggerated the importance of *Southern Pride* as a model, for it was just one of 250 such ships built by Smith's Dock between the wars.[5] But in any case, a large programme was put into execution: sixty-one were ordered as part of the 1939 programme, and sixty in 1940.

The first corvettes were ready for service in July and August 1940. They were indeed easy to build and, after the Great Depression, there was still much spare capacity in medium-sized British shipyards. By this time, the war had changed radically, with the German invasion of Norway in April 1940 and the fall of France in June. The enemy now had hundreds of miles of coastline and many excellent ports from which to launch a long-range offensive against British shipping. The corvettes, intended to protect shipping

in the relatively sheltered waters of the British east coast, where they would never be far
from bases and air cover, were to be diverted into what became the Battle of the Atlantic.

Flower-class corvette, HMS *Lavender*, off Aberdeen Beach, May 1941. (NMM P4076)

Early accounts of the performance of the corvettes were contradictory. The captain
(destroyers) at Plymouth was very much in favour of them in July. They were 'remarkably
fine sea boats in all conditions of wind and sea'. But before the summer was out, the
captain of HMS *Hibiscus* reported excessive rolling. 'In comparatively moderate weather,
as much as 50 degrees of roll to port and starboard has been registered on the Clinometer.
The roll is very short and sharp, averaging ten degrees per second.'[6] His case was taken
up by the captain (destroyers) at Rosyth, differing strongly from his opposite number
at Plymouth:

> Several complaints have been received from Commanding Officers of this class of
> vessel as to the amount they roll when in the Atlantic and it is considered some steps
> should be taken to reduce it before the winter. At present in any bad weather they
> are so busy looking after themselves that they are not of great value as an escort.[7]

In September, the Commander-in-Chief, Western Approaches (the main user of corvettes)
was aware of the problems. 'With a beam sea of 3–4 and over, corvettes roll very heavily
indeed (rolls of up to 40 degrees each way have been recorded) and under these conditions
Asdic operating is practically useless and many of the personnel are *hors de combat* from
sea sickness.'[8]

It was not just that the corvettes were being used in the Atlantic Ocean rather than
the more sheltered (if still turbulent) waters of the North Sea; the crews were not what the

original concept had demanded. The ancestors of the corvettes, the whale-catchers, had been manned by some of the hardiest seamen in the world, and the corvettes might have been crewed by fishermen who were used to working in very unpleasant conditions. But fishermen were in very limited supply. In practice the corvettes would be manned partly by Royal Navy regulars, who had spent much of their time before the war in big ships in the Mediterranean; partly by merchant seamen of the Royal Naval Reserve, who also were used mostly to bigger ships specially designed for the routes in question; but mainly by 'hostilities only' conscripts and volunteers, who had never been to sea and were not ready for such conditions. Almost the only group who adjusted well were the ex-yachtsmen of the Royal Naval Supplementary Reserve, who formed the first batch of new officers after the start of the war.

The ex-American destroyers of the Town-class were equally unsuited to the Atlantic, and in his novel *Destroyer from America*, author John Fernald puts a reaction into the mouth of the merchant navy chief engineer of one of them: 'What lucky devils these R.N.V.R. yachtsmen were, with their insides toughened by their crazy little sailing boats.'[9]

As the summer of 1940 turned into autumn and the equinoctital gales began, the problems of the Flower-class became ever more obvious. Lt.-Cdr. Robert T. Bower of HMS *Fleur de Lys* produced the severest and most detailed critique. After two ten-day voyages in September and October, he noted,

> … it was quite impossible to sit anywhere, all movables had to be lashed, and men off duty, all of whom were forced to take to their bunks, had great difficulty in saving themselves from being pitched out… The seas were more than funnel-high and the rolling was quite insupportable. Immediately, things began to break loose under the impact of seas coming inboard at the break of the forecastle and sweeping aft along the waist. Thrower charges were torn from their racks, and both after Lewis-gun shields were smashed over and the mountings rendered useless. The gripes for both seaboats carried away; in the port boat, the steadying chains were torn out; in the starboard boat, the foremost block was broken by the sea hitting the boat.
>
> … the rolling was incredible. In over twenty years in the service in every type of ship, I never encountered anything like it. Officers and men on duty became rapidly exhausted by the mere physical effort of holding on. Accurate navigation was impossible owing to the gyrations of the compass cards and the inability of helmsmen to keep the ship anywhere near her course. At times she was yawing 60 to 70 degrees. The plight of the numerous seasick members of the crew and of some of the older men became pitiable. I am myself entirely immune from seasickness, but I must confess that I felt the strain severely from the point of view of prolonged physical effort. Under such conditions, sleep, or indeed any kind of rest, is impossible, as it entails considerable physical strain even to remain in a bunk.
>
> It is impossible to escape the conclusion that these ships are unsuitable for Atlantic convoy work … I assert with emphasis that neither ships nor men will be able to stand up to prolonged severe winter weather in the Atlantic. It is not that the men lack courage or resolution; merely that the physical strain is insupportable.[10]

At first there were elements in the Navy which tried to deny the problem. Goodall claimed that the Navy did not like the Flower-class on principle. 'Moral is, don't try and force cheap ships on the Navy, which as Winston says, "always travel first class."' [11] The reports of the Captain (destroyers) Plymouth were cited several times in opposition to those of Captain (destroyers) Rosyth. Bower was dismissed as 'a pestilential fellow' by Admiral Power, the addressee of his complaints. But already the Controller of the Navy had to admit that 'There is a certain amount of truth in this, and we must try to make improvements as soon as we can'. Goodall's department was already beginning to look into the question with great concern. Mr Coats of the department dismissed the ships as 'useless' in October 1940. [12]

As well as the sea-keeping and habitability, the speed and range of the corvettes were causing concern. They could only do 16½ knots in ideal conditions, whereas the latest U-boats were believed to be capable of 18 knots on the surface. According to the Director of Plans at the Admiralty, a speed of 22 knots was needed to allow ships to pursue U-boats and then rejoin their convoys in good time. In the first phase of the Atlantic war, the convoys were only escorted as far as 12 to 15 degrees west. In October 1940, that was extended to 17 degrees, and in April 1941, to 35 degrees west, so corvettes had to spend increasingly long times in the waters of the North Atlantic.

One approach, absolutely necessary since more than 200 corvettes were already on order, was to make improvements in the design. The forecastle was lengthened to improve dryness, accommodation and stability; bilge keels were added to the lower hull to reduce rolling; and many detailed changes were made to ships under construction so that the problem was gradually reduced. Whatever their faults, the corvettes had to do the bulk of the work of convoy defence in the winter of 1940–1, in cooperation with older fleet destroyers, sloops and the ex-American Town-class destroyers. But it was clear that new ship designs were needed.

The Design of the River-class

The Origins of the 'Twin-screw Corvette'

The Director of the Naval Construction Department already knew that a larger and more suitable class had to be produced. Assistant Director of Naval Construction A. W. Watson approached Smith's Dock, which had designed the original corvettes, and asked for comments. By late November 1940, William Reed of that company had produced an outline scheme for a 'fast corvette', 320ft (98m) long compared with the corvette's 205ft (62m), powered by two sets of corvette engines. It had more than twice the displacement of a *Flower-class* corvette, but would carry the same armament and fittings.

The Royal Navy's ship design was the responsibility of the Director of Naval Construction and his staff of about 500 men, mostly members of the Royal Corps of Naval Constructors. On the outbreak of war, they had been hastily evacuated from London to Bath, and they now occupied more than twenty hotels and schools in the town, with the higher management in the Grand Pump Room Hotel and the Director of Dockyards in the Pulteney Hotel. Aged and infirm residents of the famous spa had to be evacuated, and even bathrooms were converted into drawing offices. If this was not disruption enough, the department was now very hard-pressed with orders for new types of ship. The mistake in the design of the Hunt-class occurred because a single assistant constructor was left to do the calculations unchecked, as there was not enough staff do a second set of calculations.[13]

Naval constructors could not be produced in a hurry. They were selected after four years of competitive examination from among trade apprentices in the Royal Dockyards, who were themselves carefully selected for a permanent career during an age of economic uncertainty. If successful, they went to the Royal Naval College at Greenwich for three years of professional training, followed by a year with the fleet as constructor lieutenant. They would reach the civil rank of constructor at the age of about thirty, and chief constructor ten years later. They spent time in ship design, research, repair work and study in the head office and in the dockyards at home and abroad.[14]

Meanwhile, at the Admiralty in London, a meeting was held on 27 November to draw up the requirements for the 'ideal escort vessel'. Some time was devoted to improving the destroyers of the Town-class, recently acquired from the United States, but these, even more than the Flowers, had been designed for a different kind of war, and such efforts were hopeless. It was far more fruitful to start with an almost clean sheet of paper, but there were constraints if the vessels were to be produced making the best use of scarce resources. A.W. Watson, representing the Director of Naval Construction, and F.R.G. Turner, representing the Engineer-in-chief of the Navy, reported,

> A number of alternatives for obtaining higher speed have been examined. A speed of 22 knots given by D of P [Director of Plans] involves a large increase in power with displacement limitations necessitating light hull scantlings. Mercantile vessels built to cross-channel standards and 22 knots speed would have a length of about 350 feet and turbine machinery. Many of the corvette builders have no experience with this type of machinery and their building berths are not long enough.[15]

Two possibilities were proposed by the naval architects and engineers. Alternative A had two of the engines already in use for the corvettes, which were easy to produce and had performed remarkably well in the most difficult circumstances. It was proposed to use water tube boilers rather than cylindrical boilers as had been fitted in the Flower-class and most merchant ships of the period, for even the captain (D) Plymouth had agreed that the boilers were a fault in the Flower-class design. The length would be 283ft (86m) 'between perpendiculars', that is, between the stem at the waterline and the centre of the rudder stock, which meant about 300ft (91m) overall. Alternative B would have far more sophisticated engines, geared turbines, as already used in the Black Swan-class sloops, also on 283ft between perpendiculars, almost the same as the Black Swan-class, but with a foot less breadth and a draft of 12ft (3.6m) instead of 8ft (2.4m) for ocean work. Watson and Turner recommended that Proposal A was best, 'on the basis of continuing to employ the resources in U.K. now engaged in building corvettes'. This was accepted by the meeting.

As a result, requirements were drawn up, attempting to satisfy all the departments involved. The ships were to have good sea-keeping qualities, with plenty of sheer or curve of the deck line, forward and flare (outward curve in the forward sections). The forecastle was to extend a long way aft. The propellers were to be deeply immersed in the water so that they would not be lifted out in rough seas. The ships were to have a metacentre, an imaginary point of suspension, about 2.5 to 3ft (0.7 to 0.9m) above the centre of gravity, which would give an easy rolling motion. They had a squarish hull section in midships and deep bilge keels. The bows would be reinforced for ramming. They were to have a speed of 20 knots when half-loaded with fuel, and to go for 3500 miles at 15 knots. They needed quick acceleration, which would be ensured with water tube boilers, and good manoeuvrability, which would be helped by the twin engines and a large rudder. They had to be able to go astern at high speed, which was possible with reciprocating engines.

The new corvettes were to have an armament of one 4-in. gun, with 'no elaborate fire control' for dealing with surfaced submarines. The anti-aircraft armament was to consist of two 2-pounder guns forward and two 20-mm Oerlikons aft. There would be enough depth charges to provide for a fourteen-charge pattern, which required four throwers on each side and preferably three rails to launch them over the stern – but it was found that only two could be provided alongside the minesweeping equipment. There would be a depth-charge magazine in the hold, and a workshop aft.

The anti-submarine branch suggested that a new type of Asdic could be fitted, requiring a small office on one of the messdecks. An anti-submarine hut was needed on the after end of the bridge, and possibly the newly emerging radar, which might need a space of 8ft x 6 ft. The aerial would be fitted on top of the anti-submarine hut, with searchlights for night action. A system of visual plotting was needed in the vicinity of the asdic hut.

The ships needed good habitability. Builders were to 'Provide a good warship standard of ventilation, cold and cool room, officers forward. The ship may be required to go into the tropics and awnings are to be provided for each ship'. For the moment it was agreed that minesweeping gear should consist of a winch and possibly an LL sweep, a recently designed electrical device used against magnetic mines. The electric system was to be powered by a diesel generator and possibly two steam ones. The design of the steering gear was to bear in mind 'the desirability of simplicity'.

Though the ships were not to be armoured, zarebas (low metal walls in this case) were to be erected round the 4-in. and 2-pounder guns, and the protection round the Oerlikons was to be considered. The bridge was to have its sides and front protected against small-arms fire, as well as a protected resting place for the commanding officer. Protected space for crew was to be on the same principles as in the smaller corvettes.

The Design of the Hull

The idea of a 320ft ship was not dead, and Smith's Dock produced a lines plan for one on 6 December. Meanwhile, the naval constructors at Bath were working hard and swiftly on the hull design for a 300ft vessel. The general principles were stated by Goodall a few weeks later:

> The form and dimensions have been governed by the speed requirement of 20 knots under ocean conditions. To obtain satisfactory immersion of the screws under such conditions, a normal trim by the stern of 4ft has been arranged; to provide good turning power, this involves a relatively large rudder associated with deadwood cut away aft. The long forecastle with considerable flare and sheer forward should ensure good behaviour in heavy weather.[16]

The long forecastle would help to protect the midships from breaking seas. The flare of the bows would increase the immersion as the ship pitched forward in rough weather,

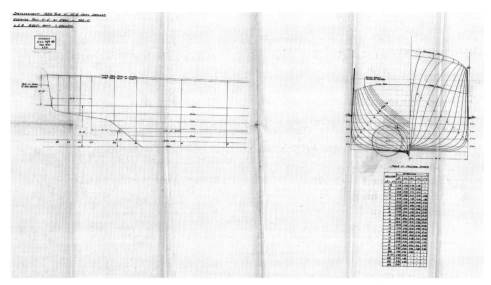

The early hull design for the River-class in November 1940, showing the shapes of the bow amd the stern to the right and left. The left-hand drawing shows sections through the body, with those forward of midships to the right. Ship Cover (SC) 645, f.15. (NMM F5140)

providing a damping motion. It would also tend to disperse the spray outward, protecting the forecastle deck to a certain extent. The sheer – the curve of the decks as seen from the side – tended to raise the bows higher out of the water. Destroyers, in contrast, tended to have less flare in their bows, as they were designed for more sheltered waters. The overall layout owed much to the experience of the Black Swan- and Halcyon-classes of sloop, though with economy and Atlantic operation very much in mind. One consistent feature running through all the design philosophy was to avoid the problems of the Flower-class. However, the new ships were to be fitted with single rudders; twin rudders could have been sited one behind each propeller, which would have helped manoeuvrability.

The lines plan of the new class, drawn by Temporary Constructor A. E. Kimberley, was ready by the end of November. The stem was raked at 12 degrees from the vertical, rather less than on a destroyer. A 4-in. gun was shown, mounted on the signal deck one level above the forecastle. The drawing showed its arc of fire when at maximum depression over the bow, suggesting that the high position was chosen to allow the gun to fire directly forward at close range in pursuit of a submarine. A $\frac{1}{19}$ scale model of the hull was made and given the serial number UE. According to instructions issued on 9 December, it was tested in the Admiralty tank at Haslar, Hampshire, on the seventeenth of the month, three weeks after the concept had been approved. In view of the problems with the Flower-class, a good all-weather hull shape had clearly been given a high priority, and Superintendent of the Tank R.W.L. Gawn was impressed. Unlike other ships, the resistance of the hull did not rise sharply until a speed of over 17 knots was reached. A maximum speed of 20¼ knots was predicted for the hull, slightly exceeding expectations. The form was 'as good as is likely to be obtained within the principal dimensions' and no modifications were suggested. As Gawn wrote later,

The first model of the River-class … had the optimum prismatic coefficient and centre of buoyancy position for the designed full speed. At cruising speed the performance was also of high standard, although a slight reduction in prismatic coefficient with a modification of the centre of buoyancy forward would be necessary to obtain the last ounce of efficiency at low speeds.[17]

The design was so good, with 'negligible change in resistance constant over a wide range of speed', that the model was kept for several years for correcting results in the tank.[18]

But the Director of Naval Construction was 'not very happy'; he regarded the design as too complicated for mass production. Watson had produced one design for ships powered with reciprocating engines, another for turbine-powered ships; Goodall ordered that only one design was to be used. Goodall had plenty of other problems: poor accommodation for his staff, gross overwork and constant interruption of sleep due to air-raid warnings. He was overseeing the construction of the new battleships of the *King George V* class, and making plans to fill some of the gaps in past ship design which had been shown up by the new kind of war, such as the first tank landing craft, and motor torpedo boats to combat the German 'E-boats' in the English Channel. Like many government officials, Goodall had to cope with the Prime Minister's more extreme ideas, including an armoured torpedo ram ironically titled 'HMS *Winston*'. On 21 December, he nevertheless found time to go over the new escort vessel design with Watson to eliminate unnecessarily complex curves, which would hinder mass production; he aimed for 'straight-line ships'. Two days later, the revised design was sent to Gawn at Haslar for his comments, and the changes were quickly agreed.[19]

The Admiralty approached seven shipbuilders who had been closely involved in the Flower-class programme: Smith's Dock on the Tees, Charles Hill of Bristol, Goole Shipbuilding on the Humber, Henry Robb of Leith, and A & J Inglis, Fleming and Ferguson, and William Simons, all on Clydeside. All were essentially builders of medium-sized merchant ships who were getting to know naval ways during the current programme. They could build the new class without straining their capacity or ability, and without encroaching on the scarce resources of the more specialised warship builders. They were asked to tender for ships of the new class, and invited to a meeting in the Pulteney Hotel, Bath, on 17 January 1941. It was also attended by representatives from Lloyd's Register and the British Corporation; the classification societies, who approved standards in merchant shipbuilding; and by men from the Admiralty: the Director of Electrical Engineering, the Engineer-in-chief, and the Director of Naval Construction, including A.W. Watson.

To save work for the hard-pressed naval constructors, it was agreed that the detailed design work would be farmed out to the shipbuilders present. The hull form was already settled, but Charles Hill would lay off the design in their mould loft, producing the necessary data and templates for the other builders to begin work; this was completed by 17 February. As to the structure, the detailed dimensions, and the scantlings, these were to be prepared in cooperation with the classification societies, using established Admiralty precedents:

Drawings of a similar vessel will be supplied by the Admiralty for the information of the builders in preparing the working drawings. These are to be considered as guidance plans only, the principal scantlings being in accordance with the structural section drawings which have been prepared by the Admiralty and accepted by the classification societies.[20]

Smith's Dock was to prepare the detailed drawings of keel framing, bulkheads and deck layouts. Builders were warned that special attention had to be paid to the area where the long forecastle ended, because the sudden reduction in structure created a possible source of weakness. As to the plating of the hull, Smith's Dock would prepare a model to be used for guidance.

The tasks of preparing the other drawings was divided among the shipbuilders present in rather a complicated fashion, the reasons for which are not always obvious. The design of the engines themselves was already fixed, adopting those used by the Flower-class, but the firm of Fleming and Ferguson was to draw the mountings for them, as well as the boilers and the auxiliary machinery. Robb of Leith would design much of the bridge and masts, along with hawse pipes for the anchors and gun supports. Inglis would prepare drawings for many details, such as guard rails, hatches, doors, skylights, boat arrangements and ladders. Robb of Leith and Hill of Bristol would divide the work of drawing the crew accommodation, storerooms, magazines, workshops and galleys between them. Most of the drawings were to be submitted to the Admiralty and the classification societies for approval, then traced on linen and sent to the other yards. Later, John Brown of Clydebank and Denny of Dumbarton, five miles apart on the River Clyde, would be brought in to help with the drawings, though they had little involvement with the building. John Brown's was famous for large ships such as the liner *Queen Mary* and many well-known battleships, while Denny was fully committed with destroyers and sloops and built none of the River-class.

The staff requirements for the type were drawn up in April – rather late in the day, for a dozen ships had already been ordered and the first one would be laid down the following month in Fleming and Ferguson's yard on Clydeside. After some debate between the Director of Minesweeping and the Director of Anti-Submarine Warfare, the priorities were finalised:

> Functions
> (a) To meet the full requirements of Trans-Atlantic convoy protection, against submarines and long range aircraft.
> (b) To have the speed and minesweeping equipment necessary to operate as a Fleet Minesweeper (first 24 ships only).
> (c) To be suitable for use at Home and Abroad.
> Sea-keeping Qualities
> To be capable of operating in any weather in which A/S escort may be required, and of operating Asdics in weather conditions in which a destroyer could so operate.

The new ships were referred to as 'fast corvette minesweepers' in March 1941, and were generally known as 'twin-screw corvettes' from April that year. They were designed for sea-keeping and speed more than anything else, and in the original concept the armament was very light – little more than a Flower-class corvette in the early stages of design, but with twice the engine power and 40 per cent greater displacement. This would quickly change, as extra guns, anti-submarine weapons and sensors were added, but the hull was well-designed and big enough to cope with this. Again, the reaction to the problems of the Flowers had ensured that the hull was designed first, with very moderate expectations of the armament it was to carry.

The Evolution of the Armament

4-inch Guns

There was never any question of the River-class ships fighting enemy surface warships. German destroyers, the smallest ships that were remotely likely to be encountered on the Atlantic convoy routes, had 5- or 6-inch guns, with ranges of up to twice that of a corvette gun, and sophisticated fire-control equipment, which would outclass anything carried by corvettes. If any larger ships should enter the Atlantic, the convoys and their escorts would be withdrawn as far away as possible, and the enemy would be chased by aircraft and larger ships, as happened with the *Bismarck* in May 1941. Therefore the River-class could be designed with guns that were intended almost entirely to fight surfaced submarines at relatively short range.

The original concept of the River-class demanded only one 4-in. gun, the same as the *Flower-class*. By 5 February 1941, the Director of Naval Conctruction agreed that 'It has been found possible to provide for two guns, and in view of the size of the ship it is submitted that an armament of two 4-inch. guns be approved.'[21]

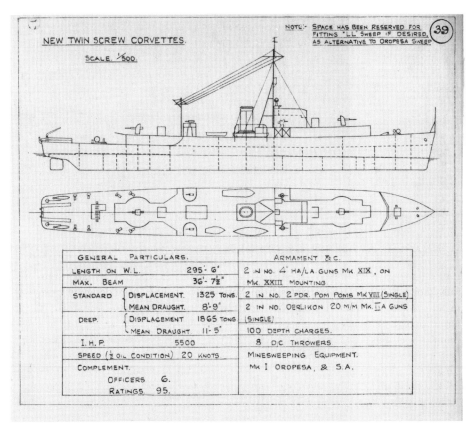

GENERAL PARTICULARS.		ARMAMENT &C.
LENGTH ON W.L.	295'- 6"	2 IN NO. 4" HA/LA GUNS MK XIX , ON
MAX. BEAM	36'- 7½"	MK XXIII MOUNTING.
STANDARD DISPLACEMENT.	1325 TONS.	2 IN NO. 2 PDR. POM POMS MK VIII (SINGLE)
MEAN DRAUGHT.	8'-9"	2 IN NO. OERLIKON 20 M/M MK IIA GUNS
DEEP. DISPLACEMENT	1865 TONS	(SINGLE)
MEAN DRAUGHT.	11'- 5"	100 DEPTH CHARGES.
I. H. P.	5500	8 D/C THROWERS
SPEED (⅔ OIL CONDITION)	20 KNOTS	MINESWEEPING EQUIPMENT.
COMPLEMENT.		MK I OROPESA, & S.A.
OFFICERS	6.	
RATINGS	95.	

The River-class 'New Twin-screw Corvette' design in an early stage of development. The second 4-inch gun has been added, but not the Hedgehog or the bridge wings. Ship Cover (SC) 645, f.67. (NMM F5139)

But there were some doubts about this, and as late as August 1941, an alternative proposal suggested that one of the 4-inch. guns be removed, presumably to save weight in favour of extra fuel. In fact, the second gun was not good value. It was mounted aft, so it would be little use in a chase – the most common method of attacking a surfaced submarine. It was only likely to be used in combination with the forward gun when the enemy was on one side of the ship. It must have been tempting for officers to allocate all the best men to the forward gun, which was the most useful.

Moreover, unlike the *Black Swan* sloops or the Hunt-class destroyer escorts, no provision was made for the accurate aiming of the Rivers' guns. At the crucial meeting on 13 December 1940, the Director of Naval Ordnance had accepted that 'no elaborate fire control was necessary' for the new class. Sloops and destroyers had a director tower mounted high in the ship and manned by gunnery officers and senior rates. It would be trained on the target and would send data to the transmitting station below, where the various factors – the relative movement of the two ships, wind speed and direction, time of flight of the shells and so on – would be fed into a mechanical computer to give a very accurate method of aiming the guns. In the Flowers and Rivers, all this had to be done by the layer and trainer in the guns themselves, who controlled the sideways and up-and-down motion of the weapon. Radar would give an accurate range at any particular moment, but the other factors would have to be calculated more or less by instinct by the gunners on the spot.

The Mk XIX 4-inch. gun was of simple construction, with its barrel moulded in a single block, rather than being made up of several parts as in more sophisticated weapons. This meant that a low performance had to be accepted, and the type was not approved by everyone. In September 1942, the Commander-in-chief, Western Approaches, complained that (among other things) there was no place for a man to set the sights on the guns.

> … great concern is expressed at the type of 4-inch gun and mounting which has been fitted in River-class corvettes. These guns are unable to engage at a range outside 8000 yards, and an additional disadvantage is the fact that no position for a sightsetter is provided and consequently the gunlayer has to carry out this duty. There have been numerous occasions recently in the Western Approaches command when it has been necessary to open fire with the existing guns at maximum gun range, and a requirement has been felt for guns having even greater range.[22]

Admittedly, the problem so far had mostly been with slower ships such as the Flower-class, which could not catch up with a submarine, but 'there are many occasions when ships have a speed greater than the submarine's surface speed, cannot afford to remain away from the convoy for the time necessary for a prolonged chase…'[23]

The fact that the ship was only armed with 'pop guns' would be bad for morale and already, it was claimed, this was being seen in courses in the training school at Tobermory. The Commander-in-chief suggested twin 4-inch. Mark XVI guns or two single 4-inch. Mark V high angle/low angle guns, each of which had more than double the range and which were also capable of use as anti-aircraft guns. The Director of Anti-Submarine Warfare agreed, but the Mark XIX had the great advantage of economy, and by this time it was too late to do anything. Twenty ships had already been launched, and dozens more, with their guns, were on order.

Anti-Aircraft Armament

Since the River-class was designed specifically for the Battle of the Atlantic, anti-aircraft armament was not a major priority. Atlantic convoys were usually out of the range of enemy shore-based aircraft, except for Focke-Wulf Condors, which were used for reconnaissance and were careful not to come within range of any conceivable anti-aircraft gun. The guns of the River-class were never intended for more than self-defence – not the protection of other ships in the convoy. More generally, anti-aircraft defence was a serious problem for the British at the time. They had no truly satisfactory light gun ready for service except the Swiss-designed 20-mm Oerlikon. Moreover, they had no efficient method of aiming, though that was not likely to affect the River-class in any case. If there was no room for a director for the main guns, they were not likely to get one for the anti-aircraft armament. Instead, they would rely on 'eyeshooting', which depended on the skill and training of the individual gun aimer.

In Constructor Kimberley's earliest plan of November 1940, the ships were to be fitted with two 2-pounder 'pom-pom' anti-aircraft guns firing aft, and two Lewis light machine guns on the bridge wings, firing forward. This was clearly a very weak defence against a head-on attack; by the beginning of 1941, the suggested anti-aircraft armament was two single 2-pounder guns on the wings of the signal deck forward, and two single 20-mm Oerlikon guns on platforms aft, with a pair of Lewis guns on the bridge.

There were difficulties with the 2-pounder, which was based on a design of the past war and had a bore of 40mm. In its initial form, its muzzle velocity of 2040 feet per second was too slow for an anti-aircraft gun, and the Mark VIII* version (the star indicating a further improvement within the mark number) was produced, with a velocity of 2400 feet per second – still slower than the Oerlikon with 2750 feet per second. There were production difficulties with the new version, and by the beginning of 1942, as the *Rother*, *Spey* and *Exe* neared completion, it was agreed to substitute twin-powered 20mm mountings on each side of the signal deck. As Kimberley, the constructor, announced in May 1942,

> It has been decided that 20-mm twin Oerlikon guns Mk V are to be fitted in *Flower*-and River-class corvettes now under construction, instead of the 2-pdrs specified. The 20-mm Mk V guns are to be mounted on the platforms originally intended for the 2 pdr guns.[24]

In July 1941, the Admiralty agreed that 'in every ship in hand for repair or refit, positions should be prepared for the maximum number of Oerlikons, as agreed by DNC, DNO and staff. The staff requirements being that if possible, every bearing should be covered by several guns'.[25]

Again, there were supply problems with the twin mountings, and most ships were completed with four single 20mm Oerlikons, one on each side of the bridge and two aft. This allowed a substantial redesign of the bridge, with the guns located on platforms abreast of the bridge instead of on a deck below. It was stressed that the substitution of single guns for twins was only temporary, but the supply situation had not improved by March 1943, for the twin 20-mm guns coming into service were being sent to capital ships and cruisers. Nine ships nearing completion were to have four single Oerlikons, and in effect this became the standard anti-aircraft armament for the class, though extra guns (mainly Oerlikons) were added over the years. In fact, the Oerlikon guns were proving to be the best guns available in the early years of the war, and were quite successful in the River-class.

Asdic

Naturally it was assumed that an anti-submarine vessel would be equipped with the latest available model of Asdic, the submarine-detecting device which relied on echoes bouncing off an underwater target. In December 1940, the Director of Anti-Submarine Warfare suggested Type 128, the latest model for destroyers, which had entered service in 1937. According to the director, it could be used in either its mechanical or electrical training version. In May 1941, development work started on Type 144, which would use many of the basic components of the Type 128, but at the same time 'heralded a new chapter in Asdic thinking'. It was part of an 'integrated weapons system' with a certain degree of automation. 'The electronics and controls were redesigned so that the last ounce of information could be extracted from the underwater sound signals, and the set was designed to be used with ahead-thrown weapons – in particular with the Hedgehog…' It was the 'First set with automatic training and with a bearing recorder; improved range recorder with optical cursor linked to bearing recorder and improved Captain's bearing repeater on Bridge'. It could operate at up to 25 knots, well beyond the maximum speed of the Rivers.[26] It was soon decided that the Type 144 should be standard equipment on the Rivers.

In April 1942, the first ship, *Rother*, had trials of its Asdic north-east of the Isle of Arran in the Firth of Clyde. As the first of the class, it was equipped with Type 128 instead of 144, but the testers agreed that it would be able to accommodate the new type, as well as its three operators, with no difficulty. The hull design was considered successful and it was concluded that 'Vessels of this class should be capable of operating Asdics satisfactorily at all speeds up to the maximum under reasonable weather conditions'. When fitted with ahead-thrown weapons and Type 144, 'the class should be excellent anti-submarine vessels'.

Radar

Robert Watson-Watt demonstrated the detection of aircraft by radar for the first time in February 1938, and later that year the naval signal school began to develop its own radar. The first sets, still intended for aircraft detection, were fitted in three of the Royal Navy's ships in 1938. By October 1940, as the U-boat campaign began to bite, a serious gap was noted in convoy defences, and this could only be filled by radar. U-boats were attacking at night, 'trimmed down on the surface' with only the conning tower and deck above water so that they would present a very small and low silhouette, but be undetectable by Asdic. When a convoy was attacked in this way, the only response was to light up the area as much as possible:

> In the event of attack, all ships on the engaged side, or on both sides if the attack is in doubt, turn 90 degrees outwards together and proceed at full speed for a distance of 10 miles from the convoy, firing star shells to illuminate the area.[27]

As early as November 1940, escort commanders were promised that,

All ships are being fitted as rapidly as the supply situation permits, with A.S.V. [anti-surface vessel] apparatus which will, it is hoped, enable the presence of any U-boat on the surface within a radius of some two or three miles to be detected at night in low visibility.[28]

Forty-six destroyers had been fitted with radar by March 1941, and twenty-three more were in hand, but the problem was that current radar sets, with their relatively long wavelengths, could not detect 'small' objects such as surfaced U-boats.

There was no mention of radar in the early plans for the Rivers, and no space was allocated for fitting it. By July 1941, plans were being made to rearrange the bridge to accommodate a set, probably Type 286 – the only small set available at the time. It had a fixed aerial in its early versions and a wavelength of 1.4 metres (about 4ft 7in.), so it was of limited value. The new Type 271 was a centimetric radar, with a wavelength of 10cm (almost 4in.) as its name implies. It was able to detect small targets, including surfaced submarines and, in good conditions, even submarine periscopes. It was first tried at sea in the Flower-class corvette *Orchis* in the Firth of Clyde in March 1941. Though the ranges achieved were slightly disappointing, the trials were highly successful in all other respects:

> In contrast to the fixed aerial type 286M – convenient for station-keeping but almost useless for A/S work because of the confusion of side and back echoes – Type 271 with its rotatable aerial and narrow horizontal beam width was just what the A/S vessel wanted, doing for surface echoes what the Asdic did for underwater echoes, capable of using the same procedures of searching and holding, which everyone was used to and could understand.[29]

Meanwhile, in May, an Admiralty committee recommended 'most strongly' that 'all work in connection with the development of R.D.F. ['Radio Detection Finding' – the precursor of RADAR] as an A/S instrument and with the training of personnel in this work should be pressed on at the highest possible priority.' In view of the success of the *Orchis* trials, an emergency construction and fitting programme was immediately put in hand, to include the River-class.[30]

Depth Charges

Depth charges were intended to be the primary armament of the River-class, as they had been in the Flower-class and all types of anti-submarine vessel for the last quarter-century. Most depth charges were simply dropped from rails in the stern of the attacking ship, and the *Rivers* were indeed fitted with a pair of such rails, so that one could hold slow-sinking and one fast-sinking charges. The River-class was conceived at a time when captains were being urged to use depth charges prolifically. Apart from larger numbers of charges in each pattern, they were advised to make as many attacks as possible. Officers were told in November 1940 that:

> Analysis has shown that sufficient attacks are not carried out in the time in which contact is held. Supplies of depth charges are ample, and there is, therefore, no necessity to economize in their use, once the presence of a U-boat is established.[31]

Despite the presence of minesweeping equipment, the quarterdecks of the River-class were large enough to accommodate quite long rails – and therefore large numbers of charges. Kimberley's original design allowed for twelve in each rail but this was soon increased to fifteen. In contrast, many destroyers, with their quarterdecks interrupted by guns, could only hold three charges in each rail, and even the Flower-class corvettes, specially designed for anti-submarine work, had nine charges per rail, with five or six more below.

In addition, some depth charges were fired short distances into the air to increase the spread of the pattern. The River-class was designed for a fourteen-charge pattern, which meant that six charges were dropped from the stern rails at appropriate intervals, while the remaining eight were fired from depth-charge throwers mounted on the sides of the ship. The ships, therefore, needed four such throwers on each side, near the stern.

Hedgehog

By the end of 1940, the inherent weakness of the depth-charge attack was becoming increasingly apparent. The charges had to be dropped over the stern of the attacking ship, several minutes after it had lost Asdic contact with the target. U-boat captains were well aware of this and tried to move unpredictably during that interval. For several years different groups of scientists and naval officers had been trying to develop an 'ahead-throwing weapon' to obviate this. If charges were fired ahead of the ship while the target was still in Asdic range, then they could be aimed much more accurately. The first staff requirements for the River-class, drawn up in April 1941, made reference to the fitting of an 'ahead-thrown A/S weapon', but no more was heard of this for some time. Meanwhile, several projects, such as the 'Fairlie mortar' and the 'five wide virgins', were under development, but early in 1941 it was decided to concentrate on the 'hedgehog' multi-spigot mortar, developed by the Admiralty Miscellaneous Weapons Department and taken up by the Director of Naval Ordnance. It fired a pattern of twenty-four charges 700ft (213m) ahead of the ship; these landed in a circle which (hopefully) would include a U-boat. They were not depth charges, but were intended to explode on contact with the enemy hull. Because of this, they were much lighter than depth charges. The designers of the weapon believed that 20lb (9kg) was enough to be effective, but the Director of Naval Ordnance insisted on 30lb (13.6kg) – and he was almost certainly right.

Hedgehog was tested from the end of Weston-super-Mare pier early in 1941 and went to sea soon afterwards. The weapon was ready for production in September 1941, and large numbers were coming forward by the spring of 1942. Early in March, the Director of Torpedoes and Mining suggested that it might be fitted to the new River-class ships, some of which had already been launched. A diagram was produced to show how hedgehog could be fitted in the space between the forward end of the signal deck and the bow, where a gun might have been sited on a more heavily-armed ship. It would involve some reorganisation of the seamen's messdeck and the storeroom below it, but it would only add a weight of 13 tons, which would not affect the stability. Watson took up the case for the Director of Naval Construction; within five days, the Director of Anti-Submarine Warfare and the assistant chief of Naval Staff (Weapons) had added their approval, provided no ships were delayed because of the need to fit them. Thus, very late in the day, hedgehog became a standard fitting in all the River-class frigates. Only the first ship, the *Rother*, went to sea without it.

As completed in the middle of 1942, the River-class corvettes had a combination of modern and well-tried, expensive and economical equipment and weapons. The Asdic and radar were the best available and both represented breakthroughs in their own fields. The 4-in. guns were to an economy design, though they did not let the ships down in practice. The anti-aircraft armament was much affected by supply difficulties. The depth charges and their equipment represented the best that was available at the time, while the hedgehog was largely untried in action, as the first ships got ready to take part in the crucial winter and spring campaigns of 1942–3.

Building the Ships

The Builders

On 4 December 1940, the Admiralty asked various shipbuilding firms what additional resources they might need to start work on new River-class ships, and when they could lay vessels down. After receiving some replies, the Admiralty compiled a list of possible builders, how long they thought they might take to start work on a new ship, and how long the building might take. None could lay the keel before February 1941, and some could not start until August that year. Most said they would take about a year to complete, Goole Shipbuilders said eleven months, Inglis of Glasgow said twelve, Simons nine to ten, and Smith's Dock could not give a definite answer. These figures, in the view of the Admiralty, were 'very optimistic'; they expected sixteen months as the average. Firms like W. Reed, Goole Shipbuilding, H. F. Craggs and W. S. Milne were unable to do anything in the short term; Craggs, for example, replied that they could not build such ships without 'disorganisation' of their yard.

In effect, the builders of the River-class ships had largely been selected during the design process. Six of the seven firms which had participated in the design – Smith's Dock, Fleming and Ferguson, Charles Hill, Henry Robb, A. & J. Inglis and William Simons – were awarded contracts on 11 February 1941 to build the first batch of eleven ships; Goole Shipbuilding was not. Since the Royal Dockyards were already fully occupied with repair and new building of major warships, it was inevitable that all the River-class work would go to private shipbuilders. The firms with large building slips were reserved for battleships, aircraft carriers and cruisers, so the River-class was built by medium-sized yards. Firms with considerable naval experience, such as Denny and Yarrow of Glasgow, tended to work on higher-specification vessels such as destroyers and sloops.

Due to the great expansion of the British shipbuilding industry in the nineteenth century or so, there were few green-field sites that could be easily developed, and none were contemplated during the war, in contrast with the situation in Canada and the USA. Later, three more firms – Hall Russell of Aberdeen, Blyth Dry Dock on the North-East Coast and John Crown of Sunderland – were also awarded contracts. The *Test* was ordered from Hall Russell in mid-March to bring the first group up to a dozen ships, with contracts for a dozen more during May and June 1941. The orders for the first eleven ships were confirmed by telegram on 10 February 1941, backed up by a letter of 13 February, which expressed the very limited financial control exercised in wartime: '...work should proceed without prejudice to price and on the distinct understanding that you agree to satisfy the Admiralty as to the reasonableness of the price to be paid…' Mere financial constraints were not to hold up urgent wartime production.

The first six builders were mostly well-established family firms, set up in the last century or even earlier. Smith's Dock could trace its ancestry back to 1768, Charles Hill to 1772, and William Simons to 1810, but all had undergone substantial management changes since then. Most still occupied sites they had taken over between 1820 and 1908, when they had seemed adequate for building large ships. But the sizes of ships had increased, and the yards found themselves increasingly constrained on land and water. Without great expense it was impossible to enlarge the river or dock into which they launched their ships, and the landward area had usually been taken over by housing development since the yards had been established. Fleming and Ferguson could build ships up to 310ft long, Charles Hill to 325ft, Hall Russell up to 400ft, and A. J. Inglis up to 425ft, so all could accommodate the 300ft of the *River-class*. Some of the yards had found a niche market over the years: Simons in dredgers, Smith's Dock in whalers, Inglis in paddle steamers.

A River-class (probably HMS *Jed*), under construction. Charles Hill Docks, Hill Yard, Bristol, undated. Yard photo no. 290. (NMM F5446)

Each yard had a number of building ships, or berths, on the banks of a river, angled at a slope of about ⅜ inch to the foot, or about three degrees from the horizontal. Inglis, for example, launched into the mouth of the River Kelvin, just before it met the Clyde. Seen from above, the four berths were angled at about forty-five degrees to the direction of the river at that point, because it was so narrow. This angle was quite common on Clydeside, less so in other areas where the rivers tended to be wider and the building slip could be set at ninety degrees to the river. Henry Robb of Leith had nine building slips, but only five of these were more than 300 ft long. Number six berth, where the frigate *Ness* was built, was

350ft long and was served by three electric cranes of a 45ft radius and a five-ton load, and a jib for a hydraulic riveting machine.[32]

Each slip was fitted with a line of blocks on which the keel of the ship would be laid. The positioning and height of these was largely determined by the requirements of launching. There had to be sufficient space between the bottom of the vessel and the groundways to get the launching ways into place when the vessel was ready, and care had to be taken that no part of the ship would strike as it slid down the ways. In standard merchant-ship practice, as used with the River-class, the blocks were at least 4ft 6 (1.4m) in high so that riveting could be carried out under the hull, and they were about 4ft (1.2 m) apart to allow workers to pass under them. Most yards derricks of modest capacity on either side of the building slips to hoist parts of the ship into place.

Labour

The British shipbuilding industry had suffered hard during the years of depression in the 1930s, and had more than sixty per cent unemployment at its worst. Few apprenticeships had been offered during these years, and the shortage of skilled labour was becoming apparent. Now there was an unprecedented need for the shipbuilder's skills, as years of naval neglect had to be made up for, warships casualties had to be replaced, new types of fighting ships had to be developed, ships were needed in place of the merchant-ship losses of the Battle of the Atlantic, and large numbers of damaged ships had to be repaired.

The labour shortage was tackled in several ways; by 'diluting' the labour force with semi-skilled and partially trained workers; by recalling workers who had been pensioned off some years ago; by the extensive use of overtime; and by employing women in certain parts of the building process. Shipyard workers were offered exemption from conscription, while women could be conscripted to shipyard work from 1942. In Smith's Dock in that year, 'There were plenty of lasses working in the yard then; you got catcher lasses, women tackers. I can remember two, if not three, women burners, not on the ship but at the end of the frame shed.'[33] Charles Hill of Bristol employed about 300 men at the beginning of the war, and 1350 men and sixty women by the end.[34]

On the face of it, the work was unattractive. It was noisy in the days of riveting, and even when that had largely been replaced by welding, a post-war recruit to Smith's Dock was taken aback on his first day:

> It was not so much heard as *felt*, like a wall of noise. Coming off the ship was very dramatic, there really was such a marked change when you came away… One of the chief complaints was tinnitus – you got a buzzing noise in your head.[35]

'During the war we worked very long hours and it was hellish black down there. The sheds, even when the sun was shining, were dark and dingy,' wrote another wartime worker at Smith's Dock.[36] The work often involved heights with minimum safety arrangements. It was often in the open in cold weather, or in confined spaces in or under the hull of a ship, or in excessive heat in forges and smithies.

In partial compensation, the men and women were fiercely proud of the finished product, and the sight of it during a launch or at sea, or reading about a warship's exploits after it had left the yard, gave a sense of satisfaction that was unusual among manual workers. Despite wartime moves to greater efficiency, a ship was not a mass-produced product like a tank, gun or aircraft and everyone who worked on it felt a personal involvement. Some of the older workers carried lists of the ships they had worked on in their pockets. The less fortunate effect was the growth of craft unionism, in which the different trades competed almost as fiercely with one another as with the management. There was a constant problem of 'demarcation' between the different groups of workers, and they were very sensitive about taking on jobs outside the strict limits of their own trade. This had effects on efficiency, as groups waited for work.

> The work in a shipyard has always been uneven in its flow. The frame bender and his squad stand idle while the frame heats in the furnace; the platers are waiting for the crane to come down with the new plates. There were lulls, there were furious rushes during the war.[37]

The shipwrights, once the sole builders of the hull in the days of wooden ships, were now confined to working the timber, the setting up of the blocks and the line of the ship. The riveters worked in groups.

> The riveter is a member of the 'black squad' – a gang of four who turn up to the job with the misleading nonchalance of a family of jugglers. They are the riveter, the holder-up, the heater, and a boy… The black squad can set up shop anywhere and begin performing their hot-chestnut act. You see one swing over the ship's side. He stands on a plank waiting with the pneumatic instrument in his gloved hands. On the other side of the plate, inside the ship, is the heater with his smoking brazier – a blue coke haze is always rising over the ship; he plucks a rivet out of the fire with his tongs, a 'boy' (nowadays it is often a girl in dungarees) catches the rivet in another pair of tongs and steps quickly with it to the holder-up, who puts it through the proper holes at the junction of the plates. As the pink nub of the rivet comes through, the pneumatic striker comes down on it, roaring out blows at the rate of about 700 hits a minute, and squeezes it flat.[38]

Materials

Virtually all major ships had been built of some form of mild steel for the previous fifty years or so. It was much stronger than the iron which had been used formerly, and less brittle than hard steel. Steel plates, as used for shells, decks and bulkheads, were measured according to the weight in pounds per square foot of area. The most common weight in the River-class was 15lb (6.8kg) plate which was ⅜ inches thick, but some plates, for example on the decks, were of 7lb (3kg).

According to classification society rules, the different parts of the structure were tested in different ways and stamped with the society's mark if they passed. Plates and angle iron as used for frames and beams were to have a breaking stress of between 26 and 32 tons per square inch. Rivets were to be tested after manufacture. Steel castings were to have a strength of between 26 and 35 tons per square inch. Stern frames, the most vital pieces of this type, were to be raised through an angle of 45 degrees and then allowed to fall onto hard ground. All castings were then to be hit with a sledgehammer of not less than 7lb , and large ones were to have holes drilled in them where flaws were likely, with the holes being filled afterwards.[39] Steel arrived at the shipyard, often by the yard's own internal railway, and was stored in the open for a time to be weathered by rusting, and to remove mill scale.

Methods of Fixing

Riveting was still by far the most common method of holding ships together in the British yards, though the Americans were already using more advanced techniques. With riveting it was necessary for the plates to overlap, causing a considerable extra weight. This surface would not be smooth in the area of the join; that needed extra work. The holes for the rivets had to be drilled or punched with great accuracy before assembly, and this needed highly skilled labour. None of these problems arose with welding, which produced a smoother surface, and some saving on skilled labour. It also provided a more watertight structure and allowed greater scope for prefabrication. But British shipbuilders were not ready to go over to welding on a large scale, though Denny, for example, had built the Firth of Forth ferry *Robert the Bruce* using welding in 1934, and the Navy had used a good deal of welding in the great aircraft carrier *Ark Royal* of 1937. Charles Hill wrote to the Admiralty in connection with the River-class in May 1942:

> We may say that we have, as long ago as 1935, built a large number of all-welded barges, three of which were for the Admiralty. In addition to this work, we have for years been welding small oil tanker and coaster bulkheads, decks, and double bottoms, all under Lloyd's Survey.[40]

They were in favour of welding some of the shell plating of the hull of their next frigate, and of welding the whole plating of the next one. The Admiralty was sympathetic to this and wrote to various firms offering to fund up to 50 per cent of the cost of any new welding equipment and training, provided it did not interfere with existing programmes.[41] British builders still felt that welding was largely untested at sea, but some provision was made for its use in the River-class, according to the faith and capabilities of the individual builder. Although there were no plans to weld the main structure of frames and plates, Smith's Dock prepared alternative plans for the welding of key parts such as the decks, engine seatings, rudder bearing and transverse bulkheads. In the event, some ships had up to 30 percent of their structure welded. According to Admiralty instructions for the *River-class*, 'The riveting is to be executed in the most careful and workmanlike manner, the rivets thoroughly fitting the holes and the work is to be carefully closed before riveting.' When joining pieces at right angles by means of riveting, it was necessary to use bars of angle iron, L-shaped in cross section, with rivets through each arm of the L into each of the surfaces to be joined.

Chapter 2: The Ships

The Hull

The Keel and Centre Girder

The keel was the first part of the hull to be constructed. The keel proper was a series of horizontal plates laid down on the building blocks. The plates were of 20lb steel, some of the heaviest in the ship, and they were only used in the midships section of the hull; forward and aft of that, the frames angled upwards too steeply to allow the use of a flat plate. Above this plate, running vertically along most of the length of the ship, was the centre girder. It was made of 15lb plate in the centre section, reducing to 12lb towards the bow and stern. It was riveted above the keel plates by means of angle iron. It was to be continuous between bulkheads, except in the area of the Asdic fitting, which had to be on the centre line; a structure was built around the hole that created.

The stem, the extreme forward part of the bow, was to be fabricated by bending a U-shaped piece of mild steel of varying cross-section. It joined the keel and centre girder between frames five and six.

Frames

The main shape of the hull was determined by the frames or ribs, of which the River-class had 131 from stem to stern. Some ships, such as recent destroyers, had their principal structure running along the length of the ship as 'longitudinal' frames, but the River-class was far more conventional in having its main structural members running across the ship, with each attached in the middle to the keel, except the last thirteen in the stern. In the midships, each pair of frames gave a roughly square cross-section; in the bows, it was roughly triangular, with sides curved inwards; towards the stern, it was triangular, with the sides curved outwards.

In the midships area where the flat-plate keel was in use, the lower part of the frame – the floor – was formed by at least a 12lb plate cut to the shape of the outside hull on one side, and with the lower edge forming a flat surface on the upper edge. Large holes were cut in each section, reducing weight and allowing liquid to drain from one area to another when necessary. In the area under the engines and boilers, 12lb plate was used, and extra members, longitudinal bulkheads, ran fore and aft to give extra strength. Except where the lower part of the hull was used as a tank for oil fuel, diesel or water ballast, plates were fitted over the floors to form a double bottom, giving extra strength and safety.

Above the floors, each was made from a piece of mild steel that was of 'bulb-angle' cross-section: L-shaped, with a thickened piece, the 'bulb', at the end of the inboard arm of the L. This arm provided the main strength, the other forming a flat surface to which the plates of the hull could be attached. This was an example where merchant-ship practice was used, for the Navy tended to regard the bulb-angle section as obsolete, and preferred a Z section or a simple L-shaped angle bar for medium-sized ships. The shape of each individual frame was drawn out full-size in the yard's mould loft, based largely on a set of dimensions known as the 'table moulded of offsets' provided by Charles Hill. The shape was then cut in wood and taken down to the bending slab: a large plate of iron with numerous peg holes. The shape was traced out with pegs and the piece of bulb-angle iron was heated and bent to conform to it. It was fixed or 'lapped' onto the floor by means of an overlapping section which was joined by twelve or thirteen rivets.

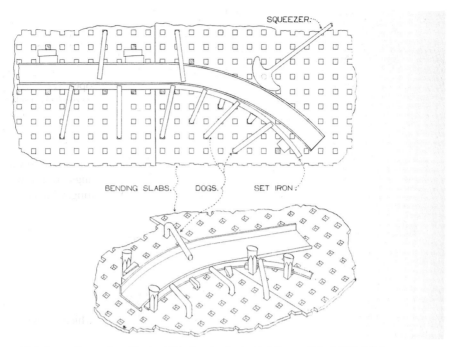

Bending a ship's frame. Diagram from Merchant Ship Construction by H. J. Pursey, 1942. (NMM F5424)

In the extreme bows forward of frame six there was no floor, and a specially fabricated steel shape formed the lower part of the hull up to about 6 ft high; the ends of the frames fitted directly into it. Aft of that, up to about frame twenty-eight, the bulb-angle frames joined across the centre line of the ship, and the floor served to strengthen the join.

Bulkheads

Twenty-one of the 131 frames were part of bulkheads, each of which formed a wall-like structure across the breadth of the ship. They served several functions. They gave extra strength to the ship against the outside pressure of the water. They divided the ship into compartments, each with its separate function; and most of them were oil- or watertight, so that in the event of damage the ship would be less likely to sink. The foremost one was at frame seven near the bows with the collision bulkhead, so-called because it would protect the rest of the ship in the event of a collision – important in ships which were expected to ram U-boats as the situation demanded. At the other end of the ship, regulations demanded a bulkhead to seal off the area where the propeller shafts met the water in order to prevent leakage into the main hull.

A few bulkheads, such as those marking the boundaries of the engine and boiler rooms, went all the way from the keel to the top of the side without interruption, though of course the one between the two main machinery spaces needed many holes for steam and other pipes. The main bulkheads in the forward part of the ship were interrupted only by holes at the level of the lower and upper deck to allow the crew to move between compartments; they were fitted with watertight doors which could be closed if the ship was in any danger. Other bulkheads, such as those sealing off the anti-magazines, storerooms and spirit room in the hold, went only up to the level of the lower deck. All watertight bulkheads were tested by filling that part of the hull with water.

Minor bulkheads, usually running fore and aft instead of across the ship above the lower deck level, had little strength or structural function, and served merely as the boundaries of cabins, messes, offices and other spaces. They were made of light steel plate of 5 or 2½lb.

The engines and boilers both needed a long space without any interruption, and at the same time they imposed heavy weights on the hull. It was necessary to compensate for this. Longitudinal bulkheads ran fore and aft under the engines to help bear the weight. Every third frame in this area was a web frame, which had extra strength created by fitting an extra bulb-angle bar inboard of the main one. Though the main strength of the frame was across the ship, longitudinal stringers running along the length were fitted about halfway between each pair of decks to help prevent 'hogging' – arching of the hull.

Plating

The shell of a ship was made up of a large number of steel plates. The classification societies made no particular rules about their sizes, except to state that 'if the breadth of plates is excessive, compensation will be required'.[1] The plates were mostly of 15lb steel, though that was reduced to 12lb just aft of the bows and forward of the stern; the bows themselves needed strength to face the possibility of ramming a U-boat, and were of 15lb steel. Thicker plate was used in selected places: for example, the area where the forecastle ended needed 24lb, as this had been identified as an area of weakness in the original design.

According to Admiralty instructions, either the plates or the frames of a ship could be 'joggled' at the discretion of the builder; this was a method of dealing with the overlaps necessary in riveting. In the older system of 'in-and-out' or 'raised and sunken' plating, one row ('strake') of plates was fixed directly to the frames. The next one was raised slightly by a 'liner' fixed to the frame, so that its edge was over the first strake. A third strake was also fixed directly to the frame, with the edges of the second strake over its edge, and so on. The more modern method was to bend or 'joggle' the edge of each alternate plate, so that all would lie directly against the frames. It needed no liners so it was cheaper and lighter, but required specialised machinery to do the joggling. Another way was to joggle the frames themselves, and the builders were allowed to do this as an alternative.

Bilge keels were fitted to the outside of the plating. As was found with the modified Flower-class, they could provide a large amount of resistance to rolling. Those of the Rivers ran from frame forty-five to frame eighty-two, less than a third of the length of the ship. Because the cross-section was already quite square in that area, they could not be very large without causing problems in launch and docking. They were 18in. wide and made from 20lb plate, with a bulbous section on the outer edge.

Though the ships were not armoured as such, protective plating was fitted in certain areas to defend the crew from small-arms fire. These areas included the bridge, wheelhouse and signal deck, the gun-crew shelters, and the zarebas around the Oerlikon guns.

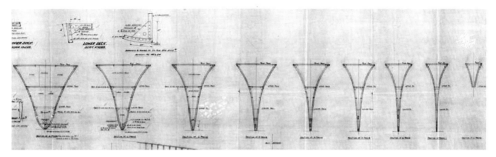

A blueprint showing the frames of the forward part of a River-class ship, with the details of the plating to the bottom right. NMM Ships Plans, Lloyd's Collection, Box LLDB0036, plan 21D, drawing 2. (NMM F5142)

Decks

Each deck was supported by beams made of bulb-angle steel of a standard size: 5 in. by 2½ inch, 8.5lb – rather lighter than the frames. The beams had two main functions: to support the decks against any weights which might be placed on them, and to help tie the sides of the ship together. They were cambered upwards towards the centre to allow water to drain away, and were fixed to the frames by means of beam knees: triangular pieces fitted in the angle between the two.

The plating of the decks varied according to the area where it was fitted. It might be as heavy as 20lb on the upper deck in the area of the engine room, with 12lb on the forecastle in the same area. Towards the stern it was 15lb where it had to bear the weight of depth charges and minesweeping gear, though it was only 7lb inside the structure. This was the weight for most of the deck structure, especially in the bows, though in May 1942 the Admiralty ordered stiffening under the hedgehog mounting. Pillars were placed between decks at strategic points to bear weights and keep the decks the requisite distance apart. Access from one deck to another was by way of hatches; their covers were 'to be fitted, generally with steel covers fitted with india-rubber strips secured in approved manner to ensure watertightness'.[2]

Painting

The painting of the ship was a progressive operation, done in several stages. Steelwork was to be 'scaled, scraped and cleaned' before it was fitted, and then was 'to have a coat of boiled linseed oil, heavy mineral oil, or thin red lead, or other substance as may be required, as soon as it is sufficiently completed to receive it, in order to prevent as far as possible the work becoming in any degree injuriously oxidized during the building of the ship'.
The final coat of paint was to be done 'after constructive work has ceased'. On the outside it was to be 'an approved colour', which usually meant a camouflage scheme. Most inside surfaces were to be painted with a coat of iron oxide and one or two coats of white oil-based paint; exceptions included the sick bay (pale green), the hammock hooks (black) and certain sensitive areas such as generator rooms, cable lockers and the steering-gear compartment. As well as the white paint, messes were to have an 18-in. dado in dark grey. It was to be 3ft wide in washplaces, WCs and galleys, and 6ft in the engine and boiler rooms. The machinery was only to be painted in areas 'as is usually painted', and not until after the full power trials had been completed.[3]

The Hull Layout

As with most ships of the day, the engines and boilers of the River-class were placed near the centre of the ship. This had a positive effect on stability, though less than in the days of coal; oil fuel could be stored anywhere in the hull and pumped to the engines, whereas coal had to be kept close. The most compelling reason to keep the engines amidships was to make it easier to site the propeller shafts. Furthermore, in a warship, engines and funnels aft would have interfered with the siting of guns and other weapons – minesweeping gear and depth charges in the case of the River-class.

From the early stages of the design, it was agreed that all officers and crew accommodation would be sited ahead of the engines. Until quite recently it had been normal for the officers to be berthed right aft, as they had been in the days of sailing ships. This proved very inconvenient in destroyers when the seas broke over the decks amidships, as Peter Gretton found in the large Tribal-class destroyer *Cossack* early in the war:

> Relieving the watch was a hazardous affair. The journey from the wardroom to the bridge was, especially at night, a terrifying ordeal. First, we climbed down onto the engine gearing room, then up and over a bulkhead and down into the engine room, and finally there was about thirty yards of upper deck to be negotiated. Then we crouched on the windward side, awaiting our chance to dash for the bridge ladder.… Once or twice, it was too rough to allow anyone on the upper deck, so a select party of officers who happened to be forrard [*sic*] lived and slept fore [*sic*] three days in the Engine Room Artificers' mess near the bridge… The other ERAs used to use our cabins aft, which were near the engine room. But we were better off than other ships, which had no passage below the upper deck, and where men had to brave the whole passage without protection.[4]

The River-class ships had the natural advantage of a longer forecastle, which would have made such hazards largely unnecessary in any case. Every part of the ship except the low quarterdeck could be reached from under cover.

In the preliminary design there was no permanent accommodation at all aft of the boiler rooms, except for the crew washrooms and toilets. The deck under the quarterdeck, used for officers' accommodation on traditional ships, was used for storerooms, magazines, minesweeping equipment and auxiliary machinery. Instead, the officers lived near their workplaces, in cabins just below the bridge. The stokers, however, were some way from the engine room, in a mess well forward on the lower deck.

This layout was gradually modified, though the basic concept remained. Soon a small stewards' mess was introduced abreast of the funnel and boiler room. There had always been a plan for 'minesweeping messes' abreast of the engine-room hatch; during sweeping operations the fore part of the ship had to be sealed off completely with all watertight doors closed in case the ship hit a mine. The minesweeping messes were never used in this role and were gradually modified to become more permanent accommodation.

Below the lower deck forward, the hull had an Asdic compartment and storerooms for cordage and provisions, a cool room and a magazine for the 4-in. guns and the Oerlikons. Aft of the engine room, the limited space below decks was initially used for workshops, depth-charge magazines, a minesweeping store and several other storerooms.

The generators took up a good deal of space, and the steering-gear compartment, right aft, was long and wide, though it had little depth and only a small amount of storage space.

The signal deck covered less than a third of the length of the hull, just forward of the funnel. Unlike other decks, it did not run all the way across the hull, for there was a passage from 6 to 8ft wide on the upper deck on each side. It had stations for the visual signallers to hoist their flags up the mast, but that was not its sole function; it supported the mast and the bridge, while at its forward end it raised the 4-in. gun 6ft above the upper deck to improve its field of fire. It also covered several important spaces which had to be close to the bridge, including the captain's and some of the officers' cabins, the ship's office and the wireless telegraphy office.

Launch

As well as a ceremony, the launch of a ship was a considerable engineering achievement. It was not just the cutting of a tape or the laying of a foundation stone, for there was a real risk that things could go wrong. Considerable preparations had to be made. Two rails known as the groundways were erected on either side of the keel blocks. The launching cradle was placed under the ship, resting on the groundways. It would take the weight of the hull when the keel blocks were knocked away, and the ways were greased to allow it to run down by force of gravity. It was usually necessary to launch at the highest-possible tide, which occurred fortnightly.

Since the times of Queen Victoria, it had been the custom for a ship to be launched by a woman, who broke a bottle of wine over the bows and pulled the lever that would trigger the ship's slide down the ways. In peacetime, the launch of a major warship would be a great event, perhaps performed by the highest in the land. With the great number of wartime ships, it was not always possible or necessary to find a high-ranking dignitary to carry out the launch. The sponsors at Charles Hill of Bristol covered a wide social range. The *Bann* was launched by Lady Burmeister, the *Taff* by Lady Hornell – both were wives of admirals. The *Monnow* was launched by the daughter-in-law of a director, and the *Avon* by the daughter of the firm's manager. HMS *Trent* was launched by Mrs Hodges, wife of a 'holder-upper', or riveter's assistant, chosen by a ballot of the workforce.[5] At Smith's Dock, HMS *Fal* was launched by Mrs Humphries, the wife of an electrical engineer in the yard; the *Moyola* by a Mrs Cook; and the *Deveron* by a Mrs Harrison. Lady Elphinstone, a local grandee and a member of a long-established naval family, launched HMS *Nith* from Robb's of Leith in 1942; but in the majority of cases the authorities did not bother to fill in the question in the ship's book about who launched the ship, suggesting that they were not especially proud of their guests.

The *Ness* was launched on 30 July 1942 from the No. 6 slip at Henry Robb's yard at Leith, near Edinburgh, in a strong breeze and showery weather. She took thirty seconds to slide down the launching ways into the Forth of Forth.[6] The ship was largely an empty shell at this stage, for most of the external and internal fittings would be put in after she was afloat.

Fittings

Fitting Out

It was desirable that the ship was as light as possible during the launch, so most of the work of fitting out was done after it was in the water. Most yards had their own fitting-out basin, in the form of an open wet-dock with one or two large cranes around it. The tradesmen involved in fitting out – 'Shipwrights, Platers, Riveters, Caulkers, Drillers, Riggers and Stagers, Fitters, Machinists, Sheet Iron Workers, Electricians, Smiths, Welders, Plumbers, Joiners, Polishers, Painters, Coppersmiths, Boilermakers, Brass-Finishers' according to the First Lord of the Admiralty – could easily find employment ashore and were in great demand there. As a result, there was a general shortage, and fitting out was often a bottleneck in many ships, including the River-class. Warships generally were expensive in labour terms; discussing the frigate-building programme in March 1943, the First Lord of the Admiralty pointed out to the War Cabinet Anti-U-boat Committee that, 'Fitting out labour required for a frigate is approximately four to five times that needed to fit out the merchant ship she displaces; consequently, every additional merchant ship taken over involves a large increase in fitting-out labour.'[7]

This created serious bottlenecks in construction, since most of the yards were geared for merchant shipbuilding. At Smith's Dock in September 1942, the facilities could not cope, and it was suggested that the yard was going slow on other construction in order not to clog up its fitting-out basin even more. Eventually it was agreed that two ships should be towed to the Thames to be fitted out in Albert Dock.[8]

Some latitude was allowed in the fittings, in order to get the ships into service as soon as possible. According to the specification for the class,

> … alternatives may be promptly considered and adopted if departures from the specification are found to be necessary for keeping within the building periods allowed. In addition, the omission of minor fittings not absolutely essential for the service of the vessel and the use of wood in lieu of steel in storerooms and messes, etc., will be permitted at the discretion of the Admiralty Overseer, if found necessary for the completion of the vessel within the time available.[9]

Most firms relied on a combination of local and regional suppliers for standard fittings. For the *Wye*, Henry Robb of Leith ordered a set of evaporating and distilling machinery, two heavy exhaust surface feed heaters, and four duplex gravitational grease extractors from Caird and Rayner; two vertical single-cylinder fire and bilge pumps from J. P. Hall and Sons; two circulating pumps from Drysdale and Co; steam-powered turbine generators from Greenwood and Batty; and a diesel generator from Davey Paxman of Colchester. Weir Pumps of Glasgow, one of the best-known firms in the business, provided two main air pumps, two main feed pumps, and two auxiliary feed pumps, as well as two oil fuel pumps, all in the area of the engine and boiler rooms. Davis and Metcalf supplied four bilge ejectors, Howden and Co. provided two forced draught fans, and Dawson and Downie supplied two steam bilge and fire pumps, while the Hamworthy Engineering Company provided two oil fuel hand pumps. The steering engine was made by Hastie and Co. of Greenock, the steering gear by Mactaggart Scott of Loanhead. The cooling machinery was made by Sterne, the anchor windlass by T. Reid and Sons of Paisley.[10]

Electrical System

The original electrical specification of the River-class was mostly concerned with lighting and instrumentation.

> The ship is to be electrically lighted throughout internally, and a sufficient number of incandescent lamps of approved pattern are to be fitted to light thoroughly and efficiently all the different compartments and decks in the ship in accordance with the Electrical Specification. The various compasses, telegraphs and instruments on the upper deck, superstructures and bridge, and anchor, stern, bow, steaming, masthead, and other signalling lanterns are to be fitted with incandescent lamps.[11]

Since 1938, it had been agreed by the Admiralty that each ship should have a ring main, below the waterline as far as possible. The Admiralty considered that steam generators were more reliable than diesel, and the former were to be given preference. The problem with this was that the steam generators would be put out of action with any hit on the boiler or engine room, though it might still be possible to save the ship using electrically driven pumps. Therefore each ship should have one diesel generator, situated above the waterline.[12] In the case of the River-class, this meant two steam generators of 60-kilowatt power, situated aft on either side of the engine room. The diesel generator was situated asymmetrically on the starboard side alongside the forward part of the boiler room. Sweeping for magnetic mines demanded a large amount of power for the LL sweep (*see* page 23), and in the earlier ships two large diesel generators were placed in a special generator room aft under the quarterdeck, with a control panel between them. They were not fitted in later ships and the space was used for storage.

Another feature connected with mines was the degaussing ring, though that was not exclusive to minesweepers. This was intended to neutralize the ship's magnetic field against mines and consisted of more than 1000 feet (305m) of electric cables round the hull, going as far as possible to the bow and stern of the ship and carrying a heavy current at 225 volts.

Boats

The *Seaman's Pocket Book* of 1943 listed five uses for ship's boats. The first three – patrolling, laying out and weighing anchors and cables, and towing and landing armed parties – had no great relevance to the River-class. The fourth use, 'Ordinary harbour duties such as landing and embarking liberty men and stores, distributing correspondence with the fleet', was important in ships which might operate from unsophisticated bases where ships had to anchor rather than come alongside. The final use was as 'Sea boats; especially seaworthy craft such as cutters and whalers, one of which is kept ready each side for lowering in the event of anyone falling overboard, or a boat being required quickly for any other purpose.'[13] This, in the case of ships in the Battle of the Atlantic, might well include the rescue of survivors from the water.

The 27-ft whaler was a common type in the Navy. Derived from the type of boats used in the whale fishery as its name suggests, it was double-ended, with both the bow and stern coming to a point. It was clinker-built, which meant that the planks overlapped one another to give greater rigidity. It could be rowed by ten men or sailed using a gunter mainmast, a fore staysail and a small mizzen sail on a separate mast aft. For sailing it had a flat drop-keel amidships to prevent it being blown sideways by the wind. For use as a lifeboat it had a buoyancy tank of 3 cubic ft in the bow and stern, to keep it afloat in the worst of conditions. In that role it could carry up to twenty-seven people. Each ship also carried a small, 15-ft boat based on types use by trawlers.

Motor boats were relatively new in the Navy. An internal combustion engine was much smaller and lighter than a steam one of similar power, and it allowed engines to be fitted in small boats, which were in turn fitted to smaller ships. Because of the difficulty of storing petrol in a warship, most engines were started by petrol and powered by paraffin, an arrangement which, according to the *Manual of Seamanship*, would 'run quite satisfactorily' if it was kept in good order and the correct paraffin was used.[14] The type most commonly issued to the River-class was 25ft (7.6m) long and had a small deckhouse well forward, and a larger one, with four portholes, aft.

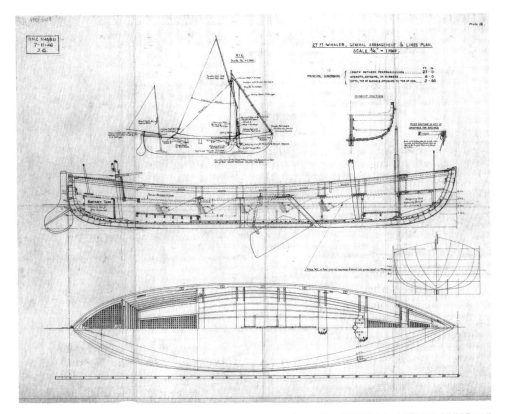

Plans of a 27ft Whaler as used by the River-class ships. Admiralty Collection, Box ADFB221, plan NPO5108. (NMM F5146)

The whaler, with lines evolved for use in open seas, was often the most useful boat in ocean warfare. In December 1944, the escort of Russian Convoy RA 62 lamented that the *Tavy's* whaler was unserviceable due to weather damage and none of the other ships of the escort had one. It proved very difficult to transfer wounded men from HMS *Cassandra* without one.[15]

Spey used its whaler in February 1944, to board the sinking *U-406*:

> The whaler had some difficulty in getting alongside the U-boat because of the slight
> sea that was running, but eventually my First Lieutenant and one Rating managed
> to scramble on board. There was one dead rating on the gun platform and the
> Commanding Officer was lying severely wounded in the stomach alongside the
> conning tower hatch. The First Lieutenant actually got down to the lower control
> room, finding the inside in complete darkness but free from fumes. At the bottom of
> the hatch was a large bag, possibly containing books, but it was too heavy for him to
> get up the conning tower; he therefore climbed up again to get a line, the Rating on
> board being fully occupied securing the whaler and keeping an eye on the wounded
> captain. The First Lieutenant had barely gained the open air once more when
> the boat began to sink and water to lap over the conning tower hatch. He and the
> Rating both jumped over the side and swam to the whaler which then backed clear
> of the disturbance caused by the U-boat sinking.[16]

The davits of the boats, apart from the whaler, were of the old-fashioned 'turn-in' type, and
some manoeuvring was required to get the boat from the stowed to the lowering position.
This was criticised at the time, for all the River's boats were intended for use as sea-boats,
and it was important to be able to launch them in a hurry. It might be possible to keep the
boats in their launching position while at sea, but few captains would countenance the risk
of loss. The pivots for the davits were outside the hull, and this, too, was criticised because
of the danger of damage when coming alongside. The later ships were fitted with gravity
davits, which could launch immediately from the stowed position. The boats were fitted
with 'Robinson's disengaging gear' to help release them after they had been lowered into the
water. This, too, had its problems, and a modified version was approved in May 1943.[17]

Navigational Fittings

Each ship was fitted with a motorised sounding machine as supplied by the Admiralty, to
find the depth of water under the hull by lowering a wire weighted with lead. A 17-ft long
boom was provided on the starboard side near the bridge to take the wire clear of the
ship and propellers when the ship was under way. More conventional sounding was done
manually when stationary or at low speed, and a leadsman's platform was provided on each
side of the hull for operating the lead.

The main magnetic compass, of standard Admiralty pattern, was of course fitted
on the bridge for use by the captain or the officer of the watch. It fitted inside a binnacle of
wood and brass, with locked cupboards containing magnets for adjusting the compass for
deviation. Hollow iron spheres were arranged on either side and could be adjusted for the
same reason. The binnacle had an electric light for use at night, and a brass hood could be
fitted to restrict the amount of light.

The gyrocompass depended on the principle that 'a wheel, when spinning at high
speed, shows great steadiness, i.e., it has a strong tendency to maintain its axis in a fixed
direction. In practice, by mechanical means, this fixed direction if made to coincide with
the true North, and consequently the gyro can be used as a compass.' It had the great
advantage that it was not subject to deviation or variation, or any magnetic disturbance.

Against this, it had to be started up at least five hours before it was required to allow the wheel to settle down. It required constant maintenance, including a daily regime of inspection, cleaning of some parts every forty-eight hours and others weekly, with further work on a monthly or quarterly cycle. It was likely to be upset by violent movement, so it was situated as close as possible to the centre of the ship, just forward of the boiler room on the lower deck. It took up much more space than a magnetic compass and needed a compartment 6ft square. The information was repeated on a dial on the bridge.[18]

Navigation lights, though rarely used during convoy escort, were fitted in the standard manner. An electric stem light was fitted at the top of the jackstaff in the bows; an electric and an oil anchor light were provided in the same area. There were both oil and electric red and green lights on the port and starboard sides of the bows, and a steaming light at the head of the foremast. Minesweeping lights, to warn other vessels to keep well clear of the gear, were fitted in the electric version only.

Masts and Rigging

Masts obviously had no function in carrying sail any more, and at this stage they did not carry radar aerials, which had to be kept close to the operator and hence the bridge. Their main function was to give height to the radio aerials and provide a viewing platform for a lookout in the form of the crow's nest. The foremast of the Rivers, situated just aft of the bridge, was by far the largest of the two. It was made of tubular steel and stood 81ft (25m) above the waterline and was 68ft (21m) long from its base on the forecastle deck. It was supported by two wooden struts placed diagonally aft of it, wire braces running aft to positions level with the aftermost side of the funnels, and wire braces which ran diagonally to join the forecastle deck just forward of the bridge. The crow's nest was a small cylinder whose base was 40ft (12m) above the forecastle deck, so that the lookout's eye was more than 60 ft (18m) above the waterline. Not content with that, Western Approaches General Orders described a way by which a man could be lashed to the head of the mast to get a longer-range view when in pursuit of a U-boat.[19]

The mast also supported a 10ft 8in. yardarm rigged near its head. This supported the four signal halyards, which ran through pulley blocks on the yardarm and down to the after end of the signal deck. It also supported the ends of four main radio aerials, running down and aft to the small mizzenmast. Access to the mast was by means of a small ladder fitted behind its aft side.

The main mast was actually much smaller, only 25ft (7.6m) high from the forecastle deck or 42ft 6in. (13m) above the waterline. It was held in place by wire rope and had a small yardarm to hold the other ends of the main aerial, and a small gaff running aft to carry the occasional signal flag.

Wire guardrails were fitted all round the hull, about 3ft 3in. (1m) above the deck to prevent the crew from falling overboard in rough weather. They were held up by iron stanchions 9ft (3m) apart and there were two other guardrails lower down on each stanchion. In warm weather in harbour, a canvas awning supported by three-legged stanchions could be rigged above the forecastle, the signal deck forward of the bridge and aft of the funnel, and part of the quarterdeck.

Life-Saving Equipment

The Navy's life-saving devices were inadequate before and during the war, perhaps because no particular department had responsibility for them, perhaps because the Navy preferred to think of aggressive action rather than the possibilities of sinking. The ship's boats, especially the motor boat and whaler, had some safety functions, but a small ship would break up and turn over quickly when torpedoed, and there was not likely to be much chance to launch them. The main device was the Carley float, three of which were carried by each River-class frigate. This had first been adopted in 1915. It consisted of an oval raft, 10ft long and 5ft wide (3 x 1.5m) and weighing 550lb (250kg). There was a grating in the middle, and 20 pints of water with a supply of signal flares, energy tablets, first-aid outfit, signalling mirror, a de-salting outfit, a torch and a Jacob's ladder. Oars, paddles and a boathook were attached to the outside when the float was stowed.

It could carry ten men sitting on its rim, and ten more hanging on the ropes from its side, though neither group was fully shielded from the weather. Even the men inside were partly immersed, and had no protection from heat or cold. The floats were stowed aft on either side of the signal deck, where they could be launched most easily without any need to manhandle them. But this was not as easy as it should have been. Often they were found to be too securely lashed, and no knife was at hand to release them; or the slips had been allowed to seize up. Across the Navy as a whole it was found that only ten per cent were successfully floated when needed. One out of three was released when the *Tweed* sank in 1944.[20]

The Flotanet provided another means of saving life. Each frigate had four of them, capable of carrying twenty-two men. Each Flotanet weighed 210lb (95kg) and consisted of rows of cork floats joined by ropes to form a net. It was first tested from the battleship HMS *Barham* in 1935 and adversely reported on. By 1939, it was accepted as 'a first refuge until the more solid support of a raft could be reached'.[21] It had the advantage of being almost invulnerable to splinters in action and free of maintenance, but in use it offered no protection at all from the elements.

Though they were not strictly part of the ship's fittings, inflatable lifebelts were issued to each man by 1942. This had not been considered until 1939, and the prototype was tested at Portsmouth in January 1940. The gear consisted of 'a rubber belt contained in a blue stockingette cover'. It had the advantage that it was 'comfortable to wear, easy to swim in, and to give fair support to the wearer. It has been found that it is possible to carry out all normal duties in ordinary temperatures when wearing it.'[22] Even so, many of the crew of the *Tweed* were not wearing them when the ship was hit by a torpedo in 1944.

The lifebelt also had many disadvantages. It was inflated by mouth, and at the Portsmouth trials it was pointed out that it did not have a non-return valve. This was never rectified during the war. Unless a man inflated it before he entered the water, it was unlikely that anyone but a very strong swimmer would be able to inflate it later. On the other hand, a man who jumped into the water from a height of more than 20ft (6m) with it fully inflated would be in danger from the belt. Once in, the man needed a fully inflated belt to keep him afloat. Lt.-Cdr. R. S. Miller, captain of the *Tweed*, attributed his survival to the fact that he kept his low on his chest, keeping him further out of the water than most people. But the lifebelt's support was 'only just sufficient to keep a man's mouth above still water' – it did nothing to keep an exhausted or unconscious man's head out of the water. 'His head invariably fell forward causing death by drowning.'[23] None of the three main means of life-saving – Carley floats, Flotanets, and lifebelts – did anything to solve the problems of cold, immersion in fuel oil, and exhaustion which killed many thousands of sailors during the war.

Pumps

Apart from floating on it and providing it for the crew to drink, a ship used water in various ways. There were salt water-ballast tanks, one in the foremost part of the bows, the other as far aft as possible without interfering with the steering arrangements. These could be emptied or filled as necessary to alter the trim of the ship and cope with varying weights of fuel, ammunition or other stores. Sea water was also circulated for cooling purposes, and sea cocks could be opened to flood magazines in the event of danger.

Water also had to be removed from areas of the ship where it was undesirable. The main arrangement was a system of 3½-in.-diameter suction piping running fore and aft under the upper deck. Branch suction pipes ran into each watertight compartment, each fitted with a strainer at its lower end to prevent it being fouled by debris. Two steam pumps were fitted to drain the engine and boiler rooms at a rate of 40 tons per hour, while one electric pump was fitted forward and one aft to work at a rate of 20 tons per hour. The same pumps could be used for fire-fighting. In addition, there were two mobile electric pumps of 70-tons-per-hour capacity. All this was enough to drain away the water which collected in the bilges through a combination of leakages, rainwater, spillages and condensation. But as the *Manual of Seamanship* pointed out, a 1-ft-square hole 25ft (7.6m) below the waterline would admit 3,500 tons of water per hour, and the pumps were useless in coping with this. Therefore the Navy relied more on efficient watertight subdivision by means of bulkheads.

Derricks and Mooring Gear

A general service derrick was rigged on each side of the ship, just forward of the platforms on the signal deck where there was room for it to swing. It was used to embark ammunition and other stores and could lift a weight of half a ton. Early ships were also fitted with a winch for using an anti-aircraft kite.

Bollards were used to attach the ends of ropes, particularly when mooring alongside a jetty or towing. According to the specification they were to be 'fitted as required'. The *Exe* had conventional double-cylindrical ones on each side of the bows opposite the anchor winch, and more further aft, opposite the shelter for the hedgehog crew. The after bollards could not be fitted too close to the stern because of the minesweeping gear, so they were fitted as far forward as possible on the quarterdeck. Ropes were rarely laid straight to a bollard, but were taken through fairleads, which held them in place. The specification demanded two strong ones well forward on the forecastle for mooring to a buoy. A second pair was fitted abreast of the hedgehog mounting. Others were fitted well aft on the quarterdeck, and further forward near the bollards. More strong bollards, known as 'bean bollards' and shaped like a squashed H, were fitted on each side to hold the ship in place during refuelling at sea.

Anchors

The Flower-class corvettes had been equipped with anchors of 21½ hundredweight (2408lb or 1092kg) each. The anchor of one of them, the *Oxlip*, had recently dragged, and the naval constructors suspected that this meant that it was too light. For the River-class, they applied the different formulae used by Lloyds and the British Corporation, which suggested anchors of 33 hundredweight and 28 hundredweight respectively (3696lb/1677kg and 3136lb/1423kg), and compromised by issuing two anchors of 30 hundredweight (3360lb or 1524kg) each. These could be stockless anchors of the standard Admiralty pattern, or the commercial Hall or Byers pattern.

To decide the weight of the chain cable attached to the anchors, the constructors turned to a treatise by W. J. Holt, one of their own number. This suggested a cable in which the iron of each link was 1⁵/₁₆in. in diameter, slightly less than used by the *Flowers*, but much more than comparable classes such as the Black Swan-, Halcyon- and Bangor-classes. It was decided to play it safe and use 1⁷/₁₆in. as with the Flowers. Chain cable in warships was invariably of the stud-link type, with a bar across the centre of each link to prevent kinking. The *Rivers* had twelve lengths of 12½ fathoms (75ft or 23m) each, plus four half-lengths; they could be joined together as appropriate, and the outfit included six joining shackles. There were more shackles for securing to a buoy, and swivels which would allow the ship to use two anchors without the risk of their cables becoming twisted together or fouled. Each ship was issued with a smaller anchor of 7 hundredweight (784lb or 356kg) known as the 'kedge', used for lighter work and small enough to be laid out in opposition using the ship's boats.

The anchor cable was stowed in the locker well forward in the ship between frames nine and thirteen, with holes in its decking to allow water to drain away. It passed up to a steam windlass on the forecastle, and then it was led forward to the hawse pipes, cast-iron tubes in the sides of the bows. When stowed, the stocks of the anchors were kept inside the hawse pipes. The anchor cable could be restrained temporarily using Blake's slips and Blake's screw-stoppers. It was secured more permanently by the brake on the windlass.[24] There was a smaller kedge anchor (*see* above) of the more traditional Admiralty pattern, with flukes and a plane at right angles to the stock. This was small enough to be slung under a ship's boat, for example, and taken out to a suitable position to be dropped. It was usually stowed vertically on the upper deck, alongside the signal deck, with its stock removed to save space. It had a steel-wire hawser rather than a chain cable.

Engines

The Choice of Engine

The steam turbine engine had many advantages over its main rival, the steam reciprocating engine. Its rotary motion needed fewer working parts, and therefore reduced maintenance. It produced less vibration than the up-and-down motion of the reciprocating engine. It was far more efficient at high speeds, allowing a fifteen or twenty per cent reduction in boiler capacity for the same amount of power. It could be fitted lower in the ship than a reciprocating engine, aiding stability, which was always important in a warship with high-mounted guns. The steam turbine had powered all purpose-built major warships, except submarines, since it was fitted in HMS *Dreadnought* in 1906.

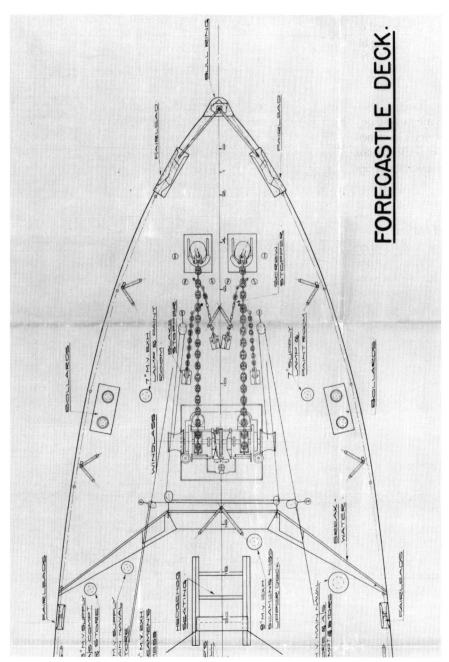

The anchor gear of the forecastle of HMS *Barle* (1942). Admiralty Collection, Box ADFB017, plan NPN0906. (NMM F5144)

It was far less common in merchant ships, except in fast passenger liners and ferries. It was less efficient at the low speeds used by most cargo ships, and its first cost was high. Cash was not necessarily a problem for the wartime Navy, which was largely free of conventional financial constraints; scarcity of materials and skilled labour were far more important issues. The blades of steam turbines required great skill and care in their manufacture, and the Navy preferred to reserve them for conventional warships – destroyers, cruisers, aircraft carriers and battleships – which needed higher speed than convoy escorts.

When the Flower-class was conceived, it was taken for granted that the vessels would be manned largely by merchant-navy engineers recruited through the Royal Naval Reserve, and such men would be more familiar with reciprocating engines. In practice, the resources of the RNR never stretched that far, and chief engineers of corvettes were usually experienced naval men, while the stokers were recruited mainly direct from civilian life.

In that respect, the reciprocating engine offered no advantage. However, the Navy was impressed with the performance of the corvette engine in service. It proved to be highly reliable in the most difficult conditions, and had low vibrations for an engine of its type. It could be built by a wide range of engineering firms, including 'inland' ones with no experience of marine work. Though it might have seemed a backward step in terms of the evolution of naval engineering, the Engineer-in-Chief and the Director of Naval Construction had no hesitation in adopting a pair of corvette engines as the main power for the new River-class escorts.

Only one change was necessary in the design: the crankshaft was extended slightly so that it now protruded through both ends of the casing. This meant that the engine could be fitted either way round, which had two advantages: a pair of engines could be mounted so that their propellers turned in opposite directions, eliminating torque, which would tend to turn a ship with a single propeller; and the engines could be fitted so that the side with the main controls was inboard on both, simplifying control and communication.

The reciprocating engine relied on principles which went back to Thomas Newcomen and James Watt in the eighteenth century. Originally, steam inside a cylinder was condensed, creating a vacuum which would pull the piston head towards it, and this was converted to a rotary motion by means of a piston rod and crankshaft. Watt's greatest contribution was to take the steam outside the cylinder to a separate condenser, thus avoiding the constant heating and cooling of the cylinder. The next stage was the double-acting engine, in which steam was fed in turn to each side of the cylinder, greatly increasing efficiency. Steam pressures were still quite low untill the second half of the nineteenth century, when stringer boilers became available. This allowed the adding of a second cylinder, so that high pressure steam would be used on the test cylinder, then its exhaust could be used again in the second, low pressure cylinder. The triple-expansion engine took this a stage further and added a third cylinder, using the higher pressures available from steam boilers. The quadruple-expansion engine was under development at the turn of the twentieth century, but its function was largely taken over by the steam turbine, so the triple-expansion engine remained the most developed form of reciprocating engine. It was the type used in corvettes and frigates of World War II.

The Engines of the River-class

In the River-class, the two engines were fitted side by side just aft of midships, mounted as low as possible above the keel and double bottom of the ship. The cylinder heads were supported by a massive structure of large pillars of square section on the inboard side and round section on the outboard side. They were mounted on the engine bearers, which in turn were bolted to the floors of the ship, with a recess in the floors to allow room for the crankshaft to rotate. Each engine was 22ft 6in. long and 8ft 5in. wide. It was 13ft 8in. high at the top of the casing, which brought it approximately to the level of the upper deck. The cylinder heads were a further 1ft 8in. higher than that and they had to be accessible for maintenance, so a space at the after end of the forecastle deck had to be reserved as part of the engine room.

Each engine had four cylinders. Steam from the boilers entered the high-pressure cylinder, near the centre of the engine with an internal diameter of 18½ in., at a maximum pressure of 225lb per square inch. At the end of its stroke it would exhaust to the intermediate-pressure cylinder, with a diameter of 31in., then after another stroke the steam would be divided equally between the two low-pressure cylinders, one at each end of the engine, with an internal diameter of 38½in. Finally, it would go to the condenser to be turned into water.

Each of the pistons had a stroke of 30in., which was the distance it travelled up or down with each revolution. The piston rod was fixed to it, and that was bolted in turn to the connecting rod at the crosshead. The connecting rod could pivot at the crosshead, and its lower end was attached to the crankshaft to translate the up-and-down movement into a rotary motion.

The function of the slide valve was to control the entry of steam to the appropriate part of the cylinder. Its movement was the opposite to that of the piston: up when the piston was down. This was controlled by means of the eccentric wheel, which was attached to one end of the crankshaft and consisted of a circular sheave with a hole some distance from its centre. The eccentric rod was fitted round the outer edge of the circle and transmitted the motion to the slide valve.

Engine Controls and Instruments

The engines were arranged so that all the major controls and instruments were on the inboard side. The throttle was the main means of controlling the speed of the engine, and therefore the ship. It simply controlled the supply of steam to the engine, and consisted of a large wheel set in the horizontal plane on the inboard side of each engine, operating a valve through which steam entered the high-pressure cylinder. Close by was a quick shut-off device for use in an emergency – for example, when the engine raced as the propeller came out of the water in rough seas.

Reciprocating engines had no gearing as such, and the engine itself had to be put into reverse for manoeuvring. This was done be reversing the operation of the slide valves, which in turn was done by altering the motion of the eccentric. A second eccentric was fitted on the same shaft as the first, with its sheave set opposite to it. The other end of the reversing eccentric was fitted inside a quadrant, and when reversing it was pulled over to link with the slide-valve rod and reverse its movement. Because of the force needed, a small engine was used to move this eccentric into place, fitted in the upper inboard part of the main engine and operated by a lever close to the throttle wheel. Alternatively, if there was no steam, the eccentrics could be moved over by means of a large hand-wheel on the outboard side of the engine.

The engine could be very difficult to start if the high-pressure piston was at the top or bottom dead-centre position, so starting steam valves were provided to supply steam directly to the intermediate-pressure cylinder. Each cylinder had a pair of drain valves operated remotely by long spindles. Their function was to let out any water that was mixed with the steam, especially during starting and warming up.

In order to monitor the speed of the engine, the pressure of the steam and the heating of the different parts, several gauges were fitted on the inboard side of the engine. Fitted close to the centre and near the throttle wheel and reversing lever, the combined revolution counter and tachometer was the most important. It was driven by a chain from the crankshaft and indicated the number of revolutions at that moment and their speed; this had to be kept at the rate ordered from the bridge by means of the engine-room telegraph. Above that, and attached to the same pillar, were three gauges indicating the pressure in the boiler and the high-pressure cylinder of the engine, and the state of the vacuum in the condenser. This gave the engineer of the watch a good idea of what was happening to the steam throughout the system.

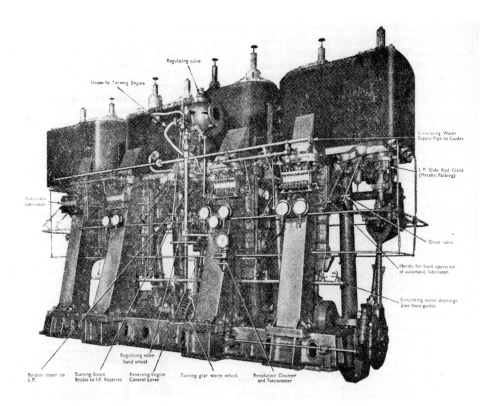

The inboard side of a four-cylinder triple expansion engine as used by the River-class, showing the engine controls. From *Naval Marine Engineering Practice* (Admiralty, 1955 – 1966 edition) (NMM F5131)

Lubrication and Cooling

With a large number of moving parts, some operating at high temperatures, lubrication was very important in reciprocating engines. The pistons, cylinder walls and slide valves could not be lubricated by means of oil, as that would contaminate the steam, but the steam itself contained enough moisture for lubrication.

Lubrication of the internal parts was automatic. There were four automatic lubricator units, one for each cylinder, fitted on the inboard pillars. Each of these contained a battery of nine pump elements which discharged oil through pipes to fixed points in the area. A sight chamber in each element allowed a stoker to check the supply of oil in it. If it was low, he would pour more in through a strainer in the top. Water pipes were fitted around the outside of the engine for cooling the guides, which directed the movement of the piston rods and connection rods. Another series of pipes led cold water towards the large end bearings, and cocks could be opened to cool them in an emergency.

The Condensers

It was necessary to condense the steam after it came out of the engine, rather than simply let it exhaust into the atmosphere, for two reasons. In the first place, boiler water had to be fresh rather than salt, which would soon clog up the tubes and machinery, so it had to be re-used. Secondly, the vacuum created by condensing a large volume of steam into a small volume of water helped to increase the efficiency of the engine. The condensers for the River-class were fitted outboard of the engines, with large pipes leading from the low-pressure cylinder to the condenser. Each condenser consisted of a shell with a large number of small tubes with seawater passing through them to keep them cool. When the steam met the cold surface of the tubes, it condensed into water and fell to the bottom of the condenser to be pumped back to the boiler.

Turbine Engines

The original concept of the River-class allowed for turbine engines. In December 1940, the constructor A.W. Watson pointed out that the turbine took up a rather different space and had different needs from a reciprocating engine. It needed higher-pressure boilers, and its higher revolutions probably needed a propeller of smaller diameter, with more trim by the stern. However, the Director of Naval Construction ruled out the idea of a separate hull design. In May 1941, at a meeting between constructors Holt and Kimberley and a representative of the Engineer-in-chief of the Navy, it was agreed that the turbines would be of 6500 shaft horsepower, on the grounds that an existing design of that type was available, though the extra 1000 horsepower would only add 0.6 knots to the speed. The same boilers as for the reciprocating engine would be used. The engines would turn the propeller at a maximum speed of 300 revolutions per minute, compared with 185 for the reciprocating engines, which would be best for the propeller in use; a bigger gear wheel could be used for lower revolutions but would take up space and cause complications. There would be a certain loss of screw efficiency due to the higher speed, reducing it from seventy-four per cent to seventy per cent. A separate turbine would also be needed for reversing. Longitudinal fuel-tank bulkheads abaft the engine room would have to be moved out sideways to clear the shaft line, and a redesign of longitudinal framing in the engine room was necessary. In all, about fifty new plans would have to be drawn. The turbines took up rather less space than the reciprocating engines fore, aft and vertically, but there was no way of using this space effectively. In all, the use of turbines on the existing hull and with existing engines was not a very efficient use of scarce resources. Only six ships – the *Cam*, *Chelmer*, *Ettrick*, *Halladale*, *Helmsdale* and *Tweed* – were fitted with turbine engines. It might have been even fewer, but Inglis of Glasgow would only build turbine ships in its first order, for the *Halladale* and *Helmsdale*.

Boilers

The Flower-class had used cylindrical Scotch boilers of a type common in merchant ships of the time. It was generally agreed that this was not a success, for they tended to react rather slowly and were not suitable for the frequent changes of speed which were necessary in U-boat hunting. According to the *Machinery Handbook* of 1941, the water-tube boiler was 'lighter, more suitable for burning oil fuel, and steam can be raised quicker. Also a water-tube boiler can be arranged to withstand higher pressures and give a higher degree of superheat.'[25] For the River-class it was decided to fit water-tube boilers based on a type which had been common on warships since they were first used in the A-class destroyers in 1925. Unlike other boilers of this type, they did not have superheaters, which were situated among the water tubes of most of the faster ships, and heated the steam to yet higher pressure. This was appropriate for turbine engines, but reciprocating engines worked better with saturated steam, which retained a certain amount of moisture to aid lubrication within the cylinders.

The River-class had two boilers, placed one ahead of the other in the boiler room, with a small gap between them and the stokehold outermost to allow work on them. Furnace fuel oil fuel from the tanks was pumped through strainers to remove impurities, and then through heaters which raised the temperature suitable for burning. Each boiler had four registers at the stokehold end. These took in air which was mixed with the fuel, and was then sprayed inside the tank to create a mixture that would burn well.

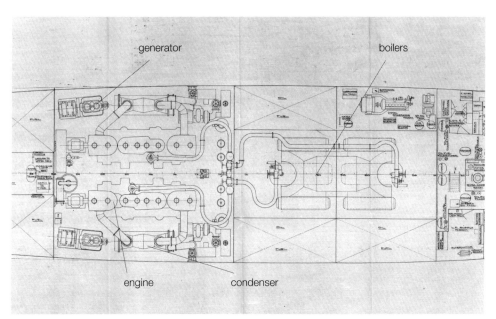

The engine room and boiler room arrangements of HMS *Barle*. Admiralty Collection, Box ADFB017, plan NPN0905. (NMM F5145)

The River-class had two boilers, placed one ahead of the other in the boiler room, with a small gap between them and the stokehold outermost to allow work on them. Oil fuel from the tanks was pumped through strainers to remove impurities, and then through heaters which raised the temperature suitable for burning. Each boiler had four registers at the stokehold end. These took in air which was mixed with the fuel, and was then sprayed inside the tank to create a mixture that would burn well.

The water-tube boiler had six main parts. There were two water drums, where the water entered from the condenser. Each was 11ft 8in. long with an external diameter of 2ft. Between and above them was the furnace, lined with fire bricks and containing four registers and sprayers. The water tubes themselves led from the water drums on each side and over the furnace and up to the steam drum. The products of the combustion of the fuel passed around the outside of the tubes, heating them to a high temperature. The final part was the steam tube above, 4ft 2in. diameter, where the steam collected and was passed through pipes to the engines, with shut-off valves and arrangements so that either boiler could feed either engine, or the various auxiliary systems.

The Funnel

Exhaust smoke and hot air from the furnace were collected by a pyramid-like structure built over the boilers, and directed to the funnel directly above them. This had straight sides with no rake and was 24ft (7.3m) in height from the upper deck. In section, it was made up of two semi-circles of 4ft external and 3ft 6in. internal diameter, joined by a short straight piece 18in. wide. Quite early in the design, an angled cap was added to protect it from head winds, and a frame was built over that so that a canvas cover could be fitted when the funnel was not in use. A rainwater catcher was fitted near the base. There were ladders up the side for inspection purposes, and gratings were fitted 2ft 6in. under the top edge. The pipes for the officers' and crew's galleys led diagonally to halfway up the funnel, then ran vertically alongside it. The whole structure was supported by guys leading sideways and aft.

Fuel

Although the rating title of 'stoker' remained in use, no major coal-fired ships had been built for the Royal Navy since World War I, and the great majority of existing ships had been converted to burn oil. Though coal-fired trawlers and other small vessels were taken on in 1939, oil fuel was standard for all purpose-built warships, including both the *Flowers* and the *Rivers*.

The first River-class ships had six main fuel tanks, situated on either side alongside the boiler room and small-arms magazine. The forward tanks extended only to the under the lower deck, but three of the tanks alongside the boiler room extended to the upper deck. The exception was the number-four tank on the port side, which was reduced in height because of the position of the diesel generator. The fuel arrangement of the *Rivers* was therefore not completely symmetrical, and they would tend to list to starboard when fully loaded. If this could make it difficult to berth the ship alongside, captains were instructed not to fill tanks seven and nine on the starboard side, but in other circumstances they were to take on as much fuel as possible. According to an Admiralty Fleet Order of

1943, 'The importance of proceeding on operational duties with maximum oil stowage should take precedence over any temporary disadvantage of a list, provided no risk of disadvantage is involved.'[26] In addition, there were six reserve tanks aft of the engine room. This gave an endurance of 4850 miles (7805km) at 15 knots – more than enough to escort a convoy across the Atlantic.

But the U-boat war looked like it would extend to the Arctic and the south Atlantic, and even greater range was needed. The space was already available in the ships ordered after the first twenty-four, which had no minesweeping gear. It was soon discovered that the gear already fitted in the *Rivers* would not be used, and this allowed the fitting of extra fuel tanks aft. In March 1943, it was noted that seventeen ships were already complete and two more complete in May, June and July, with the last of the first twenty-four in August. All later ships were completed without the gear, and the space vacated by the LL generators, in combination with a redesign of the after part of the hull, provided room for four extra fuel tanks raising the total capacity from 440 to 650 tons. The new long-endurance version had a range of 8000 miles (11,265km), though their top speed was reduced to 19½ knots by the extra weight. Other ships had the minesweeping gear removed as soon as possible and the after accommodation refitted.

The range could be extended by means of refuelling at sea, though techniques were underdeveloped in the British Navy during the war. One way was for the tanker to trail a hose behind it, to be picked up by the ship to be refuelled. Another method was for the ships to come alongside one another. In 1942, the system proposed for the River-class involved the ships being held together by means of a breast rope running 35 degrees aft from the midships of the tanker to a fairlead and a special bollard in the bows of the frigate, and a spring from midships of the tanker to a bollard abreast the bridge of the frigate. A derrick in the tanker listed a flexible hose clear of the water, and it was passed through an oil-hose trough hung from the derrick and eventually to the fuel connections on the side and bows of the frigate.

Even without this, the River-class had an advantage over destroyers and sloops in the matter of range. Convoy ONS 132 left Liverpool in September 1942, but three *S*-class destroyers had to turn back because it was too rough for refuelling. The *Rother, Spey, Exe* and *Tay* carried on and drove off an attack, though eight merchant ships were lost.[27] All the ships except the *Spey* had to refuel while escorting Convoy SC 130 across the Atlantic in May 1943: those of the Flower-class once, the destroyers *Duncan* and *Vidette* twice.[28] The *Spey* managed 3121 miles (5023km) with only sixty-one per cent of her fuel consumed.

The Propellers

The twin propellers were situated with their centres 8ft (2.4m) below the waterline in the hope that they would not be lifted out of the sea by large waves. They were 9ft 9in. in diameter and were placed under the curve of the stern to give some protection from the sea. Each was stamped with its pitch, which indicated the distance the ship should move through the water with each revolution and determined the angle at which the blades were set. Captain King of the *Avon* found that his had been wrongly marked in 1943, with a pitch that was 2ft less than what was intended, reducing the speed of the ship to 16 knots.

The shafts which connected the propeller with the engine were key components in the structure, and their correct alignment required great care and skill. They were fitted inside the shaft tubes to help keep them in place. Large castings known as shaft brackets were used to hold the tubes the correct distance form the side of the hull, and to keep the tubes straight.

Auxiliary Machinery

The boiler also fed steam to various other places throughout the ship for several purposes. It powered the pumps which fed the engines with fuel. It provided heating to all living spaces using steam at a pressure of 35lb per square inch. It fed the two steam generators at the after end of the engine room. These were usually driven by steam turbines, because there was no advantage in being able to reverse them as in a reciprocating engine. The engine which powered the anchor windlass was reciprocating, on the other hand, for it was combined with a cable holder so that it could be used to control the cable as it ran out.

Other systems of power were used where appropriate. Steering was by means of a telemotor in the aftermost compartment below decks. It was powered by two hydraulic rams operated either by the steering wheel under the bridge, or locally by a separate steering wheel which could be used in the event of damage. According to the specification, the maximum rudder angle was to be 35 degrees. It was to be tested by putting it over to full angle and back again while the vessel was going at full speed ahead and astern. Despite such trials, rudders sometimes jammed in service. In January 1943, HMS *Jed* had to leave the 42nd Escort Group and the escort of Convoy ONS 163 to go to Iceland for rudder repairs. Three months later, the *Tay's* steering gear broke down temporarily while attacking a U-boat in the vicinity of Convoy HX 231, and she used her main engines to get back to the convoy.[29] In the following month, *Wear's* gear jammed as she mounted a hedgehog attack while escorting Convoy SC 130. It was repaired in two hours, but contact with the target was lost.[30]

The reciprocating engine proved as successful in the River-class as it had been with the *Flowers*. It was adopted for the *River's* successors, the Loch- and Bay-classes. The engine itself was unchanged, but production methods varied slightly. With the River-class, it was normal for each shipbuilder to order the engine for a particular ship, perhaps from his own engine shop, perhaps from a firm he dealt with regularly. This could cause delays if the engine was ready before the ship, or vice versa. Since the *Lochs* and *Bays* were intended for mass production, it was decided that all engines should be ordered centrally, and allocated to ships as they became ready. This involved a greater standardisation of the detail, but no fundamental design change. In all, around 1150 engines were built for all classes between January 1940 and December 1944.[31]

Entering Service

The Names

The idea of naming a class after British rivers was not entirely new. There had been a River-class of destroyers, built between 1903 and 1909. As the first destroyers with forecastles, they had been a great advance at the time and were far more seaworthy than their predecessors, but they were quite slow. They were soon outclassed by the first Tribal-class vessels, built between 1907 and 1909, which were 10 knots faster. The River-class ships were largely obsolete by the time war broke out in 1914, and they were relegated to secondary duties away from the Grand Fleet. None survived the mass scrappings after the war.

The choice of river names for the new class had several advantages. The names came somewhere between the unmilitary gentleness of the Flower-class, and the slightly aggressive masculinity of the Captain-class frigates built in the USA for the Royal Navy, named after commanders of the age of sail. Though some of the river names were very obscure, they did not invite the obviously embarrassing names possible for the Flower-class. It was quite late in the day when the Admiralty decided not to use *Pansy* but *Buttercup; Wallflower* and *Dahlia* did not hint at martial virtues. The river names, on the other hand, tended to suggest flow and movement and had obvious associations with water, if not with the oceans. Some of the greatest rivers, the Thames, Clyde and Severn, had already given their names to a small class of submarines, while the *Forth, Medway* and *Tyne* were in service as depot ships. Mersey and Humber were never used in this period for some reason, but the River-class frigates were to include some quite well-known rivers, such as the *Tay, Avon* and *Tees*; others which were better known for the towns named after them such as *Plym, Exe* and *Chelmer;* and many which were known only to locals, including the *Moyola, Barle* and *Evenlode.* Since most of the names represented small country rivers, they tended to evoke memories of bucolic charm rather than industrial might, and perhaps reminded the seaman of the idealised Britain he was supposed to be fighting for. Unlike their successors of the *Loch* class, the *Rivers* could represent all areas of the United Kingdom, including the *Bann* and *Lagan* in Northern Ireland. It also allowed the dominions of Canada and Australia to use their known river names, though the Canadians did not take the opportunity as they had already named a class of destroyers after rivers, so they used the names of towns.

As to the class as a whole, the title 'twin-screw corvette' was clumsy and did not convey the radical difference between the *Rivers* and the Flower-class they were intended to replace. 'Sloop' would have been an obvious title, as it would have said something about the origin of the design, but in the meantime the Royal Canadian Navy began to refer to its own ships as 'frigates' in March 1942, before any of them were in service. The Admiralty in London disapproved of this use of an historic title. In the age of sail, frigates had been substantial warships, second only to ships of the line in the naval pecking order, and the ancestors of the cruisers of the modern Navy. The 'twin-screw corvettes' were much smaller than that, and in some ways inferior to sloops, which were smaller than frigates in sailing terminology. In April 1942, the secretary to the First Sea Lord wrote to the Canadian naval headquarters,

> 1. The introduction of a new class name can only be justified on account of marked change in function or type.
> 2. In addition to the Twin-screw Corvettes, the American built British Destroyer Escorts will soon come into service.
> 3. Twin-screw Corvettes and British Destroyer Escorts have the same function as the present corvettes, namely convoy escort, and they only differ in type as regards size, speed and endurance.
> 4. It is, therefore, considered insufficient justification for the use of the term frigate and it is therefore, intended that all ships shall be designated corvettes...[32]

But the name caught on, and on 25 February 1943, the Admiralty issued an order re-classifying the new ships as frigates. This was publicised on 3 March when A.V. Alexander, the First Lord of the Admiralty, told the House of Commons during the debate on the Navy estimates,

> The special new, faster type of corvette with greater armament, some of which are already in use, is being given a new name, to distinguish it from the previous corvette, and I hope the House will approve it. We propose to call it the frigate.

Any dramatic impact was lost on Mr Tinker, the member for Leigh, who asked, 'What is a corvette?'[33] But the name proved popular, perhaps because it featured in C. S. Forester's *Hornblower* novels which were being read by many people with naval connections, from the Prime Minister downwards. Since then, the name has become almost universal, and Royal Navy surface ships are referred to by the press and public, often mistakenly, as 'frigates'.

Trials

HMS *Rother*, the first of the River-class to enter service, was completed at Smith's Dock on 3 April 1941. It sailed round the north of Britain to the Firth of Clyde to carry out speed trials on the deep-water measured mile off the Isle of Arran on 8 and 9 April. The trials were slightly disappointing, in that the ship made only 19¾ knots rather than the 20¼ which had been predicted. The staff of the test tank at Haslar were unperturbed by this. The ship had been out of dock for a month, allowing some weed to accumulate on its bottom; and it now displaced 1900 tons instead of the 1400 tons at which the form had been tested. Their report concluded, 'The propulsive efficiency anticipated in the design stage has been realised, the reduced speed being entirely due to the greater displacement and time out of dock.'

HMS *Fal*, a typical ship, had been ordered from Smith's Dock 13 December 1941 and was launched nearly a year later on 9 November 1942. After completion and commissioning, it sailed south to Blackwall Dock in London, owned by Green and Silley Weir, for docking and tests. It was in dry dock between the 26 May and the 5 June and it was found that the anti-fouling composition on the ship's bottom was poor.

The report of the inspection on 29 June stated that the *Fal* was 'complete and properly fitted' regarding hull and fittings, rigging and derricks awnings and canvas gear, main engines and auxiliary engines; the order suggests that the form, though recently reprinted, was a relic of the age of sail. There were a few minor outstanding electrical items, such as the starter for the lathe in the engineers' workshop. The naval officials answered seventy-eight questions on the hull, plus many additional sub-questions, plus fifteen on the machinery, concluding with, 'Has the specification been read over article by article as required by the Contract, and all details as to fittings, & etc., found to be in accordance with the specification and approved drawings?'[34] The answer was yes, and it was signed by various dockyard and naval officers, including the captain, navigating officer, gunnery officer, signal officer, chief engineer and boatswain of the ship.

Gun trials were carried out on 10 July, under the supervision of the gunnery school at Chatham. Four rounds were fired from each of the 4-in. guns, but the officers stated that the recoil of the forward gun was longer than intended, and that of the after gun was too short. It was found that the ammunition hoist was not able to lift two shells at once.

The Oerlikon guns fired sixty rounds each with no problem. The radios were tested by calling stations at Whitehall and Chatham, and the echo sounder was found to work at speeds up to 10 knots, in depths of 5 to 15 fathoms.

On 12 July, under the supervision of Lloyds Register, the *Fal* carried out its full power trials in Barrow Deep in the Thames Estuary. The average number of revolutions achieved by the main engines was 177.8. The chief engineer commented that they were satisfactory, but that 'a little difficulty was experienced in maintaining full steam pressure at boilers'. He suggested that 'this was due to the new ship's company having had little time to become fully acquainted with the most satisfactory working of the oil fuel units'. The auxiliary machinery was satisfactory except for the distilling plant, which was overhauled and repaired by the ship's company.

The trials were not always successful. Despite many modifications, the engineer officer of the *Nith* reported,

> The performance of propelling machinery has not been satisfactory. After failure to carry out a successful full power trial on two occasions during the previous quarter, the main engines have failed to do so on one occasion during this quarter, also after readjustments had been subsequently carried out, bearings overheated during a run at 140 revs: and a proposed trial was abandoned. It has been found that the alignment of the bed plates is not satisfactory and at least partial rechecking of the engine is necessary.[35]

The problem was never solved in this ship, and it found a new role as a landing-ship headquarters, where speed and endurance were less necessary. Ironically in the circumstances, the builders, Robb's of Leith, took pride in the *Nith*'s new role. 'To H.M.S. "*Nith*," a frigate, fell the distinction of being selected as a Headquarters ship for D-Day operations', reported the firm's postwar brochure.

Another ship that was initially unsuccessful was the *Avon*, built by Charles Hill of Bristol and commanded by Lt.-Cdr. P. G. A. King in 1943. There was no measured mile to do a speed trial in the Bristol Channel and the Admiralty was keen to get the ship through as quickly as possible. The full power trial, according to King, was meant to establish that the engines developed the power they were intended to, rather than test the speed. King complained that the ship was only doing 16 knots instead of 20, but this was put down to inefficiency in the engine room and ignored. King signed for the ship, 'the most valuable object, in terms of money value, that I have ever signed for …'

The *Avon* escorted a fast 16-knot convoy of troopships to Gibraltar and through the Mediterranean, but could only keep up by running the engines for dangerously long periods at full power. Eventually, in a dry dock in Colombo, it was established that it had been fitted with propellers of the wrong pitch which had restricted its speed. After that was rectified, ten months after the ship was commissioned, there was no problem.[36]

Performance

For all the praise in some quarters, there are signs that the *River* class never quite lived up to its designed performance. Peter Gretton suggested that they had a maximum speed of 18 knots, though that was written twenty years later and might have been caused by a lapse of memory.[37] King suggests 19, even after the problems with *Avon*'s propellers had been dealt with.

In sea-keeping, the evidence also has its contradictions. The naval constructor W. J. Holt took passage in the *Spey* on its maiden voyage from the builder's yard at Middlesborough to Tobermory in May 1942 and was quite impressed, though the ship was never really tested. There was very little sea during the passage up the east coast, but after Dunnet Head, in the north of Scotland, the ship encountered a moderate swell of force 4-5 and 'began to roll and pitch easily', average 5 degrees in each direction, occasionally 12 degrees. The period of the roll was nine seconds, the pitch was five seconds. Holt wrote,

> Generally speaking I was very favourably impressed by *Spey*. The motion of the ship is easy and reminiscent of a destroyer. The accommodation is exceptionally good. The general layout of instruments and the functioning of fittings associated with a/s work appears to be good. The good accommodation, combined with the easy motion, should be of great value in keeping the ship on efficient operational work in a seaway.[38]

Peter Gretton went further and suggested that 'These frigates were more comfortable than destroyers.'[39] Nicholas Monsarrat was pleased with the *Ettrick* in harbour:

> The impression was, again, one of solidity and strength: in a corvette the Oerlikon and two-pounder mountings made an appreciable difference to the top-weight; here they could be planted almost at will, like candles in a birthday-cake of the pre-war, majestic sort. This ship was a steadfast platform, for guns, for men, for fighting enterprise or rocklike endurance: the sort of thing a sailor likes to have beneath his feet.[40]

At sea it was less solid; 'though she rolled more slowly than a corvette, she was just as good at it really, and all that night we were chucked about as brutally as I ever remembered'.[41]

In the spring of 1943, the captain of the *Spey* complained that the low quarterdeck was very wet and asked for bulwarks, at least 4ft high, to be built around it. The Admiralty decided to retain it as it was.

> The freeboard aft compares reasonably with that of other types of warship of similar size, and this, together with a good width of upper deck which has been maintained right aft to give space for minesweeping and other equipment, gives the form adequate for reserve of buoyancy at the stern. The addition of bulwarks is not recommended.[42]

The official postwar report on the class claimed that

> Reports from sea stated that these ships were comfortable, very good sea boats and capable of maintaining better speed in bad weather than the ships built on destroyer lines. High freeboard made for a dry ship forward and amidships, but the quarterdeck was wet and some pounding was experienced even at quite low speeds.[43]

According to one report, a new River-class frigate cost £140,000 for the hull and £80,000 for the machinery, compared with a Black Swan-class sloop, which cost £181,000 for the hull and £105,000 for the turbine machinery. By another report of early 1941, a River-class ship was expected to cost a total of £325,000, compared with £120,000 for a *Flower*.[44]

Appearance

There was no doubt that the River-class were good-looking ships. Captain Humphrey Boys-Smith wrote of the *Spey*, 'A very beautiful ship she was, too, and I was inordinately proud of her.'[45] Nicholas Monsarrat wrote of the *Ettrick*, 'The ship behaved as well as she looked, and that was saying a lot.'[46] From the lower deck, Sidney France of the *Evenlode* thought that 'The River-class were a good-looking ship.'[47]

The gentle sheer produced a pleasing curve, not too extreme as in the Flower-class. The long forecastle gave an impression of solidity that was absent in destroyers. The armament was light and did not detract from the appearance, as in the Black Swan-class which was similar in other respects. The hull lines were fine and fair, without making the ship look too fragile. The whole impression was a series of levels rising in a pyramid shape to a peak at the radar cabin, and then descending equally regularly to the quarterdeck. The proportions were not unlike those of larger ships regarded as the ideal of beauty by Cdr. D. A. Rayner RNVR who thought HMS *Hood* was 'to my eyes the most beautiful steamship that man ever devised'.[48]

The appearance of the *Rivers* was very different from that of 1920s battleships *Rodney* and *Nelson* as described by Lt.-Cdr. Benstead of the *Rodney*. They had 'not the faintest suggestion of the low pyramidical profile and jutting armament that gives so truculent an air to previous design'. With a low, flat deck and a high and prominent conning tower aft, the lower deck called them 'The Ugly Sisters' or 'The Pair of Boots'.[49] The *River* class reverted to an earlier phase of design, *circa* 1920. In view of the pressures of the time, it is unlikely that the designer had any intention to make them look good, but he did so. Yet it was not difficult to mar the beauty of the ships. After the war, many of the Canadian ships were converted to have a flush deck with no quarterdeck, a taller funnel and a larger bridge. Their new appearance was undistinguished, to say the least.

The Bridge

Origins and History

In the days of sail, the captain or officer of the watch stood on the quarterdeck or poop towards the stern of the ship, where he was close to the steering position and had a good view of the sails which were essential to the ship's motion. The first steamships were paddle steamers in rivers and estuaries, and they were far more likely to do intricate manoeuvres such as coming alongside a pier or jetty. The captain needed a high position near the centre of the ship where he could have a good view of the sides and move easily from one side to the other; a 'bridge' was built between the heads of the paddle boxes for his use. As screw-propelled steamships became more common in the second half of the nineteenth century, sails became less and less important and there was no need to fear that elaborate superstructures might interfere with them. A large structure could be built about a third of the way along the ship, forward of the engines and their funnel smoke, where the captain could have the best view. Mechanical means of steering meant that movements could be transmitted a long way through the ship, so the wheel could be sited forward near the bridge.

Bridges were usually open to the weather for the first half of the twentieth century, for sailors felt that they had to feel the wind in their faces. This conflicted with their reliance on paper charts for navigation, and arrangements had to be made to allow them to look at charts or plots without going too far from the exposed position of the bridge.

The Evolution of the Design

From the start, the bridge of the River-class ships was planned to be two decks above the forecastle deck and therefore about 32ft (10m) above the waterline to give an adequate view for the captain and the officers of the watch. The bridge deck was above the much longer and somewhat misnamed signal deck, which included the mounting for the forward 4-in. gun. The compass platform on the bridge, from where the ship was controlled, would be placed well forward, and the design meeting of 13 December 1940 decided that an asdic hut should be fitted at the after end of the bridge, so that the captain or officer of the watch could check any reports of submarines personally, or follow the progress of an attack in detail. A searchlight would be fitted above it. This was revised at a further meeting on 27 January 1941. Cdr. St. J. Taylor and Mr A. L. Lawford of the Admiralty indicated that they preferred the Asdic to be at the forward end of the bridge. Therefore the compass platform was moved aft, leaving 6ft (2m) along the whole front of the bridge, sufficient to accommodate the Asdic on the port side, while on the starboard side there would be a shelter for bridge personnel, and a trunk through which officers on the bridge could view a plotting table below. The roof of this structure was to be sloped forward and a low glass shield was to be built round its after edge 'to afford wind protection for the bridge personnel'.[50]

Early in March, the Director of Anti-Submarine Warfare proposed further changes:

> It is considered that the space allocated on the bridge should be reduced by 2ft in depth namely from 6ft to 4ft when it would measure 8ft x 4ft. This reduction, while leaving ample space for present and future equipment, is necessary in order to bring the operator and components within easy reach of the Control Officer, who will normally be on the raised platform in the centre of the bridge.[51]

It was also suggested that the pelorus, used to take bearings of objects at sea or on shore, should be placed in front of the compass, and this was discussed with Director of Navigation.

In July 1941, the decision to fit Type 271 radar meant much alteration to the after end of the bridge. Since it was impossible at the time to transmit a radar image any distance, the only way the captain or the officer of the watch could refer to it was to have the full outfit, including aerial and cathode-ray tube, situated on the bridge itself. It had to be fitted on the centre line some feet above the bridge deck, in a space which had been planned for a 20-in. 'projector' or searchlight. This was still necessary for hunting U-boats in the dark, among other things, but there was no alternative site high enough. To maintain the full range of coverage it was decided to fit two projectors, one on each side of the radar.

A mock-up of the suggested bridge design was constructed at Fairlie, the anti-submarine research establishment on the Firth of Clyde. By September 1941, trials with this had produced several changes. The Asdic office was moved from port to starboard; the plotting table was placed on the centre line and separated from the Asdic by a sliding door. Curtains and doors were placed round the Asdic office to prevent leakage of light, either in or out. A 'view plot trunk' was no longer needed to look onto the plotter from the bridge and was replaced by eyepieces in the roof of the shelter. The pelorus was moved a foot aft, the depth-charge release gear was moved to starboard, and a signalling table was to be fitted into the port side of the shelter in the space vacated by the plotter.

Meanwhile, a much greater change in layout was under consideration. The 20-mm Oerlikon gun was proving to be the most effective available anti-aircraft weapon in practice, and in July 1941 it was agreed by the Admiralty that 'in every ship in hand for repair or refit, positions should be prepared for the maximum number of Oerlikons, as agreed by DNC, DNO and staff. The staff requirements being that, if possible, every bearing should be covered by several guns.'[52] It was now decided to put Oerlikons instead of 2-pounders on the sides of the bridge of the River-class, and at some stage it was discovered that the 20mm guns, weighing only 150lb (68kg) instead of more than 700lb (318kg) for a 2-pounder, could be raised one deck without adverse effect on stability. This would bring them under greater control from the captain, and it would help to achieve the staff requirement which implied that each gun should have the greatest-possible range of bearing. The actual details of this redesign are not covered in the papers, but the draughtsmen at John Brown's yard were pleased. In August 1941, they wrote to Goodall about the 'Twin screw-corvettes (modified)',

> Many thanks for your letter of the 7th instant regarding alternative positions for the smaller armament on the above vessels. I am glad to know you approve of the higher position with the exchange between the Oerlikons and the pom-poms. This will certainly meet the criticism and I hope will prove to be justified in service.[53]

It was quite an important redesign that created a large space around the bridge proper, which could hold lookouts as well as the Oerlikon guns and their crews, with plenty of space for signallers. The new bridge wings were supported by two pairs of crossed beams on the outside, above the crosses which supported the wings extending from the signal deck. The four crossed beams beside the bridge structure gave the class one of its most obvious recognition features. The sides of the new structure sloped downwards towards the outside to allow the Oerlikons to be fired downwards if necessary, but this tended to make the position rather draughty and wet in bad weather. The wings of the signal deck below were retained, presumably for structural reasons, though they were little used.

The Bridge Deck

The compass platform, occupied by the officer of the watch or the captain, was now a relatively small area in the centre of the bridge deck. It contained a standard Admiralty magnetic compass, with a pelorus just forward for taking bearings on ships or points of land. It had numerous voice pipes to connect with the other parts of the ship. It was enclosed in a low partition made of wood so that it did not interfere with the magnetic compass. During HMS *Spey's* maiden voyage in May 1942, the constructor W. J. Holt reported that the bridge was

> Operationally … a very effective design, the arcs of fire of the Oerlikon guns are very good and the gunners are under the direct control of the captain. The captain can investigate what is going on in the asdic office and view the automatic plot with

the minimum of delay. The signalman and the rating in the Type 271 office are also under complete control of the captain.

But it tended to be rather exposed, especially on the wings:

> The small sort of platform on which the gyrocompass and standard compass are mounted is enclosed within a small wooden screen structure [to prevent deviation]. Standing on this compass platform, a man's head and shoulders are above the glass screen on the front of the bridge and considerably exposed to wind, spray or driving rain. By sitting on a chair inside this wooden screen, a good degree of comfort is obtainable as the screen protects the legs and backbone from a pronounced back draught. ... The low sides to the bridge associated with the Oerlikon platforms result in a very exposed bridge.

The captain paid a price for the compactness of his control position. The main manoeuvring controls of the ship, the wheel and the engine-room telegraphs were situated in the wheelhouse a deck below, and communication was by voice pipe. Holt was shown the problem in the most effective way possible, when the *Spey* put into the Firth of Forth to take on stores. On the way through the anti-submarine boom, the inexperienced helmsman turned the wheel the wrong way and hit one of the trawlers operating the gate. It 'made rather a mess of the stem' according to Holt, and temporary repairs were carried out in Rosyth Dockyard. He concluded:

> At present, all orders which are necessary when manoeuvring the ship are passed by the captain through a voice pipe to the wheelhouse, where all the controls are situated. The captain is at the mercy of whoever happens to be at the wheel, and any mistakes of the helmsman, due to incompetence, are not visible to the captain until too late. There is something to be said in favour of having a wheel and engine-room telegraph on the bridge to ensure that when the ship is in difficult circumstances, major mistakes of helm or in orders to the engine room are obviated.[54]

The other element of control of the ship's movements was achieved by means of the engine-room telegraphs which sent orders to the engine room. The standard merchant-navy type consisted of a quadrant of a circle mounted at the top of a pillar and marked with speeds such as 'slow', 'half speed' and 'full speed' for both astern and reverse, with 'stop' and 'finished with engines' in the centre of the quadrant. A lever and handle could be moved over one of these sectors, which rang a bell and indicated the same sector in the telegraph in the engine room, ordering the engineer of the watch to change the speed or direction of the engine. The exact numbers of revolutions per minute for 'slow' and 'half speed' had been arranged in advance. The frigates had a slightly different version of this: the 'wind on' type rather than the lever type. Changes were made by turning a wheel on the side of the telegraph in either direction, one revolution per step in speed, e.g. and slow speed to half, half to full and so on. Holt felt that the lever type would have been more appropriate, since it was familiar to the RNR officers who commanded most of the frigates.

There were three engine-room telegraphs, all situated in the wheelhouse, so the captain or the officer of the watch had to communicate by voice pipe. There was one for each engine, for it was quite common to have one engine in reverse and the other going forward when manoeuvring. The third was used to indicate revolutions per minute for both engines and was useful when involved, for example, in intricate station-keeping with a convoy. Holt suggested that two RPM telegraphs might be more appropriate, since there were times when differential speed might be useful.

Monsarrat describes the bridge of the *Ettrick*:

> From the bridge, once I had it in a tight grip, command could be fittingly exercised … It was of the authentic destroyer type: open, properly shielded by glass dodgers, with batteries of voice-pipes and telephones lining two sides of it, and a grand array of instruments – Asdic repeater, log, compass, gunnery indicators, and other more discreet products – on the forward end. My chair was centrally placed, high up behind the gyro-compass: there was a solid chart-table close at hand, and a view of the plot (an instrument for recording the ship's movements as she goes along, by means of a track-chart) without walking twenty yards and turning two corners to get it. The flag-deck and signalling platform were separately sited, well clear of the main stream of activity; and there was, to finish off, a covered approach leading up from the sea-cabin.[55]

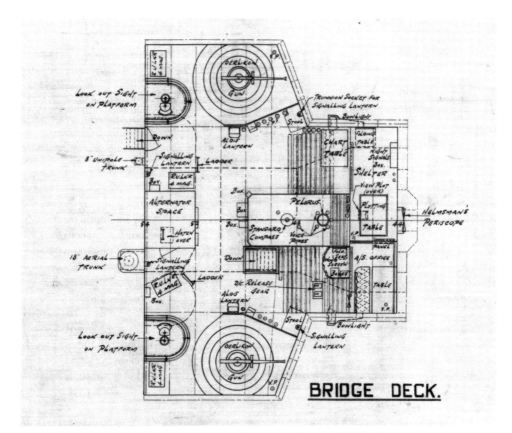

The bridge of HMS *Exe*. Admiralty Collection, Box ADFB130, plan NPN8287. (NMM F5148)

Communications

For normal communication, the bridge was fitted with nine voice pipes, including one
to the captain's cabin for the officer of the watch to call him when needed; one direct to
the engine room and one to the charthouse, where the steering wheel and engine room
telegraphs were operated; the crow's nest for the lookout to make reports; another to the
wireless telegraphy room; one to the signal deck on each side; one to the gyrocompass room
deep in the ship; and the last to the emergency steering position near the stern. There were
six more for use in action to each of the 4-in. guns and Oerlikon guns fore and aft, port
and starboard. All were made of galvanized steel except within ten feet of the compass,
where they were made of copper.[56] To Monsarrat, it was rather too much to handle.

> [The Bridge] was as well equipped and finished as any I had seen, with a system of
> inter-communication between the various parts of the ship which (I could see) was
> going to take some time to master. (It was all right in daylight: it is in the pitch dark
> that one must assess the urgency of a report from the voice-pipe that relays it, to put
> one's hand unerringly on an alarm-gong or a "stand-by" buzzer…[57]

The Wheelhouse and Sea Cabins

The wheelhouse, just below the bridge, was shaped like a pentagon with its longest side
facing forward. The helmsman stood on a small platform in the centre, with a magnetic
compass just in front of him so that he could steer by it as ordered by the officer of the
watch. There were portholes on each side of the wheelhouse, but any forward view would
have been restricted by the gun crew's shelter just ahead. Instead, the helmsman had a
system of mirrors – in effect, a large periscope – which led to a level about halfway up the
bridge shelter, and allowed him to look over the gunner's shelter. It could be useful even
when steering by the compass, for sight of an object ahead often gave an indication that
the ship was swinging rather more quickly than looking at the compass. It might also have
been some help in preventing the helmsman from making a silly mistake, turning the wheel
the wrong way when it would obviously lead to a collision, though clearly it was not enough
when *Spey* entered the Forth in May 1942.

Just aft of the wheelhouse proper was a rectangular space with three compartments.
Forward on the starboard side was a lobby with stairs leading up to the bridge deck and
down to the officers' cabins, wardroom and wireless office. To port was the captain's 'sea
cabin', where he was likely to spend most of his off-duty time on operations, perhaps sleeping
and reading light fiction like the captain of the destroyer *Eskimo* in the Atlantic in 1941.[58]
Accommodation was very simple: just room for a bunk, a chair and tiny desk and a few
cupboards. Aft of that was the chart house, with a large table and equally large drawers to store
the numerous charts of all the areas where the ship might be expected to serve. There was a
bookcase for pilot books and other essential publications, and a bunk so that the navigating
officer could snatch some sleep during periods when his services were less in demand.

Chapter 3: Weapons

Guns

The 4-inch Guns

The 4-inch gun was one of the smallest practicable for anti-ship use. It had only fifty-seven per cent of the range of the 4.7-inch gun as carried by modern destroyers, and its projectile weighted seventy per cent as much. In size it was barely a match for the 105mm (4.1in.) guns carried by some U-boats, and its range was inferior to the 88mm (3.4-in.) guns carried by others. However, a U-boat was not likely to stay and fight on the surface against an escort which might well call on reinforcements, and slight damage to a U-boat was far more serious if it prevented it from submerging. In theory the gun could be used in an anti-aircraft role, but its maximum elevation of about 40 degrees and its low muzzle velocity made it ineffective in this role; it was too slow to track an enemy aircraft at short range, and a River-class ship had no equipment to help aim it at long range.

The 4-in. gun was a quick-firing weapon, defined as one in which the propellant charge was made up in a brass cylinder instead of a consumable silk bag. This could be used with smaller guns in exposed positions; the disadvantage was that the brass cylinder had to be taken out after each shot. Fixed ammunition was used, with the shell inserted into the mouth of the cartridge to form a single unit. Like practically all naval guns of the age, it was loaded by opening the breech and had a rifled barrel for greater accuracy. The Mark XIX on the Mark XXIII mounting, as used by most of the River-class, had a barrel 166.6 inches long, of which 161.84 inches were rifled with a twist of one in thirty. The barrel was moulded in a single piece with the breech ring shrunk on to the end. The breech was opened by sliding the block horizontally across it, using a system of levers and grooves. A plunger and spring at the bottom of the breech ring was pushed down as the cartridge was inserted, and sprung back up to retain until the breech was closed. The block contained the firing pin which was operated by a series of levers to fire the cartridge. The breech itself included the extractor which ejected the spent cartridge after firing.

The aftermost end of the gun barrel was fitted inside a round brass or steel cradle, within which it recoiled. The cradle was fitted with trunnions on each side. These allowed the gun to pivot near its centre of gravity in order to elevate or depress it. When fired, the gun could recoil for a maximum of 18in. (46cm), and this was controlled by a spring within a cylinder above the cradle, which would automatically return the gun to the firing position after each shot.

The cradle was attached by means of the trunnions to the mounting. This was a pyramid-like structure of riveted steel plates which raised the barrel 5ft 6in. (1.7m) above the deck. It included a platform on which the gunlayer and trainer could operate. The mounting in turn was on the upper racer plate, which revolved above the deck with the aid of spring rollers. There were electric cables going into the mounting, and a device prevented it from turning through more than two complete revolutions in order to prevent fouling them. Another device, the training stop, prevented the gun being trained in a dangerous direction. Both the elevating and training mechanisms were operated by hand through a system of gears, as was common in smaller naval guns.

The shield was strong enough to protect the crew from light gunfire and shrapnel. It was rectangular at the rear and angled towards the front and upwards so that it gave protection from the front and overhead. There were apertures on each side to allow the gun sights to be used. Later versions had a wider shield with doors to the apertures, which could be held open by spring clips. When the gun was not in use, a canvas cover was fitted over its rearmost part.

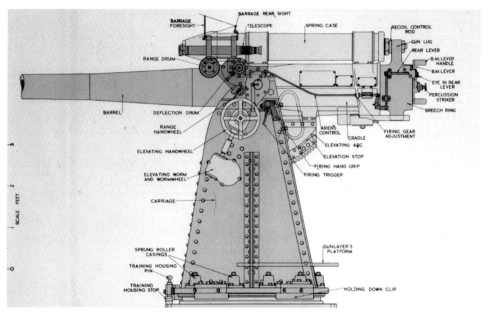

The type of 4-inch gun used on the River-class frigates. (TNA ADM 234/161)

The Gun Crew

The crew of a 4-inch gun consisted of six to seven men, of whom three would be fully trained gunners: the gun captain, the layer and the trainer. As the *Pocket Book* put it, 'The crew does not consist of seven men doing seven jobs but is a team doing one job.' The value of drill was emphasised.

> The gun's crew in action must work with the regularity and accuracy of a well-adjusted machine, since if damage or casualties occur, the crew must display a good knowledge of the gun and its capabilities in order that it shall be kept in action if humanly possible. Since there is no point in firing the gun at all unless it is correctly aimed, this, under all conditions, must be the crew's next consideration.[1]

When on standby, at the second or third degree of readiness for action, all or some members of the gun crew could take refuge in the gun shelters. These were quite large spaces just aft of the forward gun and forward of the after one. The forward one was more than 7ft across and 10ft wide (2.1 x 3m). They were interrupted by ammunition hoists and served as stations for ammunition handling in action. Otherwise they were quite sparse as fitted out, but the crew had the opportunity to make them more comfortable.

Since there was no director to control the firing centrally, each gun was under local firing, which meant that the aiming was done by the gun's own crew. The layer and the aimer were the key men in this process. The trainer sat on the right of the gun and was responsible for the accurate aiming of the gun in all conditions by turning it in the horizontal plane. He looked through a telescope attached to the gun, keeping it constantly fixed on the target. He also had a barrage sight consisting of two concentric rings, for conditions (such as close quarters) when the telescope was inappropriate.

The gunlayer was 'responsible that the gun is accurately aimed for elevation in all conditions'.[2] He sat on the left-hand side of the barrel, and like the trainer he had to elevate the gun; he used the elevating hand-wheel by his right hand. But his duties did not end there. On more sophisticated guns there was another man known as the sightsetter, but on the Mark XIII mounting his duties were taken over by the layer. He had to set the range hand-wheel, placed just in front of him on the distance tube, according to information supplied to him by the radar office. He also had to set the deflection hand-wheel at the left end of the deflection drum, using an estimate of the target's speed, bearing and movement. As was complained in 1941, there were serious difficulties in aiming the gun in certain conditions:

> At night, the fact that the gunlayer has to remove his eye from the telescope in order to set his sights is unacceptable. Not only will there be every chance of the target becoming lost, but the 'night adaptation' of the gunlayer's eye will also suffer after looking at an illuminated dial.[3]

In later versions, known as the Mark XXIII* and XXIII**, a sightsetter was added to the crew and he was given a seat on an enlarged gun platform.

Ammunition

The main ammunition for the 4-in. was the ordinary high-explosive shell, of which 150 were carried per gun. There were also 100 star shells per ship. These were fired high and a flare descended slowly by parachute to illuminate the area at night. There were twenty rounds of shrapnel per gun. This was a group of small balls in a light casing, which could be exploded in mid-air over a land target or in front of an approaching aeroplane. There were twelve rounds of practice ammunition for high-angle or anti-aircraft fire, and ten for low-angle fire. There were ten rounds per ship of blanks for saluting purposes, though these were not usually carried in wartime.

The magazines for the 4-in. guns were sited as low as possible in the ship, partly to lower the centre of gravity, partly to reduce the danger of being hit by enemy fire. The forward magazine was under the forward part of the bridge, where the hull was wide enough to allow it some space, but it was separated from the heat of the boiler room by fuel tanks and the small-arms magazine. The after one was just aft of the engine room. Each could stow rounds in bottle racks, in which they were stowed horizontally, and each magazine had a valve to allow it to be flooded with water in an emergency. Building contractors were to supply locks and keys of the latest approved Admiralty type, which were not to be used for any other compartments in the ship.[4]

There were ready-use lockers beside the two guns, where shells of different types were stored in secure, flameproof boxes. The forward gun had one on the fore edge of the signal deck, where it must have interfered with the original intention to let the gun fire forward at short range. It had two slightly smaller ones aft, just forward of the bridge. The after gun had three lockers, placed forward of it near the gun-crew shelter.

Ammunition was supplied from the magazine by means of electrically driven pulleys known as cruet or bollard hoists. Each could carry four rounds of ammunition at one time. The hoists were operated from the crew shelters and the shells were unloaded there, partly for safety and partly because of the siting of the magazines some distance from the guns.

Anti-Aircraft Guns

The early design of the River-class had included several 2-pounder 'pom-pom' guns; two of the first ships, *Rother* and *Spey*, were actually fitted with these. They were used in four- and eight-barreled mountings in larger ships, but mostly in single mountings in the River-class. The pom-pom fired a 40-mm shell, but its main fault was its low muzzle velocity as the shell left the gun. Some of the early ships – *Deveron, Mourne* and *Towy* – had 6-pounder guns using a design first introduced in 1884.

The 20-mm Oerlikon light anti-aircraft gun was one of the most prolific weapons of the naval war. It was used by most warships and many merchant ships, and formed the main anti-aircraft armament of the River-class. Compared with other British weapons, it was unusually simple. It operated on the blow-back principle, in which the recoil of one round forced back the breech block and allowed the next one to enter the chamber. It had an effective range of about 1000 yards (914.4m), and could fire up to eight rounds per second. About 55,000 were used by the British and Dominion navies during the war. Early River-class ships had four Oerlikons in single mountings, one on each bridge wing and one on each side of the raised gun platform aft of the funnel. More guns were added later, especially for the Pacific war. Sometimes single mountings were replaced with twins or guns in other places such as right in the bows. Space became available in the stern after the removal of minesweeping gear.

The Oerlikon was operated by two men, at least one of whom was a trained anti-aircraft gunner, or AA3; the other was a slightly less skilled loader. The Admiralty would have preferred two AA3s for each gun, but supplies were not always available, and often the loader was a seaman without a gunnery rating. Each single gun was mounted on a conical pedestal so that it could be trained in any direction and elevated up to 80 degrees. At the rear of the gun were two shoulder rests which the gunner placed himself under, and he was held in position by a harness. He would aim the guns by moving the shoulder rests, leaving a hand free to operate the trigger. Aiming was dependent on good footwork, which required constant practice. AA ratings depended on 'eyeshooting' – aiming the guns themselves. They used sights with two or three rings, each representing 100 knots of an aircraft's speed.

> The method of using the sight is very simple. Look at the aircraft, note its direction of flight and estimate its aim-off speed. Point the gun so that the aircraft is flying towards the centre of the sight, with its nose the distance from the centre corresponding to your estimate of its aim-off speed. As the attack develops and the aim-off speed increases, bring the nose of the aircraft further and further out from the centre,

always adjusting direction of aim-off to keep the aircraft flying towards the center of the sight.[5]

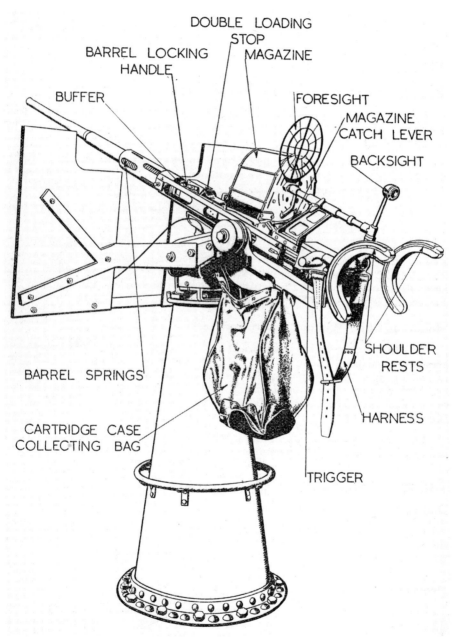

20mm Oerlikon Gun as used by many ships including the River-class. Diagram from *The Gunnery Pocket Book* (Admiralty, 1945) (NMM F5130)

The loader had to deal with the sixty-round circular magazine, six of which were provided with each gun. He would place it in position with the forward end first and swing the rear part down to lock it in position. The first two rounds in each firing were practice rounds without explosives, one to carry away the muzzle cover and the other as a spare. The gun needed some care in operating. Partly loaded magazines needed special tensioning. All rounds had to be greased to ease the loading. The magazine had to be removed daily, the bore sponged out and the breech lubricated.

Other Weapons

The PAC (parachute and cable) rocket was designed before the war as an anti-aircraft device, but was unsuccessful in that role. Its launcher was adapted to fire rockets known as snowflakes to illuminate the area round the convoy in case of a night U-boat attack. Two launchers were fitted on platforms just aft of the bridge on either side. Forty-eight snowflake rockets were carried, plus four PAC projectiles. Each ship also carried a set of signal flares to attract attention or transmit simple messages by day or night – three dozen each of red and green 1-in. flares and twenty-four white ones. Other flares were used to provide target practice for anti-aircraft gunners.

 The original plan called for Lewis light machine guns; these were replaced by Oerlikons, but one was supplied for each of the ship's boats. The ship also had six .303-in. rifles as used by the army for boarding parties and for shooting surfaced mines; four pistols; two signal pistols for the ship and one more for each boat; and a line-throwing gun to project a rope towards another ship or the shore.

The Guns in Action

Captains were given guidance on when to engage U-boats with gunfire. It was to be avoided in low visibility at night, when the U-boat might be unaware that it had been detected. Opening fire too fast could blind the crews of other ships. When the enemy was in a position to fire torpedoes at an important target, however, gunfire could cause him to dive and break off the attack. Tracers were useful in illuminating the target so that other ships could see it.[6]

 Gun action was relatively rare in anti-submarine frigates, compared with the prevalence of depth charge and hedgehog attacks, and it was subject to much less analysis. The Royal Navy's Anti-Submarine Branch naturally paid much attention to the performance of depth charges and hedgehog, but the Gunnery Branch was far more concerned with its weapons on big ships and destroyers.

 HMS *Spey* was in action with a large Italian submarine at around 0700 in the morning of 6 May 1943, in support of Convoy ONS 5. The enemy was sighted by radar at a range of 5200 yards (4.7km), closing rapidly. *Spey* pursued, but the submarine turned round to attempt to escape. The range eventually closed to 800 or 900 yards (732–823m) when the enemy could be seen through the mist in the growing daylight, crossing from starboard to port. The *Spey* altered course to port to get on a collision course and opened at once with its 4-in. gun, pom-pom and Oerlikons. Five 4-in. shots were fired, and at least two of them were observed to hit the enemy – good shooting in the circumstances. Both hit the conning tower, one on its aftermost edge and the other in its centre, putting up 'a good shower of debris.' But the submarine crash-dived when the range had been reduced to 400 yards (366m). Hedgehog and depth-charge attacks were carried out, but the attack failed to destroy the submarine, despite the damage to the conning tower.[7]

Spey was in action again on 18 February 1944. *U-406* was detected and attacked by depth charge, forcing her to surface in the middle of a pattern, 500 yards (457m) astern of the frigate. The port bridge Oerlikon opened fire immediately, followed by all guns that could be brought to bear. The U-boat answered and did some damage to the *Spey's* bridge and radar equipment. However, as the frigate approached, her crew could see 'the shambles that our gunfire had made of her upper works and also could see the number of men in the water to leeward of her, it was obvious she had no more fight in her and all fire was checked'.[8] The U-boat sank despite the *Spey's* efforts to keep it afloat.

The following day, *Spey* had another encounter with a U-boat on the surface. Again, the enemy broke surface after a depth-charge attack, this time at 600 yards (549m) off the bows. It was the starboard bridge Oerlikon which opened fire first. The frigate manoeuvred quickly to prevent the U-boat getting inside her turning circle, getting the submarine on her beam, and the 4-in. guns scored several hits. The submarine's bows reared out of the water then she sank 'saluted with one last direct hit from each 4-in. – one on the pressure hull and one on the bows – before they sank from view'.[9]

The anti-aircraft guns were not particularly successful in their designed role. Direct aircraft attacks were rare in the open Atlantic, though rather more common on Arctic convoys or in the Mediterranean, where the *Rivers* rarely operated. In July 1943, off Portugal, *Swale* and its convoy were attacked by a Focke-Wulf Condor flying at 10,000 to 15,000 feet, well out of range of the Oerlikons. One of the merchant ships was set on fire and lost her steering gear. Officers and men from the *Swale* went on board to fight the fire, and the ship managed to travel 500 miles (805km) to harbour without effective steering. The captain of the *Swale* lamented that the 4-in. guns had no effective aiming system against this. 'Yet again, the accuracy of the Fock-Wulfe [*sic*] high-level bombing is evident. Escorts without an H. A. [high angle] Fire Control are unable to contend with this form of attack.'[10]

In June 1944, while serving as a landing ship (headquarters), the *Nith* was at anchor off the coast of Normandy when she was attacked by a Junkers 88 bomber flying very low. Her Oerlikons opened fire and there were some hits near the cockpit from the starboard forecastle Oerlikon. The Junkers dropped a bomb which landed very near the ship, then the aircraft exploded, showering the *Nith* with debris, which killed nine men and wounded seventeen.[11]

At four in the morning of 9 June 1944, the *Tavy* was escorting a small convoy from Falmouth when it was attacked from starboard by a low-flying Heinkel 177. Sub-Lt. Ian Bailey took charge of the gunfire and Able Seaman George McCullough of Glasgow aimed his Oerlikon. He 'marked the approaching aircraft: and, on the word of command, was in a position to open accurate and instant fire. The guns then, following the direction of his tracer, got the target, and heavily engaged the aircraft.' It was seen to bank, slip sideways and touch the surface of the water, but it recovered and flew on. Some bombs were dropped near the convoy, to no effect. Such action was rare in the Atlantic escort force and Bailey and McCullough were recommended for awards. The authorities were dismissive. 'They all did well in dealing with attack but it was a comparatively light one. This sort of thing was constantly going on in the Med last year without special award.'[12]

In August 1945, the *Nadder* was serving in the East Indies when it was attacked suddenly by several Japanese planes. At first, it was taken by surprise as no hostile aircraft were expected in that area. The first attack, by a twin-engined Dinah bomber at 5000 or 6000ft, met no response from the ship's guns. The second, by another Dinah, was answered by the 4-in. guns at a range of 3000 yards (2743m) and by the 20-mm Oerlikons at 2200 yards (2012m). All guns were under the local control of the officer of the quarters, the normal way of doing things when the ship had no director. There were three more attacks, during which the guns, particularly the twin Oerlikons on the bridge, were fired with great accuracy, but neither side suffered any casualties.[13]

Depth Charges

Principles

Since World War I, the depth charge had been the main means of attacking and destroying submerged submarines. In principle it was quite simple. A charge of explosive was placed inside a container, with a weight to aid its rapid sinking, and a fuse or 'pistol' which could be set to explode at a prescribed depth. Initially the depth charge was simply dropped over the stern of the attacking vessel, and this remained common from 1939–45; but it could also be fired a short distance as part of a pattern of charges which would cover the area where the submarine was expected to be.

Asdic equipment of the time was not completely accurate, and at first there was no easy means of determining the depth of a target or tracking it as the ship passed over it, so it was far better to fire depth charges in groups rather than singly. Nor was it desirable to fire off groups at random – at best, that involved a waste of effort, at worst the explosion of one charge interfere with another. Thus, charges were fired in standard patterns to maximise their effect.

Charges and Patterns

At the beginning of World War II the standard depth charge was the Mark VII, which had been in service since 1935. It had a charge of 290lb (132kg) of amatol and a total weight of 420lb (191kg). Its initial sinking rate was 7ft (2.1m) per second, rising to almost 10ft (3m) per second after it had gathered momentum. Its blast effect on a U-boat with 7/8 in. plating would be lethal at 20ft (6m), and there would be severe shock and psychological damage at 82ft (25m). It was designed to be fired in a pattern of five charges 40ft (12m) apart in a cross shape, with depth settings ranging from 50 to 500ft (15 to 152m). This was adequate for war in the relatively shallow North Sea, but the war in the Atlantic and the greater depth of modern U-boats caused the adoption of the Mark VII Heavy in 1940. The weight of ballast was increased by 140lb (64kg) to make it sink at 16ft (4.8m) per second. It had a new pistol, the Mark IX, in which the 50- and 500-ft orifices were blocked off so that charges could not be set to these depths, and a new one at 140ft (42.6m) was introduced. However, there was often leakage with the blocked 50-ft orifice, which could cause the charge to detonate prematurely, endangering the ship which dropped it.

As mentioned earlier, a depth charge was simply a cylindrical container filled with explosive. It was detonated by the pistol, which could be set to operate at a specific hydrostatic pressure, and therefore at a specific depth of water. This operated a primer, which instantaneously set off a detonator, which then exploded the main charge. Pistols were removable and were kept separately from the charges in the magazines. Once fitted and set, there was a danger that they might go off if the ship sank, greatly increasing injuries to survivors; this happened with the loss of the *Tweed* in January 1944.

The new types of depth charges allowed the introduction of the ten-charge pattern, which was simply the five-charge pattern of Mark VIIs with a layer of Mark VII Heavies under it. In November 1940 it was hoped that 'improvements in attack will be effected by the larger depth-charge patterns now carried by some ships. In this way, the large effect of the unknown factor of depth will, to some extent, be counterbalanced.'[14] Therefore in December the fourteen-charge pattern was introduced. This added four more charges, fired from the quarter throwers at 45 degrees from the movement of the ship. In a shallow pattern, depths were set at 100,140 and 225ft; in a medium pattern, 150, 225 and 300ft, and in a deep pattern, 150,300 and 385ft.

The River-class was designed specifically for the fourteen-charge pattern, with two rails which could drop three charges each, and four throwers on each side which could fire the other eight. One rail was intended to be fitted with heavy charges, the other with light. It was not long, however, before the fourteen-charge pattern came under some criticism. In November 1942, trials were carried out with the destroyer HMS *Skate*, and these showed that the charges interfered with one another, and some failed to explode because of this. Furthermore, the effect of the four extra charges did not justify the weight of the throwers and their equipment on the decks of a ship. The fourteen-charge pattern was abandoned before the majority of the River-class had come into service, and the ten-charge pattern became standard.

Meanwhile, there were some improvements in the charges. At the beginning of the war, they had been filled with amatol: a mixture of TNT and ammonium nitrate. In December 1942, minol was approved for use in depth charges. This had an addition of twenty per cent of aluminium powder which increased the blast effect by fifty per cent; a charge was lethal at 26ft range instead of 20ft (8m instead of 6m). Very large depth charges, such as the Mark X with 2000lb (907kg) of explosive, were not used by the River-class, for, unlike destroyers, they had not the speed to get out of the way of such a huge explosion.

Rails

The simplest method to deploy a depth charge was to drop it over the stern. Most pre-war destroyers and other escorts carried short rails at the stern to hold three depth charges each. This would require quick reloading during an attack, and was far too few for intensive anti-submarine warfare. The Flower-class had two rails each to hold nine charges on top and six more below, ready to be raised after the first ones were expended. Originally it was suggested that the River-class should carry three rails – one each for shallow, medium and deep charges – but this got in the way of the minesweeping equipment, so two were fitted. Again, the long quarterdeck allowed some space, and the racks were able to hold fifteen charges each, enough for five fourteen-charge patterns in conjunction with the throwers.

Each rail had a gauge of 2ft 4¼in., just wide enough to hold the standard depth charge, with a further 5⁹⁄₁₆in. on one side for the fuses. It was made in six sections, of which three were 4ft 8¾in. long, to hold three charges, and the fourth was slightly longer.

The edges of each section were supported by a 12.5lb (5.6kg) flanged plate, and a smaller piece of steel continued upwards to support another rail which helped keep the charges in position. Fittings for portable bars were placed in each of the verticals; these could be put in place to restrain the charges if needed. This part of the rack was angled at 1½ degrees from the horizontal, to allow the charges to roll aft. The last two sections, to hold three charges between them, were angled at 10 degrees to allow a faster roll on the last part. They were fitted with a release mechanism, the Depth Charge Trap Mark I* or Hand Trap Mark I*, which was hydraulically operated and could be controlled either from the bridge or the side of the rack. It was arranged so that a pair of 'toes' would spring up when one charge was released, to prevent the next one falling accidentally. It also incorporated a mechanism to prevent the second charge hitting the toes too hard and causing a jam, but this never worked successfully and was removed by orders of December 1943.

At the inboard, or forward, end of each rack was a removable pair of rails angled at twenty-five degrees for use in reloading. Charges were raised up the ramp by means of 'parbuckling': a standard naval method of lifting roughly cylindrical objects such as barrels. One end of a rope was attached to each rail and the ropes were passed round the depth charge. The other end of each rope was passed through a sheave above the rail, and hauling on them would raise the change, giving a good mechanical advantage and keeping it under control without direct human contact.

Throwers

The frigates were fitted with eight throwers Mark IV, two on each side at angles of approximately 90 degrees to the line of the ship (the beam throwers) and two more at approximately 45 degrees (the quarter throwers). First tested in August 1940, the Mark IV was a version of a machine which had been in use for some years. It could fire a standard depth charge 67 yards (61m), and a heavy charge 51 yards (47m). It differed from earlier models mainly in that the barrel was 4ft (1.2m) longer to give greater range, and the carrier which held the charge was expended in the earlier version, while the Mark IV retained it. A Mark V version was developed slowly during the war, but was not accepted for service until after May 1944. It was smaller and lighter but had a greater range.

One of the biggest problems was reloading the throwers, which often had to be done in action, for, unlike the racks, they could only hold one charge at a time. A depth charge weighing up to 430lb (195kg) had to be lifted into place, often as the ship rolled or pitched fiercely. The answer in 1942 was to construct racks beside each thrower to hold five charges each. A small derrick was fitted on each side and was used to hoist the charge into place. The initial arrangements on the *Rivers* were not entirely satisfactory.

> The depth-charge [DC] racks fitted for loading the throwers are not completely efficient in design. It is a heavy job getting a depth charge from the rack onto the thrower, so that the lifting of one tier in the rack to the next tier above could be improved by extending the rails slightly inboard and curving up the ends so that when the load is taken off the davit with the DC resting on the rails, there is a decreased possibility of the depth charge rolling off the rails due to the motion of the ship.

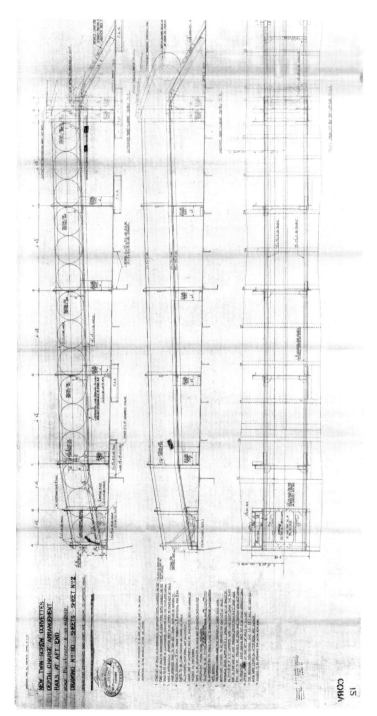

The depth charge rails of the River-class
Lloyd's Collection, Box LLDB0015, plan 257, drawing 110. (NMM F5141)

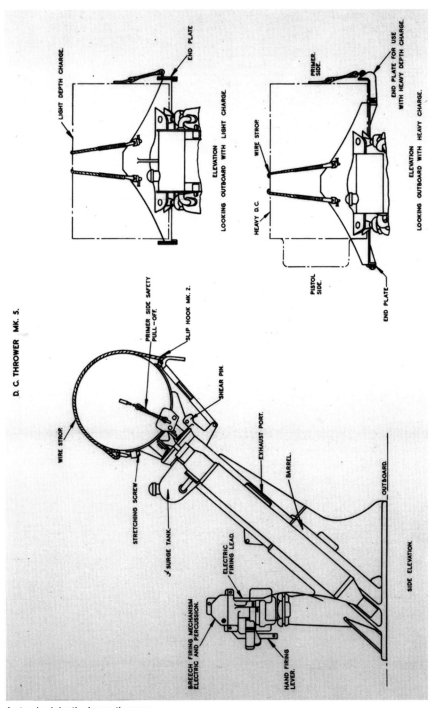

A standard depth charge thrower
(TNA ADM 234/292)

This was never entirely satisfactory, even in the relatively stable River-class, and, after trials in February 1943, a system of parbuckling by means of a hand winch fitted at the top of the rack was adopted.

As the fourteen-charge pattern was discarded, the full complement of throwers was no longer necessary. Two were removed from each side on later ships, to be replaced by a long rail holding extra charges.

Release Mechanisms

A ship had to undertake a depth-charge attack at a reasonable speed if it was not to blow off its own stern. The accurate release of a pattern required very careful timing. In 1940, for example, a fourteen-charge pattern could be timed in one of three ways: using a log which recorded the distance travelled in a few seconds; a Chernikeeff log, which recorded the distance since the last charge was fired; or by a stopwatch. On a signal from the bridge, one normal and one heavy charge were dropped from the rails at the same time as a heavy and a normal charge were fired from a beam thrower on each side. After the ship had travelled 40 yards (37m) or four seconds had passed, similar charges were dropped from the rails and fired by the quarter throwers on each side. After a further 80 yards (73 m) or eight seconds, the last charges were fired.

Shorter response times, and therefore greater accuracy, could sometimes be achieved by controlling the firing from the bridge, and a hydraulic pipe of 3/8-in. bore linked a position on the starboard side of the bridge with the throwers and rails. After 1941, this included a means to fire hydraulically, with push-button buzzers to signal to the depth-charge crews as well as telephonic communication. Later, in order to get more accurate patterns by keeping release times consistent within half a second, the depth-charge clock was developed. It could be operated directly from the Asdic range recorder, or by a button on the bridge.

Magazines

The original depth-charge complement of the *Rivers* was 100, with fifteen on each rail, six stowed beside each thrower, and one on the thrower. This made eighty-six and only left fourteen in the magazine. The magazine was situated aft on the lower deck, among the workshops and storerooms. It was fitted with a system of overhead rails to transport the charges round the magazine, and a trolley was provided to take the charges to their loading positions. The magazine looked very empty with only fourteen charges, and it soon became clear that it could hold more. The total complement was increased to 150, including ninety-eight on the upper deck and fifty-two in the magazine. According to Nicholas Monsarrat, the 'full complement of depth-charges made one blink one's eyes'.[16]

In later ships, the magazine layout changed somewhat. It was extended some way aft, displacing the naval store and the gunner's storeroom, but the spaces on each side were taken up with fuel-oil storage, so the room was now much squarer. In addition to the magazine there was a depth-charge workshop on the upper deck, under the very aftermost part of the signal deck immediately above the magazine. It was fitted with a bench and a sink with a supply of fresh water and was used 'for the preparation, testing and overhaul of depth-charge pistols'.[17]

The River-class was quite fortunate in its depth-charge arrangements. The large forecastle partly created by the need for minesweeping; the long rails; the extra throwers intended for the fourteen-charge pattern; and the large magazine spaces released after minesweeping was abandoned all combined with the experience already gained in the *Flowers* to give the ships an impressive underwater armament. Perhaps this was just as well, as other types of underwater weapons were less successful than hoped, and depth charges remained the principal weapon of the class.

Depth-Charge Attack

The newly commissioned HMS *Spey* had the first success for the River-class on 11 July 1942, while escorting Convoy OS 33 to Freetown. It sighted *U-136* on the surface 18 miles (29km) away and immediately the submarine sent home a sighting report, then dived. In good Asdic conditions, *Spey* carried out two fourteen-charge attacks, with the charges from the traps set at 100 ft (30 m) and those from the throwers at 140 and 225ft (43 and 69 m). After the second attack, half a kapok lifebelt floated to the surface, and a piece of wood, but this evidence was not conclusive, and a hedgehog attack was launched. *Spey* was joined by two more ships and ordered to continue attacking as long as she had contact. The frigate dropped two more patterns of fourteen charges each, while the others launched five separate attacks. The group commander wrote, 'If the object were destruction of U-boats, then the apparent failure – in so far as there is no conclusive evidence – after some handsome chances is pertinently admitted.' But in fact, *U-136* had been destroyed.[18]

Three days later the *Spey* found itself on the attack again. Just before midnight on 13 July, the radar picked up a submarine at a range of 6200 yards (5669m). The ship pursued, and at 1800 yards (1646m) the wake of the U-boat could be seen with glasses. When *Spey* was within 1000 yards (914m) the submarine dived. No Asdic contact was made because the *Spey* was going too fast, but it dropped a five-charge pattern, set to 100ft, as close as possible to the diving position. Speed was then reduced and *Spey* began a sweep. Contact was made, and a fourteen-charge pattern was dropped, though one thrower failed to operate. But the captain had been too impatient and the charges were fired too soon. The anti-submarine officer reported that the U-boat was 'making the most extraordinary noises, whistling effect, rattling effect and a roaring noise. I think she is blowing tanks and is going to surface.' The plotting officer agreed and a five-charge pattern was dropped at 150 ft. Suddenly, a scraping noise was heard all along the port side and the propeller was fouled as the U-boat's jumping wire came into contact. The propeller was cleared by stopping the engine and putting it astern, and three more attacks were made. In all, the *Spey* dropped five patterns in an hour and a quarter, one fourteen-charge and four five-charge, with a minimum of ten minutes between attacks. Ten seconds after her last attack, a mysterious charge exploded close to the ship, causing a shock and slight damage. But she had not sunk the submarine and had only four depth charges left when the sloop *Pelican* arrived to take over the pursuit. The *Monthly Anti-Submarine Report* featured the episode under the heading 'A Three Hour Hunt of a Wily U-Boat'. The submarine escaped and the River-class would not chalk up another success for nine months.[19]

A well-aimed depth-charge attack was devastating to its victim. The crew of *U-536* had been at sea for nearly two months under Rolf Schauenburg, a traditional naval officer who insisted that his men shave and wear regular uniforms. On 20 November 1943, they were part of an attack on convoy SL 139/MKS 30 when *Nene's* depth-charge pattern crashed unexpectedly around them and threw them into confusion.

> It was also so accurate that the crew thought the charges contained a new explosive. The boat went badly down by the stern, though there was apparently no entry of water. The Engineer Officer spent an hour endeavouring to regain trim; when at last he gave up his efforts and reported his failure to the captain, the order to surface was given.[20]

U-536 was the ninth kill in which the River-class participated, and the first for four months. Dropping depth charges could sometimes be dangerous to the attacker. In the early evening of 18 July 1944, the *Cam* was attacking a presumed submarine contact, without calling her crew to action stations. In fact, it was a sunken ammunition ship, which went up with a huge explosion, raising the *Cam* bodily into the air. The surgeon, relaxing in the wardroom was thrown 3 ft into the air and hit his head on a fan above. The cook was in the galley when the stove exploded and he suffered severe burns. The sick-berth attendant was hit in the chest by a spar, but went to tend the injured. One stoker was hit in the abdomen by a 50-lb (22.6-kg) tin and was in inconsiderable pain with intestinal damage. Most of the crew suffered from injuries to their heels, spines and knees because of the shock.

The electrical system failed until the diesel generator could be got into action. Most of the food and drink in the galley was destroyed, so the canteen manager opened his stock. Two other ships came alongside and took off the most seriously wounded, and the surgeon tended the rest in the officers' cabins. Fortunately, the ship was not far offshore and the wounded were landed to hospitals within a few hours. For days the remaining ship's company was dazed, apathetic and in a state of extreme nervousness. When a seaman dropped a bucket of broken crockery, the sudden noise made everyone jump, and one seaman fainted.[21]

Hedgehog

The anti-submarine mortar hedgehog was only added to the River-class armament at a late stage in the construction of the first batch of ships, and its fitting was improvised. This was part of a cut-throat competition between two design teams within the Admiralty to get ready weapons, in circumstances of appalling conservatism, obstruction and office politics.

Only *Rother*, the first ship of the River-class, was not initially fitted with hedgehog. Many corvettes and destroyers were also fitted with hedgehog, but not universally, and the weapon was identified with the *River* class more than any other type of ship.

Description

The hedgehog was designed to fire a projectile which was 38in. (96.5cm) long, of which about 23in. (58.4cm) formed the head, 7in. in diameter. Initially this was filled with 31½lb (14kg) of TNT, but after May 1942, 35lb (15.8kg) of Torpex were carried. The projectile was fitted with a fuse at its forward end, and an arming propeller forward of the head. The after end of the projectile was simply a tube which fitted over the spigot in the mortar. At its upper end was the cartridge of 260 grains of cordite which projected it through the air. The projectile was fitted with tail fins to stabilize it during its short flight. The whole projectile filled with Torpex weighed 63lb (28.5kg), and 144 rounds were issued for each

River class ship, plus twenty-four practice rounds.

The mounting consisted of six rows of 1-in. diameter spigots, each four deep. They were fired in pairs at approximately half-second intervals, and arranged so that they would form a circle 100ft in diameter with the charges 15ft (4.5m) apart if fired dead ahead. The weapon could also be angled to fire up to 20 degrees to either side to compensate for the wind or the ship's head being off course, in which case they would form an elliptical pattern on striking the water. Firing all twenty-four charges at once would cause severe strain on a deck, so they were fired two by two in a ripple pattern with one to one and a half seconds between each firing. If the ship was moving at 8 knots, the pattern would land 230 yards (293m) ahead of it. The range would be longer if the ship was moving faster, though speeds of more than 12 knots were not recommended.

A cross-roll gyro was fitted to stabilise the mounting during firing. This was important because the salvo was fired over ten to sixteen seconds, during which time the ship might roll considerably; it was much less necessary for a gun, which fired instantaneously. An operator used a hand-wheel to keep a pointer lined up on a small gyroscope, keeping the spigots horizontal if required, or at the correct angle if firing to either side was needed. A sloping shield was provided at the after end of the mounting to protect the crew from flying splinters of cartridge during firing, and to keep the electrical equipment as dry as possible.

A cross-roll gyro was fitted to stabilise the mounting during firing. This was important because the salvo was fired over ten to sixteen seconds, during which time the ship might roll considerably; it was much less necessary for a gun, which fired instantaneously. An operator used a hand-wheel to keep a pointer lined up on a small gyroscope, keeping the spigots horizontal if required, or at the correct angle if firing to either side was needed. A sloping shield was provided at the after end of the mounting to protect the crew from flying splinters of cartridge during firing, and to keep the electrical equipment as dry as possible.

Officers were instructed to keep quiet about the new weapon when it was fitted to their ships. If they were pressed into explanation, they were to say it was an anti-aircraft device.[22] The authorities expected a success rate of 50 or 60 percent for the hedgehog in service. It was, in the words of the Monthly Anti-Submarine Report, 'a weapon of precision which requires for success a skill that can only be obtained with adequate training and practice'.[23] Unfortunately, the weapon was rushed into service too quickly, and there was no real provision for any such training.

Hedgehog in Action

Commander Donald Macintyre was delighted when his destroyer *Hesperus* was fitted with hedgehog in 1943, for he 'had long felt the need of a weapon of this sort which would enable us to deliver an attack while still in Asdic contact', though he regretted that a near-miss was literally 'as good as a mile', which was not so with a depth charge. But the first use in action turned out to be a fiasco.

Then Bill Ridley's voice – 'Fire!' It is with a feeling of shame that I have to record that nothing happened! A hasty check with the crew of the Hedgehog revealed what had happened. Unfamiliar with our new weapon, it had not been realised that the Hedgehog bombs, which had a complicated set of safety pins to be removed one by one, would take so long to prepare. With twenty-four bombs to arm, this took some time, and the crew had not had time, between 'contact' and the order to fire, to complete the operation.[24]

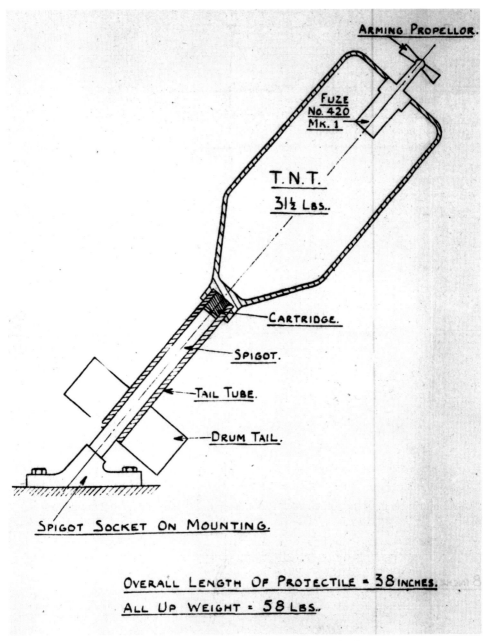

Cross section of a Hedgehog projectile mounted on its Spigot. (TNA ADM 239/612)

Failures like these were common, and there were problems at several levels. The anti-submarine officer of each ship was trained while the weapon was being fitted, but there was no training for the rest of the crew. In the preliminary manual, the duty of operating the weapon was allocated to the crew of the forward 4-in. gun, though gunnery branch ratings traditionally despised other callings within the Navy. Often, fire-control equipment was not fitted on many ships due to a shortage. There was no standard drill until November 1943, and no proper operating manual was issued until December 1944 – until then, operators had to make do with a 'very inadequate' handbook of January 1942, which 'contained very little information concerning the fire-control gear, and a most inadequate drill'.[25] A supplementary handbook was issued in July 1942, dealing mostly with fire control. In January 1944, it was complained that 'few of the responsible torpedo ratings knew of the existence of the Hedgehog Handbook'.[26]

An extra leading torpedoman was appointed to each ship for maintenance of the hedgehog, but the loading and firing was to be done by the crew of the forward 4-in. gun. This probably did not help morale, as the gunnery branch tended to regard itself as superior and to undervalue any but gunnery work. When on the hedgehog, the gunlayer was responsible for firing, and the breechworker, trayworker and projectile supply number for loading. The trainer operated the hand-wheel, the cartridge supply number operated the communications and assisted with the loading, while the sightsetter worked at the bearing transmitter on the bridge, giving the orders regarding the angle at which the spigots were to be set.

Both aiming and firing were quite complex. The moment to fire was decided by the anti-submarine control officer on the bridge, using a formula involving fixed factors such as the position of the Asdic dome and the mounting on board ship, the expected underwater advance of the projectiles after leaving the surface, and the times of flight through the air (average eight seconds) and the water. These could be set into the recorder in the Asdic, but variables such as the speed of the ship, and the speed and relative bearing of the target also had to be taken into account for each attack. A wind of 20 miles (32km) per hour would deflect the projectiles by only about 3 yards (2.7m), but more than that had to be taken into account. The weapon could be fired directly ahead in a stern chase, but it worked best when the submarine was crossing, with the target at an angle of between 45 and 135 degrees.

Before the ship got into a firing position, the crew on the forecastle had to prepare the hedgehog. Three states of readiness were prescribed by an order of May 1943, after some experience of the weapon in action. In cruising stations it was a five-minute notice for action. The crew was not closed up, the safety pins were in, the fuse caps on, the mount loaded and uncovered and the control gear and safety switch were off. When called to anti-submarine action, the roll-corrector took his station on the hedgehog but the rest of the crew went to the 4-in. gun until needed. The fuse caps were taken off but the safety pins remained in. If called to immediate action the crew came down from the gun. They took out the safety pin but the safety switch remained off until the order 'salvoes' was given at 350 yards (320m) from the target. Then, on hearing a buzzer signal from the bridge, the weapon would be fired – but that, too, was complex.

> The rounds are fired by switching the ON and OFF switch to ON, setting the selector knob so that READY appears on indicator, and then pressing the firing handle in, and turning it as fast as possible away from you (clockwise).[27]

Another problem was the unreliability of the ammunition. When the destroyer *Keppel* fired a salvo in March 1942, five of the charges misfired and one landed on the ship's forecastle. The remainder was very irregular and no explosions were heard. This was put down to 'damp impulse charges and to jamming down of certain spring-loaded firing pins in the spigots'.[28] It was noted by September 1942 that some projectiles exploded soon after hitting the water. To test this, all hedgehog-fitted ships were ordered to fire a salvo using the oldest ammunition on board, in depths of not less than 250 fathoms, in an area where it was clear there was no target. They were issued with pictures showing how explosions at 10ft, 30ft and 40ft should look.[29]

Hedgehog was difficult to reload. A charge of 63lb (29kg) was not easy to handle, and it had to be manhandled into position with some accuracy to fit on its spigot; this often had to be done on a pitching deck. *Tavy* was able to carry out five attacks in just over an hour and a half while sinking *U-390* in July 1944, and this was regarded with pride.[30]

Hedgehog did not have the psychological impact of a depth-charge attack. A pattern of ten depth charges would lead to the explosion of 2900lb (1315kg) of amatol, whether the submarine was destroyed or not. At most, a hedgehog attack would explode two or three charges of 35lb (16kg) each – and then only if it was successful. The huge bangs and the boiling seas around depth charges had an important moral effect on the crews of the escort vessels, and just as much on the crews of the merchant ships nearby. Near-misses could do much structural damage to a U-boat and terrify the crew, perhaps forcing them into surrender, whereas a miss by hedgehog went unnoticed by both sides.

As a result of these factors, hedgehog was little used during its early months in service. Until November 1942, only sixteen salvoes had been fired against confirmed U-boat targets, with no apparent success. Then the corvette *Lotus* used its hedgehog after all its depth charges had been expended, and sank *U-605* off Algiers. The Director of Anti-Submarine Warfare issued instructions that hedgehog was to be used in preference to other weapons in certain conditions. This was partly caused by fear of the German naval acoustic torpedo, or GNAT. Ships could avoid it by attacking at 8 knots or less, but at such a low speed, the ship was in danger of being blown up by its own depth charges. This was not a problem with the hedgehog. Captain Bob Whinney of the destroyer *Wanderer* reluctantly obeyed his orders to use hedgehog in January 1944, although he 'disliked this weapon and distrusted it' after ammunition failures. When the attack produced an indecisive result, he commented, 'Bloody useless weapon. Theory no damn good.'[31]

The matter came before the Anti-U-boat Committee of the War Cabinet on 24 November, chaired by the Prime Minister. It was reported that 'Owing to the speed with which this weapon was got to sea, it is not yet clear of its teething troubles…' Captains had been told that 'even with the present incidence of unaccounted explosions of some rounds of the salvo, the probability of success in the Hedgehog is very much greater than that of depth charges dropped astern.'[32]

On 12 May 1943, HMS *Lagan* took part in an action on a U-boat that had already been attacked by aircraft from the escort carrier *Biter*. The destroyer *Broadway* joined the hunt with an unsuccessful hedgehog attack. *Lagan* fired its hedgehog four times after that, but it was *Broadway's* second hedgehog salvo which destroyed *U-89*.[33] The attack was described in the *Monthly Anti-Submarine Report* under the heading, 'Some Recent Successful Hedgehog Attacks'.

Yet the hedgehog was actually slightly more successful than was recognised, and perhaps the method of assessing claims acted against it. On 17 May 1943, HMS *Swale* attacked U-640 while escorting Convoy ONS 7, firing two hedgehog salvoes between depth-charge patterns. There were two quick explosions during the second salvo, apparently premature, and a third thirty-three seconds after firing. In view of the lack of firm evidence, this was assessed as a U-boat 'probably sunk', but after the war it was confirmed as a kill.[34]

Between April and July 1943, there were four more recognised successful attacks out of a total of seventy-three hedgehog attacks, of which forty-seven were definitely on U-boats. This was apparently a success rate of less than seven per cent. Three failures were caused by attacking in seas that were too rough; eight more were due to losing contact at over 350 yards (320m); and another eight to technical failures, including cases where four or more bombs misfired. When the conditions were suitable and there was no technical failure, the success rate was eighteen per cent, still well below expectations.[35] The failure rate reduced confidence in the weapon still further. In the second half of 1943, a total of fifty-three salvoes were fired to destroy four U-boats, a kill rate of 7½ per cent – only slightly better than the depth-charge rate of 5.3 per cent.[36]

Another difficulty, relating particularly to the River-class, was the position in which the hedgehog was fitted. Clearly, as an ahead-throwing weapon it had to go on the forward part of the ship rather than the spacious quarterdeck. By the time it was first planned for the River-class in March 1942, the most obvious place on the signal deck had already been taken up by the 4-in. gun. It was impossible to move this without considerable disruption, as it would have meant moving the magazine and ammunition hoist as well. Instead, the hedgehog was put on the only available place: the forecastle. It was placed behind a breakwater, and the designers had done their best to keep water off that area by flaring the hull, but it could never expect to be dry in the waters of the North Atlantic. The hedgehog, unlike the 4-in. gun, relied on a great deal of electricity and it was quite a delicate machine.

There were strong complaints about this in March 1943. As the Director of Torpedoes and Mining pointed out,

> The anti-submarine weapons must be considered the primary armament of Escort Vessels. Of these the Hedgehog, providing a probability figure of some sixty per cent, is by far the most effective, yet in a large number of our escorts, the mounting has had to be placed on the forecastle, as bad a position as one could choose for a weapon of this type, not only from the point of view of maintaining it, but also from the difficulty of manning any armament in an exposed position of an Escort in the North Atlantic.[37]

It was proposed to fit another version, the 'split' hedgehog. This had two separate launchers – one on each side of the ship. But the only available position was on the signal deck on either side of the gun, and that would restrict the gun in its field of fire to 90 degrees on each side. Only the *Monnow* was fitted in this way.

The Londonderry Trials

Early in 1944, a small team was set up at Londonderry to carry out an analysis of hedgehog attacks. Ships between convoys were sent there for a few days to be tested. Three anonymous River-class ships took part. A 'clockwork mouse' submarine was employed as a target, and each ship carried out three attacks. The first one, straight from the working-up base at Tobermory, had its equipment in good condition, though the firing buzzer was not wired up to the recorder firing bar of the Asdic as it should have been, and there was trouble with the electrical system.

The three Asdic operators were naturally inexperienced. They had only been together for a week, and had used their equipment only three times in practice. Their first attack was a complete failure as the Asdic operators 'wandered into wake', confusing the water disturbance caused by the submarine with the real thing. The range was in error by 25ft (7.6m) and the bearing by 85ft (30m). The second attack was more successful. The submarine was on the edge of the ellipse, and one projectile hit its conning tower, though the operator had used too much deflection and the range was 20ft (6m) short. The third attack was marginal. The bearing deflector was set at too low a value, too much deflection was allowed, and the operator fired late. In theory, the edge of the pattern should have touched the submarine, but in fact no hit was recorded.

The second ship came from Escort Group B7, based at Londonderry. The hedgehog was in excellent mechanical condition and good electrical state, and the Asdic team was quite experienced. Its leader, the higher submarine detector (HSD), had been working on Asdic for three years and the two submarine detectors (SDs) for fifteen months and a year, respectively; they had been together for about three months. Their first attack was not perfect; too much deflection was used and the range was 25ft short, but a hit was achieved in the after part of the submarine. The second was marginal. The edge of the pattern should have touched the submarine, but no hit was reported. The traces from the Asdic were very good, and there was disappointment that a relatively experienced crew should have done so poorly in the circumstances. The third attack was a complete failure, because the HSD became confused by some wake echoes just before firing; the projectiles were 65ft (19.8m) off the correct bearing.

The next ship, from Escort Group B6 at Liverpool, was also quite experienced – five years for the HSD, two years and fourteen months, respectively, for the SDs. The Asdic was in good condition, though the recorder was not linked up and the crew did not know how to operate it. Even worse, the hedgehog was 'nearly completely seized up. Flexible drive operating rod sheared. Roll unit connected wrong way round.'[37] Like many other ships in Western Approaches command, this crew had become completely cynical about the value of the hedgehog. It is no surprise that all three attacks failed. The last one was the worst of all. 'Pattern fell away to the right. This was due to H/H receiver flexible drive breaking during the attack. This was due to lack of maintenance.'[38]

More generally, it was noted that the drill was at fault.

> Ships varied considerably in their drill, but the work of the hedgehog team was not in the least helped by the orders from the bridge being sent either too early, too late, or not at all, or misleading and redundant. In some cases the order 'Salvoes' was sent so early that the firing number of the hedgehog crew, who should thenceforth be instantly ready to fire, put his hands in his pockets to keep them warm. The firing delay which ensued is obvious.[39]

The team concluded that some ships used hedgehog efficiently, others did not. Thirty-six ships carried out ninety-five attacks, but thirty-seven of the attacks scored no hits at all, while the remaining twenty-one carried out fifty-six attacks with twenty-eight hits: a success rate of fifty per cent, which lived up to expectations. Better training and improvements in procedure were suggested, and courses were set up at the main bases. There was special emphasis on maintenance; a driller with a realistic rolling movement was installed ashore and linked with a mobile training unit so that proper control orders could be practised; and commanding officers were given lectures on the use of the weapon. Each ship carried out at least two practice attacks. 'The results were remarkable. Within a very short time, the percentage of hits obtained at sea during exercises rose from ten per cent to fifty per cent.'[40]

The success rate in operations also began to improve. There were thirty-seven attacks in the second half of 1944, of which thirteen were successful, or thirty-seven per cent. *U-390*, for example, was probably sunk by *Tavy's* first hedgehog attack on 5 July, though five more hedgehog attacks were made by the ship and its consort just in case. No other weapons were used during the engagement.[41] On 12 August, *Findhorn* attacked with hedgehog despite some long-standing technical difficulties, and hit *U-198* with its first pattern. Another attack was made without result, but it was considered that the first salvo had already destroyed the U-boat, and this was confirmed after the war. *Findhorn's* captain was recommended for an award, as was Leading Seaman Earnest Vaughan, who was 'a keen type' who had 'taken great interest in his job as Hedgehog trainer, and by his careful operation contributed to the success of the attack'.[42]

By this time, the hedgehog's rival, the squid, was in service and was proving very successful. It consisted of a three-barrelled mortar firing depth charges rather than contact charges. The squid had been considered as a possible armament for the *Rivers*, and a drawing was produced in July 1942 showing twin mountings on the forecastle deck, but this was never pursued. Nor were they fitted retrospectively, for the new ones were reserved for the ships of the Loch-and Castle-classes. Learning from the mistakes made with the hedgehog and exploiting the time which had not been available during the crisis of the Atlantic War in 1942–43, the squid was fully tested before entering service, and crews were well trained. This gave them a very high success rate in action. During the last months of the European war twenty-one attacks were made with twin squids, with a success rate of forty per cent.

It was not the weapons that made the River-class successful, but the good design of the hull and sensors, asdic and radar, which were the best available at the time.

Minesweeping Equipment

The River-class ships were designed so that they could double up as fleet minesweepers when required. Unlike the much smaller coastal or ocean minesweepers, fleet sweepers needed the speed, range and seaworthiness to cross oceans with the main fleets. They were not likely to be needed as sweepers in the deep water of an ocean passage, but might use their specialised skills in the shallower waters close to an enemy coast. It had long been common to combine the roles of anti-submarine warfare and minesweeping. It had been done with the original Flower-class in World War I, and with most of the interwar sloop designs. Both roles needed medium-sized vessels with moderately high speed, good endurance, and a low quarterdeck aft, from which either depth charges or minesweeping gear could be handled. But anti-submarine vessels preferred a slightly deeper hull to make the Asdic more effective, while minesweepers were best with the hull as shallow as possible to allow them to operate closer inshore. The River-class ships were about 2ft (0.6m) deeper than their minesweeping counterparts, the Algerine-class.

Contact Mines

Three different types of minesweeping had to be considered by 1940. The traditional contact mine had been in use in one form or another since the Crimean War in the 1850s. The standard type of World War II, used with lethal effect by the Germans and others, was attached to an iron sinker which descended to the bottom of the sea. A length of wire was let out – just enough to let the mine float under the surface of the water. The mine itself had several horns filled with acid. On contact with a ship, one of them would break and cause the mine to explode.

The standard method of sweeping, evolved in World War I, was to tow a float known as an oropesa sweep, after the trawler which first used it. HMS *Exe*, for example, had two of these, stowed on the upper deck on each quarter. Each was of a streamlined shape with a rudder set to keep it some distance from the ship which was towing it. Also provided were 'otters' (towing devices that displaced themselves sideways to a predetermined distance) and kites, looking rather like giant letter racks. These were also attached to the cable, and the kites would keep the oropesa sweep at the right depth underwater while the otters displaced it from the ship's track to spread the sweep. They, too, were stowed on the quarters. The cable was fitted with wire cutters at intervals. When in use, it would catch the wire of a mine and pull it towards one of the cutters, which would release it. The mine would float to the surface where it could be destroyed by gunfire.

Early River-class ships were fitted with a large steam-driven geared winch in the centre of the quarterdeck, placed on a teak bed 4 in. thick. Operators could work the steam valve and the brake and had a clear view astern of the operations going on. The ships also had large davits on the quarters for hoisting the floats overboard and recovering the float. Danbuoys were provided and dropped into the water to mark the position of swept channels, each with a pole and flag high above the water.

Influence Mines

The magnetic mine was considered a vital weapon in the attack on British shipping until ways were found to neutralise it. As its name implies, it did not have to touch its target directly but was set off by the ship's magnetic field. It could only be used in relatively shallow water, but it could be dropped by aircraft as well as by ships and submarines.

The first countermeasure was to neutralise the magnetic field of one's own ships by a process known as degaussing. This was obviously most important in a minesweeper, which would have to go close to the mine before destroying it. Ordinary ships could simply be passed over a degaussing range to provide temporary safety, but the early River-class had a series of cables fitted all round the interior of the hull. When current was passed through these, the magnetic field would be neutralised.

For the actual sweeping of magnetic mines, the more common system of oropesa sweeps was useless, as the mines lay on the bottom of the sea. The usual technique was to detonate them by creating an intense magnetic field some way aft of the ship so that the explosion would be harmless. The gear for this, code-named LL, consisted of 575 yards (526m) of electric cable and a shorter, 225-yard (206-m) cable, both towed astern. Ships would operate in pairs in line abreast. A strong current was passed between them at timed intervals and created the magnetic field, exploding any mine within the corresponding rectangle. This required even more equipment than the conventional minesweeping gear. Two large diesel generators were provided on the lower deck under the quarterdeck so that sweeping could be done on both sides at once. A large cable reel was fitted on the quarterdeck just forward of the steam winch, capable of holding 750 yards (686m) of cable, 3.58 in. in diameter and weighing about 4 tons.

River-class frigates were also capable of carrying SA equipment, which was used to deal with acoustic mines, setting them off by a sound similar to that of a ship. The specification merely demanded of the builders that 'Arrangements are to be made to fit SA gear, particulars of which will be supplied on application to the Admiralty'[43]. It is not clear how many were actually fitted.

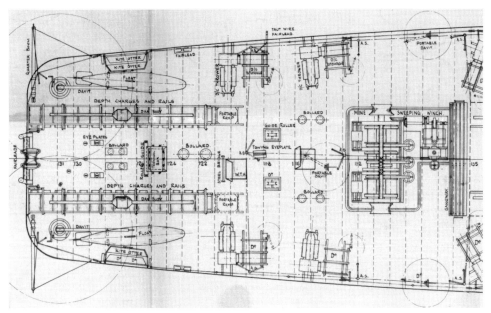

The arrangement of the minesweeping gear on HMS *Exe*. Admiralty Collection, Box ADFB130, plan NPN8286. (NMM F5149)

The End of the Minesweeping Role

As it turned out, none of the *Rivers'* minesweeping gear was used in practice. Though the first twenty-three ships were fitted with the equipment, as they entered service the minesweeping position began to improve with the building of the Bangor-and Algerine-classes. Furthermore, the *Rivers*, which were larger and deeper, were in great demand as ocean escorts and could not be spared. Five of the class were set aside for minesweeping operations late in 1942 in preparation for Operation Torch, the invasion of North Africa. They formed the Tenth Minesweeping Flotilla and did some training in the Firth of Clyde, but it remained a shadow organisation and was never used as such. As John Palmer, anti-submarine control officer of the *Exe*, recalled, 'Fortunately we never had to do it [minesweeping]. I remember the exercise which I fear made it pretty clear that we would have been in danger of making a mess of it.'[44] It was commented,

> The frigates appear to be much too valuable as escorts to be available for minesweeping and the minesweeping-fitted vessels are now so scattered that it might require a month to assemble eight ships together and a further month would be required for minesweeper work up and flotilla training.[45]

The situation was considered at an Admiralty meeting in March 1943. The Director of Dockyards pointed out that they were not likely to be spared for minesweeping because of their other duties, and that the extra space for the minesweeping equipment was worth up to 2000 miles (3218km) of extra range. The Director of Minesweeping proposed the removal of all LL and SA gear, as it could be used elsewhere. But seventeen ships had been completed by that time. Six more would be completed in the next three months. It was too late to make any changes in layout by this time or to add extra fuel tanks, but they would be sent out without the gear fitted. Only the last ship of the first twenty-four was completed without any provision for minesweeping at all. Finally, in April 1944, the remaining eighteen ships were ordered to land any remaining equipment. It had still never been used in action. But the original plan for minesweeping had one fortunate effect: it meant that the *Rivers* had more room for extra fuel and accommodation, which became urgently needed as the range of the submarine war increased.

The GNAT and the Foxer

In September 1943, the Germans first used their homing torpedo, the T5, *Zaunkönig* or 'wren', known as the German Naval Acoustic Torpedo or GNAT to the British. Unlike other torpedoes which were usually aimed at the merchant ships of a convoy, the GNAT was more effective against escorts. Its target needed a speed of at least 10 knots, which was faster than most merchant ships. Its own speed was about 25 knots so it could only catch a ship doing 18 knots or less. Destroyers, therefore, were fast enough to escape. The River-class was particularly vulnerable to this, and the GNAT's first success was against HMS *Lagan* in September 1943, when it was hit in the stern.

> Bulkhead at 100 station is holding, and structure is generally still present, but badly damaged from approximately 100 and the cut-up at 118. Abaft 118 everything is missing – this portion included the rudder and shaft brackets.… There is extremely little damage forward of 100 bulkhead, and from the statements of the ship's officers, it appears that the shock of the explosion was very slight…[46]

However, the ship was not sunk as the U-boat believed. It was towed home, though never repaired. The first of the River-class to be sunk was the *Itchen* a few days later. Just before midnight on the 22 September, it was chasing a U-boat via searchlight when other escorts observed a largetongue of flame from the frigate amidships as it broke in two and sank. It was carrying survivors from two other ships' companies, but only three from the combined crews were saved.

The Admiralty had been predicting the acoustic torpedo for some time, and had the answer ready. 'Foxer' was a noise-making device, based on ones already used against acoustic mines, which could be towed behind the ship as a decoy. It was quite heavy and consisted of two parallel steel pipes in a frame, arranged so that they would clang together when towed at a suitable speed, though it could not be used at more than 14 knots. Two were normally streamed at once, so that if the torpedo missed one it would almost certainly hit the other rather than going onto the ship's propeller. It was effective enough in its job, but it had several disadvantages. It was difficult to handle, and any residual minesweeping gear must have been useful in this respect. It greatly reduced the speed and manoeuvrability of the ship towing it.

It was far noisier than a real ship, from ten to a hundred times, according to the U-boat captains, and this might actually attract U-boats to the vicinity of a convoy while blocking out the escorts' asdics. The Canadians developed single noise-makers which were much easier to use, but British experiments – for example, with devices that could be launched by the hedgehog's spigot mortars – were too late to enter service.

Chapter 4: Sensors

Asdic

Principles

Asdic (later known as sonar) was the most important detecting device in anti-submarine warfare. It was based on the principle that sound travels at about 1500m (1640 yards) per second in water – faster than in air – and it is much easier to control and direct. A sound could be sent out on a fairly precise direction and its echo would give a good indication of both the distance and direction of a target. It was essentially an active device, in that it sent out signals and waited for a reply; a passive device such as the hydrophone of World War I, relied entirely on noises made by the enemy's crew, engines, movements or propellers.

At the centre of Asdic operation was the oscillator or transducer. This was a heavy disc about 2ft in diameter containing layers of quartz crystal. A current of high voltage was passed through it at between 14 and 24 kilohertz to produce a cigar-shaped sound wave with an average range of about 2500 yards (2286m). If the echo hit anything solid – rock, wreck, fish, whale or submarine – an echo would be sent back. The sound wave and its echo could be heard by the Asdic crew, and the distance and bearing of the echo could be measured.

The so-called Asdic 'dome', where the transducer was situated, was in fact a pod with vertical sides. It was streamlined so that any water disturbance that might interfere with the asdic signal was minimized. The River-class used the Type 15 dome with a frame made out of a material known as 'alpex' and a 'staybrite' steel skin designed to reduce drag. It could be retracted within the hull at speeds of over 21 knots, although this was not necessary in the River-class, which could only do 20 knots.

Possibly this model of dome was used so that the ship could have a shallow draught in its projected minesweeping role, for the ship's depth could be reduced by 4ft 5⅜in. (1.4m) by raising the dome. It was wide enough to allow the transducer to rotate, and rather longer than that because of its streamlining. It was situated under the hull with its centre about 36 feet (11m) from the bow, about as far forward as possible due to the narrowing of the hull. Its forward position and its location with its centre about 3ft (0.9m) under the hull kept it free from the effects of the ship's own wash. Above it was the space to which it could be retracted, containing the motors to raise and rotate it. Above that, on the lower deck, was a compartment holding the asdic instruments. The signals from the Asdic were transmitted to a compartment known variously as the asdic hut, office or cabinet, far above in the bridge.

Features of Type 144

The Type 144 Asdic, introduced in 1941 after trials in HMS *Kingfisher*, used all the standard features as developed over the previous twenty-five years. The method of sending and receiving the sound was not unusual, but the device brought in two new features. The first was automatic training. In earlier models, the operator had turned a large wheel to rotate the transducer. In the Type 144, this was done automatically through 5-degree steps, with a ping sent out on each. The operator merely had to reset the instrument at the end of each sweep and the process would begin again.

The second feature was the bearing recorder. Previous sets had been fitted with a range recorder, which gave a visual indication of how far the target was from the ship, but the bearing recorder gave extra information to the operator. Like the range recorder it consisted of a number of styli over slow-moving pieces of impregnated paper. When an echo was received, the operator pressed a button to make a mark on the paper. During trials in 1942,

> The bearing recorder was found to be of the greatest assistance in keeping contact with a target. The plot will show at once if the target has a high rate of change of bearing, and in such a case the oscillator is trained so that the Bearing Recorder stylus is moves 10-20 degrees off the target and in the direction in which the target is moving. The oscillator is then allowed to step back to meet the target and, if the plot again shows that the target is still changing bearing rapidly, the process is repeated.[1]

Typically, the range recorder was marked with dots which formed a kind of funnel shape as the ship got nearer the target. It often showed a curve as the range closed and the target moved across the path of the ship. The bearing recorder also had settings for the various factors, such as the speed of the ship and the sinking time of the projectiles, which had to be taken into account in a hedgehog attack.

The Asdic Office

The Asdic office on a River-class frigate was situated just forward of the bridge on the starboard side. It was 7ft wide and 4ft 4in. (2.1 x 1.3m) deep, giving just enough room for three operators. It took up about two-fifths of the width of the bridge, with the plotting table on the other side. Within the office, the table was situated to starboard, taking up about two-thirds of the width. On one side of it was the range recorder, with various controls above and a radiator below for heating. The bearing recorder was at the other end of the table, with the Asdic training control between the two. Seats for two operators were placed opposite the instruments. The area on the other side of the office was vacant, except for a junction box on the bulkhead. It was reserved for new depth-determining Asdic as soon as that became available, and provided room for a third operator to sit during an attack.

Searching

The escorts of a convoy were arranged as far as possible to cover likely areas of attack. By the time the *Rivers* came into service, it was usually possible to provide a sufficient number of escorts to give reasonable cover, though this could be reduced by temporary shortages or ships being detached to pursue U-boats or rescue survivors, as happened disastrously with Convoy HX 229 in March 1943. Asdic was most important in daytime, as U-boats were unlikely to attack on the surface. Each escort swept ahead, about 80 degrees on each side, as a submerged U-boat was slow and was unable to pursue from behind. Asdic had a range of about 2000 yards (1829m) in average conditions, and the warships might be up to 3000 yards (2743m) apart in a convoy with eight escorts, so it was difficult, but not impossible, for a U-boat to penetrate the screen.

At night, surface attack was far more likely, and anti-submarine officers had to decide whether to use the Asdic passively, with its transmitter switched off, listening for the noises made by an attacker. This was far more likely to detect a U-boat on the surface, though it was agreed that in these circumstances radar would be likely to detect it first.

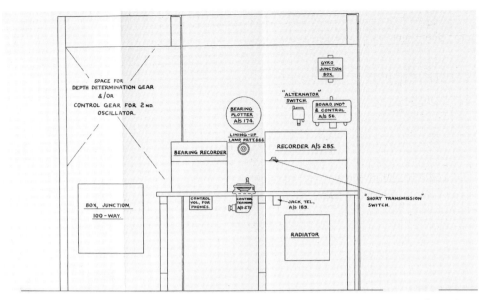

The office for a Type 144 Asdic set on the bridge of a corvette or frigate. Diagram from *Monthly Anti-Submarine Report*, July 1942. (NMM F5423)

During normal escort duties the Asdic was usually manned by a single operator in half-hour spells, with another one not far away on the bridge, resting between spells and ready to close up if a likely echo was detected. Officers worried about the concentration levels of operators on long voyages, and attempted to maintain their interest in their work. One way was to involve them in the tactical situation, emphasising the importance of keeping a good watch. Another was to interest them in the non-sub echoes they found, thinking about the underwater world of fish and whales. They recognised that there was a difference between the 'aural fatigue' caused by long watches on the Asdic (though that was not a great problem on frigates, which had an adequate supply of operators) and the 'physical tiredness and boredom induced by long periods at sea'. It was also suggested that 'all ships should keep their loudspeakers permanently switched on. This gives more people a chance of hearing an echo and certainly enables the officer of the watch to keep more in touch with his operators' performance.'[2]

Sometimes officers could be excited by the noises they heard from the sea, even during a great convoy battle like ONS 5, when the escort passed through 'the Western Ocean Whales Spring Mating Ground' in May 1943:

Numerous fish echoes of exceptional clarity were obtained, and frequently the recorder markings would show a pair of fish [*sic*] coming together and separating. Echoes of every varying amplitude on the R.D.F. scan gave evidence of the great beasts thrashing on the surface in amorous ecstasy. Before the situation was appreciated, J.E.D. interrupted one romance with a ten-charge Minol pattern. I myself have witnessed a pair of whales once performing the procreative act. It is a rare and impressive sight, but I can only conclude that it was the illusion of privacy fostered by the fog coupled with the unwonted spring heat that gave rise to the surely unparalleled orgy on this occasion.

It was suggested that BBC radio's *Brains Trust* discussion programme might be interested in the phenomenon.[3]

Identification of Echoes

On hearing an echo, the first task of the operator was to classify it as 'submarine' or no-sub' – which might be a movement in the water caused by the tide or an enemy decoy, a rock, a wrecked ship, a mass of debris, a school of fish or a whale. The size of an echo for a given range was a key factor in determining this, relying largely on experience. The operator could also use the 'Doppler effect'. If the target was moving towards the ship, the echo would be slightly higher-pitched than the original transmission, in the same way as the pitch of a train whistle changes as it passes through a station. Conversely, if the target was moving away, then the echo would be lower-pitched. This could give the operator some indication if the target was moving through the water at a likely speed for a submarine, though of course he had to take into account the ship's own movements, and it was no use against a stationary submarine.

Another device was the hydrophone effect, or HE. Apart from its active role in sending out sounds, the asdic could detect sound in the water on a particular bearing. This could be very useful in assessing the noise made by a target, whether from its movement through the water, the noise of its propellers or engines, or even sounds made by the crew during an intensive search. HE could sometimes be detected between pings of the Asdic, or during certain operations the transducer could be switched off to allow the operator to listen for it. It was also useful against submarines on the surface, unlike Asdic in its active mode. Since an Asdic could sweep faster than radar, it might be used against a submarine which was believed to be retreating on the surface. In 1942, officers were advised, '… it should be borne in mind that a U-boat, having fired a torpedo and knowing that escort vessels are near, will probably move away either on the surface or submerged at highest possible speed and be most susceptible to detection by H.E.'[4]

The Type 144 was also fitted with the automatic volume control (AVC) receiver. This automatically altered the amplification of the signal according to the amount of background noise. It was claimed,

> Automatic control of amplification by background is advantageous for detection of echoes, but it would impair observation of hydrophone effect; in consequence, it is arranged that automatic control is effective for only about five seconds following any transmission, after which the amplification remains constant at its highest value. If, then, water noise sounds unpleasantly high, the volume can be reduced by operation of the speaker and telephone controls.
>
> The high normal amplification of the receiver permits detection by hydrophone effect at long ranges under quiet conditions, automatic control renders it especially suitable for echo detection of submarines and mines, and high volume in the speaker facilitates detection by the officer of the watch.[5]

The sound of pings and echoes was usually broadcast on the bridge of the ship so that the officers of the watch could have an opinion on assessing an echo. The anti-submarine control officer (ASCO) would have an important role in this. Lieutenant A. H. Cherry found that his course at HMS *Nimrod* was dominated by this aspect of the work. 'It was echoes from morning to night. We slept, ate and drank with the sound of echoes of varying frequencies buzzing from ear to ear; we were a world apart from the natives on the streets … our every thought was in terms of sound and its echoes.'[6]

Attack

On finding an echo and identifying it as 'submarine', the operator held the contact while the spare operator took up his station immediately. Meanwhile, the ship was brought to action stations and the senior Asdic operator, the higher submarine detector, also came to the hut and took his position.

The Asdic beam filled a sector of 2½ degrees, and a target at close range might occupy 10 or 15 degrees itself, which meant that a single echo did not give a precise bearing for the target. With a series of echoes, an Asdic team could establish a reasonably precise bearing in the middle of them. From early 1941, the standard method of following a target was for the operators to identify the edges of the target, producing echoes and marks on the bearing recorder at either edge (the 'cut-on'), and then moving outwards by a further 2½ degrees to where there was no echo.

> At the beginning of the approach stage of an attack, after the bearing-recorder had been lined up, the First Operator trains across the target, stopping at the 'cut-on'. If an echo is heard, the echo-push is pressed to mark the record and simultaneously to step the oscillator 2½ degrees off the target. On the next transmission, if no echo is heard, the oscillator automatically steps back 2½ degrees onto the 'cut-on'. A second echo on this bearing confirms the 'cut-on' and permits the operator to train across immediately to the other side. The time taken to cross the target is, in the early stages of the attack, inappreciable, and the first echo on the other boundary may be obtained with the next transmission.[7]

Thus the extent of the target was defined. Unlike older procedures of taking a bearing on the centre of the target, it helped prevent inexperienced operators following a wake instead of the submarine, and it made it less likely that officers would misjudge the submarine's movements. This worked reasonably well, but in poor conditions there were two problems. Because of the minimum number of echoes used, the range record tended to be sketchy and unsatisfactory; the first operator needed to concentrate quite hard on the bearing recorder, and so was unable to look at the range recorder to help him distinguish between submarine and non-sub echoes. An alternative approach was devised in which the operator continually stepped across the target 5 degrees at a time, pressing the echo-push every time there was an echo. He then went 5 degrees beyond the boundary of the target, where there was no echo. The direction of operation was reversed automatically, and the oscillator stepped 2½ degrees in towards the target, then resumed its 5-degree steps until the other boundary was found. The equipment was modified so that the oscillator would step forward by 5 degrees on each echo, rather than reversing its direction as in the older system. The new method was easier to learn, and it was claimed that a man with no experience of the Type 144 could learn it in half an hour.

Asdic operators were encouraged to report as soon as they had lost contact with the target:

> The report 'lost contact' is also frequently misinterpreted by the A/S Control Officer to mean that the submarine's position cannot even be estimated. It is hoped that these faults can be overcome by the initial report after losing contact being altered to 'no echoes', and by the operator being allowed to start the procedure whenever he is in doubt about the contact. … After reporting 'no echoes' the operator therefore cuts a big step of 20 degrees aft and investigates the last bearing. Unless contact is regained the investigation is continued through a total arc of 40 degrees, and if contact is not regained the operator then reports 'lost contact'.[8]

As the ship got to a range of 1000 yards (914m) from the target, the operator changed to a larger scale. By this time the captain had decided whether to attack by hedgehog or depth charge.

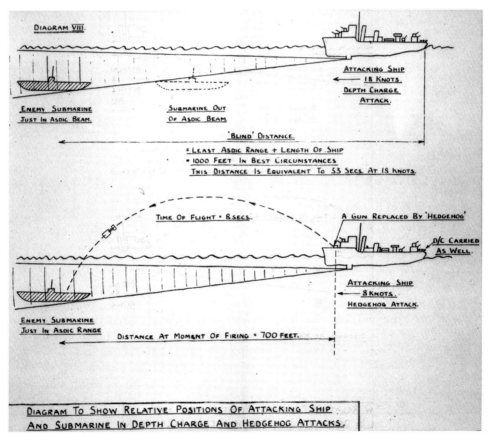

The use of the Asdic in attacking by depth-charge and Hedgehog, showing the blind area of the Asdic.
(TNA ADM 239/612)

Operating with Hedgehog

During a hedgehog attack, the captain merely had to order the helmsman to follow the indicator, so that the captain could give his attention to the general fighting and safety of the ship. HMS *Findhorn* carried out an attack on *U-198* on 12 August 1944, though not all the features of the Asdic worked perfectly. The target was found by another ship at 1800, and *Findhorn* prepared for a hedgehog attack at a speed of 10 knots. The range recorder was set for this and for a sinking time for the projectiles of 7½ seconds, while the bearing recorder was set for 10 knots. At 1808, the submarine was at a range of 1300 yards (1189m) and the bearing recorder was lined up. The commanding officer ordered the helmsman to 'steer by Asdic', but the helmsman's indicator was soon out of action, and it was noted that the captain's bearing pointer had a 5-degree lag, so helm orders had to be shouted from then on. The depth-finding Asdic found that the submarine was at 300ft, so the sinking time was reset to fourteen seconds. As the submarine drew to the left across the frigate, a hedgehog pattern was fired at a range of 250 yards (229m) and several projectiles were heard to explode. Another attack was made eighteen minutes later on an indistinct echo, but that was almost certainly disturbed water from the previous attack; it was considered that the first attack had already destroyed the submarine, and this was confirmed after the war. The captain and several members of the crew were decorated, and the senior officer of the group commented, 'It is particularly gratifying that "FINDHORN" should be the ship to score this success, as she had for some time been fighting a determined battle against an accumulating series of major defects.'[9]

Sometimes this was too complex to use in practice. When *Spey* attacked a U-boat at 0615 on 19 February 1944, an 'otherwise ideal attack' was spoiled by a failure to apply the corrections for slant range and to switch on the Q attachment (*see* below). The anti-submarine control officer was distracted at a critical point by having to 'make abstruse mental calculations to decide on a depth and sinking time setting for the Recorders'. A list of sinking times had been made on board and hung up beside the operators, but the depth of the U-boat, 500 feet, was 'off the map'.[10]

Later Developments

The beam of a conventional Asdic covered a range of about 15 degrees in the vertical plane. This meant that as the ship approached the target, a deep submarine was likely to disappear beneath it. After experiments in 1942, the 'Q Attachment' was devised to counteract this. It was a small additional oscillator, 12in. across and 1.6in. deep, fitted under the normal oscillator in order to deflect its beam lower through an angle of 15 degrees below the horizontal, and able to detect targets up to 45 degrees below the horizontal. It required some modification to the Asdic dome, but it was generally fitted during 1943. It was not needed during normal watch-keeping, as it was confined to a very narrow beam in the horizontal plane, and any target would be detected at long range. It could be switched on during the later stages of an attack, at a range of about 1000 yards (914m). In February 1944, *Spey* attacked *U-386*. Her depth charges had been set to 50 and 140ft, when at a range of 700 yards (640 m) the Q was switched on and gave a depth of 350ft. The depth-charge crews had seconds to reset all their charges and there was no time to apply all the corrections. A ten-charge pattern was dropped. The U-boat was forced to surface and then sunk by a shallow pattern. *Spey* was complimented on 'good seamanship, efficient use of Asdics and the highest standards of depth-charge drill'.[11]

Since pre-war exercises had assumed that submarines would operate in relatively shallow depths, Asdic had no direct means of determining the depth of a target – hence the unsuccessful fourteen-charge pattern which tried to cover all possible depths. In addition to Asdic, ships had depth-sounding gear for navigational purposes, and it was suggested that this could be used to find the depth of a submarine in certain circumstances. However, it would interfere with the Asdic and could only be switched on after the Asdic had already determined the course and bearing of the target; it would only work when the target was directly underneath, which was useless in an ahead-throwing attack and not much help with depth charges, since the ship would attempt to pass ahead of the submarine rather than above it.

Type 147 Asdic was available in late 1943, though priority for its fitting was given to the new Loch-class frigates which needed more accurate depth determination to use their squids (*see* page 95). It required a separate Asdic system, generally fitted forward of the Type 144 dome. It transmitted a fixed fan-shaped beam dead ahead in the horizontal plane, for Type 144 could be used to find the bearing and range of the target. The Type 147 beam was very narrow in the vertical plane and could be rotated up and down to find an angle by which the depth of the target could be measured. Depth-finding allowed much more accurate use of anti-submarine weapons. With depth charges, it allowed the best depth setting to be used. With hedgehog, it was a factor in calculating the time to fire, in calculating the movement of the target and allowing time for the projectiles to sink.

The Effects of Underwater Conditions

Scientists had always been aware that water conditions were variable, and this had much effect on Asdic performance. This was less important during the middle stages of the Atlantic war which were fought in the open seas, but it had much importance during the Arctic convoys to Russia, where layers of varying temperature could confuse the signal. It became vital during the final stages of the U-boat campaign as the enemy, forced out of the North Atlantic, was able to deploy his new snorkel, which allowed his diesel engines to operate when submerged, and he began to attack in shallow waters. As early as November 1942, officers were told about how range might vary, and echoes might be affected by the speed of the ship, the inclination of the target and the weather.[12]

During 1944, anti-submarine officers began to receive more information, based on American research, on the effects of underwater conditions on Asdic. They were told that where the water temperature decreased with depth, the asdic beam was bent downwards, creating a shadow zone which sound could not penetrate, and a submarine a few hundred yards inside the zone could not be detected. If the temperature increased with depth, a positive gradient, the effective range against a shallow target might be increased to 2 to 4000 yards (1.8 to 3658m). If there were layers of temperature in shallow waters, the effect was more complex. A shallow target could be detected at long range, a deep one only at short range. In shallow water (increasingly important as the U-boat campaign changed its nature during 1944), the roughness and texture of the bottom might affect the issue. Range might be increased with a smooth bottom such as sand or mud, and reduced among rock, coral and stones. All this could have an effect on stationing escort vessels the correct distance apart, though it was admitted that 'Our knowledge of the effect of water conditions on Asdic performance is still sketchy and we cannot afford to be dogmatic.'[13]

Radar

Early History

Radar was developed simultaneously in several countries, including Britain, Germany and the United States, in the late 1930s. It depended on recent developments in radio, such as the ability to detect and measure the tiny reflections from a transmitted wave, and the cathode-ray tube. Originally known as radio direction finding or RDF in Britain, it consisted of bouncing a radio wave off an object such as a ship or an aircraft and measuring the time it took to return, giving an accurate measure of bearing and distance. The first British set was demonstrated by Robert Watson-Watt in 1935, and in the second half of 1938 the battleship *Rodney* and the cruiser *Sheffield* were fitted. Though shore-based aircraft-detection radar had priority for home defence in the run-up to war, the Navy's signal school at Portsmouth was developing sets of its own to detect ships.

Type 271

The general principles of radar were described in the handbook to the equipment:

- The action of the set depends on the fact that, when wireless waves in the course of their travel encounter any object, a certain amount of energy is reflected back along the original path, somewhat as sound is reflected in an 'echo'.
- Energy is sent out from the transmitter in the form of a narrow beam, the receiver is also most sensitive in the same direction.
- The bearing of an object is found by rotating the transmitter and receiver around until the receiver signal is a maximum.
- The range of an object is determined by measuring the time interval which elapses between the departure of a very short signal or 'pulse' from the transmitter, and the arrival of the reflected energy or 'echo' onto the receiver. This time is measured on a cathode-ray tube.[14]

According to the handbook, 'The aerial assembly is trained on the target by turning a crank in the office, which turns the shaft through a series of bevel wheels and a worm wheel, about 40 revolutions of the crank turning the aerials through 360 degrees.'[15]

Anti-U-boat radar was, in many ways, one of the most difficult to develop. 'The U-boat is one of the smallest targets which radar is required to detect operationally...'[16] The first set able to do this, the Type 271, used waves of 10 centimetres (4in.) or less, and was known as the centimetric set. It was the biggest advance since the invention of radar itself. It was first tested on the corvette *Orchis* in March 1941, and was available in time for fitting to the ships of the River-class.

One difficulty with fitting the Type 271 was that the cable between the aerials and the transmitter had to be kept as short as possible. The whole system had to be kept close together in a radar hut, which had to be mounted high enough to get a good range, but not so high as to affect stability, and it must be where the officer of the watch could look at the screen without leaving the bridge. Early in February 1942, the naval constructors met in Bath to discuss the practicalities of this. It was agreed that, in regard to the twin-screw corvettes,

> Those building in the United Kingdom will be fitted with prefabricated huts. These huts will be exactly the same as the 271 PF huts now being fitted in destroyers, except that the foremost bulkhead of the office will be made of brass. DNC estimated that these huts could be introduced from about the fourth ship to be built. DSD will arrange for the huts to be built. [17]

Up to that time it had been planned to fit Type 286 alongside the new Type 271, but it was agreed that the older set was no longer required in corvettes.

In the earliest ships – *Rother*, *Spey* and *Tay* at Smith's Dock and *Exe* at Fleming and Ferguson's near Glasgow – the builders were to construct the huts themselves from plans supplied. But already, this type of teak lantern-like structure with sand-blasted flat perspex windows was causing problems in service, for the heaviness of the structure interfered with the radiation. A new, lighter, prefabricated structure was designed – essentially a moulded perspex cylinder – and large numbers were ordered from W. H. Smith Ltd. of Trafford Park, Manchester. These were to be supplied to the remaining thirty-seven River-class ships by an order of March 1942.

One great advantage of the Type 271 was that its beam covered a relatively narrow angle – about 2 degrees compared with about 4 degrees for a decimetric set and up to about 20 degrees for a metric set. This led to much greater accuracy in finding the bearing of a target. It also had almost no back lobes – reflections which interfered with the main picture. As fitted in a frigate, the set could detect a surfaced U-boat at a range of 12,000 yards or nearly 7 miles (11km) in good conditions, and a submarine periscope at about a third of that distance. With the A display that was standard in the middle years of the war, it was accurate within 200 to 500 yards (183 to 457m) of range, and less than 2 degrees of arc. It could pick up low-flying aircraft at a range of up to 12 miles (19km).

Operating the Set

Switching the set on and off involved twenty-one separate operations when the set was cold, and they had to be done in the right order. It could take up to twenty minutes to warm up. Ordinary Seaman Lindop described his initiation:

> First impressions were that it appeared to be of bewildering complexity with a mass of coloured knobs, dials, meters, switches, co-axial cables, handles and cathode-ray tubes. It was the size of a bulky wardrobe, and the transmitter, buried in the basement, the size of a small room. The Instructor gave details of how the instrument was switched on and gave a practical demonstration with the CRT [cathode-ray tube] lit up with a vivid emerald-green tinge, on the left side a large blip caused by the ground returns and the top of the trace, an 'A' trace, looking like grass, which was the term for it – this was the equivalent of noise in a radio set plus odd returns from mountains and the like. Turning a large wheel in the front of the

set rotated the aerial so that it was pointing at the mountains of the Lake District some 60 miles away and on the CRT appeared a large blip on the 60-mile range: our first echoes.[18]

In early radar sets, the cathode-ray tube used the 'A system' to show a target. The distance of the object was indicated by a blip on a straight line running across the cathode-ray tube, and range scales of 0–15,000 yards, 0–75,000 yards and 0–150,000 yards were provided (0–13.7, 0–68.6, and 0–137.2km); the 15,000-yard scale was in normal use. The operator had to read the bearing of the target separately, and it was shown by the position of the aerial. This in itself gave no indication of the direction of the echo, so the operator had a periscope which showed him the scale of a direction indicator. According to the handbook, 'The relative bearing of the aerials is read on a scale at the bottom of the shaft. The true bearing of the aerials can be estimated by means of the direction indicator (when fitted). The direction indicator is a simple form of gyrocompass which, however, drifts slowly and must be reset frequently.' It was gyro-stabilized so that it could maintain a bearing despite the movements of the ship. As the manual put it,

> The principal object of the Indicator is to indicate (roughly) the bearing of the aerials, relative to a fixed direction in space so that the operator, when observing a particular 'echo', is assisted in keeping his aerials continuously trained to the target despite the ship's yawing or altering course.[19]

It was an awkward arrangement for the operator, who had to use two instruments at right angles to one another. It was difficult tactically, because only one object could be kept in view at a time, and its relative position was not obvious without plotting on paper. It was fairly easy to keep track of an echo, such as a marauding U-boat, approaching the convoy from inside. It was far more difficult to spot an intruder among the convoy itself.

One of the most difficult tasks was to eliminate interference from the set. This was often a matter of maintenance as well as adjustment, for early sets were delicate and broke down easily.[20] Operators were also warned about various types – tramlines, criss-cross pattern, double echoes, telegraph poles and railings, for example. In the old-style A-scope set, a spot indicated the movement of the beam. If the spot was stationary, the operator had to carry out a six-stage procedure, including;

> 2. With the Brilliance Control adjusted to give a spot on the C.R.T. remove the Sync connection and note if spot disappears.
> 3. If spot disappears time base is not working and the trouble will probably be due to failure of the 400 volts supply, or to a defective V3.
> 4. If 3 fails to achieve results, check components and diodes in grid and anode circuits of V3.[21]

The aerial was rotated by hand at a rate of 90 degrees per minute in the early stages, though trials were conducted to test rotation at 180 degrees per minute. The faster figure became standard in good weather, though 90 degrees a minute was retained in bad conditions. It could only rotate through 400 degrees or a little more than a revolution, before the wires became tangled – after that, it had to be rotated in the opposite direction.

The pulse rate of the radar set could be varied to suit the circumstances. A long pulse rate gave the maximum detection range, while a short one gave better discrimination at short range once a target had been picked up.

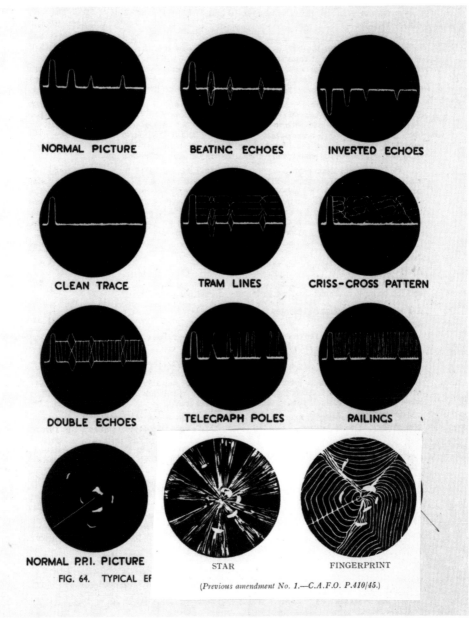

NORMAL PICTURE   BEATING ECHOES   INVERTED ECHOES

CLEAN TRACE   TRAM LINES   CRISS-CROSS PATTERN

DOUBLE ECHOES   TELEGRAPH POLES   RAILINGS

NORMAL P.P.I. PICTURE   STAR   FINGERPRINT

FIG. 64. TYPICAL EF

(Previous amendment No. 1.—C.A.F.O. P.410/45.)

Problems with radar displays. The top four rows show the A-scan, the bottom row is for the Plan Position Indicator. (TNA ADM 239/307)

Sweeping

A radar set could carry out an all-round sweep, or it could be used to search a particular sector from which danger was expected. Early sets had a slow speed of rotation, which was done by hand and was not continuous. An all-round sweep was advised if there was a chance of a U-boat surfacing inside the escort screen, or if the number of escorts equipped with radar was inadequate, so that one might slip through before it was detected. The set would sweep from aft to forward alternately on each side, with a 20-degree overlap on the bow. Otherwise a sector sweep should be used. It might start at the edges of the convoy, or from the next escort in line. One advantage of sweeping the empty area of sea was that the operators would detect new echoes more readily.[22]

The officer of the watch would instruct the radar operator on which areas to search, which pulse to use and any policy on interrogating contacts. He was to be given any information which might be useful in interpreting contacts – 'the position and movements of ships in company (or the bearing limits of the convoy), whether any ships or land are likely to be met with, and details of the zigzag if in force'. Normally the operator was instructed to report all echoes except those of ships in company; other identified echoes and any others he might be ordered to 'disregard'. If there were too many to report, he should be told on which ones to concentrate. Once a target was reported, the operator was to give amplifying reports every two minutes. He might be ordered to hold, or concentrate on a particular target, but only if it was clearly identified as likely to be hostile, for the benefits of the all-round sweep were lost. He might be ordered to investigate, to carry out a search over a particular area from which attacked was expected imminently.[23]

Radar could be used to direct gunfire, though the types fitted to frigates did not offer any great accuracy. During the battle for Convoy ONS 5, 'in low visibility when starshells are useless, effective 4-in. H.E. was used to force U-boats to dive by training the gun fore and aft with sights set to zero, firing when R.D.F. reported the U-boat dead ahead. This obviated the necessity of a long chase'.[24]

The Plan Position Indicator

The plan position indicator, or PPI, was introduced from 1942, and was fitted in large numbers after the middle of 1943. It showed the situation as a plan, with any ships or land in view. 'In this, own ship is the centre of the [cathode-ray tube] and the beam sweeps round like the hand of a clock, showing "blips" which fade at relatively slow speed.'[25]

> As the aerial sweeps round, echoes are traced out (or "painted") not only at their correct range (from the centre of the tube) but also on their correct bearing, leaving a bright arc to mark their position. An after-glow tube is used, so that the echoes do not immediately die away, and provided the aerial is kept rotating at a reasonable speed the result is a complete picture or plan display of the relative opposition of all objects within radar range.[26]

The head of the screen was always orientated to true north. The screen had range rings around its centre, and both range and bearing could be seen at a glance. Most important of all, multiple targets could be spotted at once, and the relative positions of different objects could be seen without any trouble. A U-boat which had got among a convoy, for example, would be much easier to pick out. It was easier to hold on to a target among the ground waves with a PPI than with an A display. However, it was less accurate in bearing and range than the A display, which was sometimes still used when a specific target was being attacked.

When sweeping with a PPI with the Type 271 set, the aerial was rotated at 360 degrees per minute. Once one revolution had been completed, it was swept back in the opposite direction.

Later Developments

Early radar sets had no means of telling friend from enemy, which caused many false alarms. One way round this was to fit an 'identification, friend or foe' (IFF) device. Friendly ships or aircraft carried a transmitter set on a specified wavelength, and the Type 271 radar was fitted with a small U-shaped aerial above the hut, following the movements of the main aerial. This would produce a signal under the main scan of the A-frame, identifying the object as friendly.

From mid-1944, *Rivers* were fitted with the new Type 277 radar. The set itself was similar, but the aerial was radically different, saucer-shaped and constantly rotating under power. This was much more convenient for the PPI display. Its beam was only 1 to 2 degrees wide – even narrower than the 271 – and the slightest displacement would cause confusion, so the aerial was stabilized in the horizontal and vertical plane. It was mounted at the top of a mast, and lattice masts began to come into use to support such aerials, greatly altering the appearance of warships. In addition to its other advantages, it was able to determine the height of approaching aircraft to a certain extent.

Signalling

Visual Signalling

At the beginning of the war, the Navy still placed most of its faith in visual signals for most of its short-range traffic. By day, messages could be sent by semaphore or by pre-arranged flag signals hoisted from the masthead. By night, lights could flash Morse code. Visual signals had the great advantage that they could not be detected by the enemy. If radio was used, it was in the form of wireless telegraphy in Morse code, rather than radio telephony using voice. For signals within the fleet, it was possible to use low electrical power which an enemy could not detect at a longer range. Signals from base were transmitted over specified areas using an elaborate worldwide system.

The peacetime battle fleet was relatively compact, operated close to shore and had highly trained signallers. A wartime convoy might be spread over a distance of many miles, and a thousand or more miles out into the ocean. The Atlantic was notorious for its rains and fogs, and signalmen were hastily trained. Often they had to communicate with merchant ships where a different language was spoken, or knowledge of Morse and signalling flags was minimal. Nevertheless, visual signalling was only slowly replaced in the Battle of the Atlantic, and voice radio came into use gradually.

The River-class frigates, like all fully fledged warships, were equipped with masts for flag signalling. The mainmast of the *Exe*, for example, was fitted with a yardarm carrying two pulley blocks on each side for signal halyards. The *Barle* had three per side, and this was as in the specification used for most ships. The lower ends of the halyards went to the after part of the signal deck, aft of the bridge and among the legs of the tripod mast. The flag locker was situated there, containing a full set of flags. The Navy used its own system of flags for signalling, though a full set of the internationally recognised code of signals also had to be carried. The naval signals included twenty-six rectangular or triangular flags to represent the letters of the alphabet; twenty-six flags for specialised naval purposes, indicating types of ship, squadrons and divisions, etc; ten numeral pendants; six substitute flags to repeat other flags; and fourteen specialised pendants to indicate courses, bearings, answering and interrogative pendants, etc. The ship also carried a full complement of national flags, including at least three white ensigns to be flown in battle, in case one was shot away.

In practice, escort groups relied on more dramatic and unmistakable signals in action, especially if it was urgent. If a U-boat was sighted in a dangerous position, the ship was to fire tracer shells to indicate its position and try to force it to dive. In sighting a torpedo attack at night, an escort was to fire 'snowflake rockets', which discharged many white 'falling stars' that outlined an enemy submarine on the surface at night. In the earlier stages, two white rockets were to be fired in the event of a ship being torpedoed. Ships could also communicate by loud-hailer if one steamed close to another.[27]

The original specification for the River-class allowed for a semaphore with arms on each side of the bridge with a clear working space around it, but these do not show on plans and were probably omitted. There was nothing, however, to stop signalling by flags if it was necessary. Each ship was fitted with a 6-in. signalling lantern ('projector') on either side of the bridge, with another two facing aft. These operated by means of a shutter arranged like a Venetian blind, to open and shut to transmit Morse code. Each ship also carried two large 20-in. lamps, or 'projectors'. One was planned in the original design but was displaced from its central position by the radar, so one was needed on each side of the Type 271. They could be used for long-range signalling, but also to illuminate a U-boat at night. The *Itchen* was using her 20-in. projector to chase a U-boat 300 to 400 yards (274–366 m) ahead on the night of 22 September 1943, when she was sunk by torpedo.

Wireless Telegraphy and Radio Telephony

Before 1939, the Navy had paid little attention to voice radio. When wireless had to be used at all, it preferred Morse telephony in which an accurate record was kept of the signals, rather than less formal methods using voice. Ships kept radio silence except in the presence of the enemy, but listened for messages sent out from headquarters. During the Battle of the Atlantic these often included urgent matters such as reports on the position of U-boats. These were sent out on high frequencies (3000 to 30,000 kilocycles) so that they could bounce off the Heaviside layer in the upper atmosphere (a layer of ionized gas that affects the propogation of radio waves and enables them to follow the curvature of the earth) and be transmitted across the ocean. They could, of course, also be picked up by the enemy. They were sent in cypher, but the Germans had much success in breaking the British code.

The standard set for the early River-class was the Type 49, designed around 1930. Like most sets of that period it lacked frequency stability, for the Navy had relied on its highly trained operators and neglected to use crystal control. This allowed a set to be rapidly trained to a particular frequency and to remain accurately tuned for a long period. It made it much easier to transmit the message through a loudspeaker on the bridge and reduced the need for skilled operators. Mass production of crystals was begun and most sets were fitted with them.

By 1940, it was clear that a constant intercommunication circuit was needed for ocean escorts. Wireless telegraphy needed a large number of trained operators working in watches, and these were not available. Radio-telephone sets, which used speech rather than Morse code, were therefore fitted to all escorts by the end of 1941. The Navy had done little to develop its own, but it was able to get models developed by commercial firms, the RAF and the Americans. They used low power so that their transmissions could not be heard over a great distance, but they were not totally secure. Transmissions could be heard via a loudspeaker on the bridge, so that less-specialised radio watch-keeping was needed. They operated on the universal convoy frequency of 2410 kilocycles, though other frequencies were available for emergency use and to avoid misleading transmissions by U-boats. This was a high-frequency (HF) waveband, in which the signals bounced off the upper atmosphere and back to earth. It was useful when the convoy was spread out between visual range, but could only be used sparingly for fear of giving the position away.

Often the communications system was under considerable stress: for example, when support groups joined a convoy escort:

> The convoy R/T wave was heavily loaded from the time the convoys joined p.m. the 20th until Westomp mid-day 25th, but at no time did any important signal fail to get through.
>
> There was nothing unusual in the amount of R/T taking into consideration the number of escorts present and the weather conditions. Besides the three groups, totalling at first 18 ships, there were two convoys, each with their own Commodore, a Rescue Ship, and a merchant HF/DF ship. The convoy R/T wave was used for HF/DF intercommunication, as HT 11 was found to be indistinct, very noisy, and much interfered with by Convoy R/T. Most of this period was spent in thick fog, and the short periods of comparatively good visibility found the convoy and escorts covering anything up to 40 square miles of ocean.
>
> The conduct of the entire operation, therefore, depended on this one wave, and although it would have been possible to have made use of another, I considered that the advantages of having everyone, including the air, on the same wave outweighed the disadvantages provided it could take the strain. This it did.

This type of action did impose a good deal of work on the radio staff:

> The entire coding and ciphering staff, together with the more senior telegraphist staff, were working at very high pressure in very cramped conditions and with remarkably little sleep throughout the period.
>
> One of the worst bottlenecks is the fact that only one set of books for Naval Code is supplied so that when immediate "In" messages are being dealt with all "out" work has to cease and vice versa.[28]

Later in the war, the American system 'talk between ships', or TBS, was introduced in some groups. This was a VHF set which was much more secure, as the signals could only be heard within visual range. Captain Donald MacIntyre, whose escort group included the *Mourne*, was enthusiastic about it.

> The transformation the TBS worked in the cohesion of the group dispersed around the sprawling convoy was wonderful. Instead of the tedious process of call-up by lamp and the laborious process of spelling out an order, or the shorter but insecure communication by HF radio, each ship was in immediate touch with the others simply by speaking into a telephone handset, the message coming through a loudspeaker on the bridge.[29]

It did have drawbacks when officers tended to talk too much, jamming the airwaves with trivia at vital moments. Also, 'The differing accents of two signalmen on TBS could produce moments of misunderstanding which would have brought the house down as a music-hall turn.' But as a whole, 'the efficiency of the group as a team rose tremendously'.[30]

One senior officer of escorts regarded TBS as a 'regular goldmine for a Group Leader, especially with a remote-control "telephone" at his elbow on the bridge. All we need now is for all V/S ratings and all officers of the watch to grasp the RT procedure and become loudspeaker-conscious. Rather too much devolves on the RT operators at present.'[31]

Ships did keep logs of their RT conversations, despite the fears of the pre-war officers, as in that kept by HMS *Tay* during a single eventful hour in command of the escort of the crucial Convoy ONS 5 on 5 May 1943:

Time	From	To	Signal
0110	Tay	Northern Spray	11 survivors from no 34 trying to find no 13 and 81
0111	Tay	Vidette	In position D
0116	Northern Spray	Tay	Can U explain flash?
0118	Tay	Northern Spray	Cannot explain flash
0120	Offa	Tay	Request you cover the front of the convoy as close screen
0124	Offa	Tay	Can anyone explain flash Oribi at 0100
0124	Tay	Offa	Flash seen but cannot explain
0126	Tay	Offa	Flash sighted BG 030 but no explanation
0126	Tay	Snowflake	J 9 o'clock 6
0142	Tay	Snowflake	Chasing sub unable to overtake
0143	Offa	Tay	Request destroyer assist Snowflake
0147	Oribi	Snowflake	My position 120ZZ9
0154	Oribi	Snowflake	RU joining me
0156	Offa	Oribi	Snowflake Sub ½ mile ahead of me

The U-boat crash-dived and in this case a depth-charge attack was unsuccessful though the escorts sank two U-boats later in the day.[32]

An ordinary escort vessel needed to keep radio watch on two frequencies: the area broadcast, which sent tactical and administrative signals over a wide area; and the convoy R/T wave, used for immediate operation purposes. Escort group leaders, and ships used for guard operations would also use the air wave for communication with long-range shore-based aircraft, and perhaps the naval air wave, if naval aircraft were operating with the convoy. Selected escort vessels would also keep watch on the commercial wave, used by merchant ships in an emergency.[33]

The W/T Office and Aerials

The wireless telegraphy office of the River-class was situated on the upper deck, two decks under the bridge. Its fittings consisted of the radio equipment in question, with desks and at least four seats for the operators on the port, or outer, side.

Naturally the equipment tended to become more sophisticated over the years. One of the first ships, the *Exe*, had the Type 49 MR as the main W/T set, a medium-power type more common in destroyers. Its panels took up a large amount of space in the centre of the office. The direction-finding set was mounted forward on the port side, as in most ships. The *Barle*, launched in Canada in September 1942, had the American RBJ receiver. The *Nadder*, built in Smith's Dock a year later, had the Type 89, also used by the RAF, for communication with aircraft; TBS for VHF telephony; the Marconi TV5 set, mostly used in auxiliary craft; the CDC receiver; and the FM 12, the latest model of HF/DF set (*see* below). The latest equipment was more compact, and the *Nadder's* operators had two extra seats, facing aft in the office.

An elaborate aerial arrangement was needed, especially for transmitting. One of the main functions of the masts and yardarms was to support this. Four insulated copper wires were stretched between the 18-ft main yard and the 10-ft main yard.

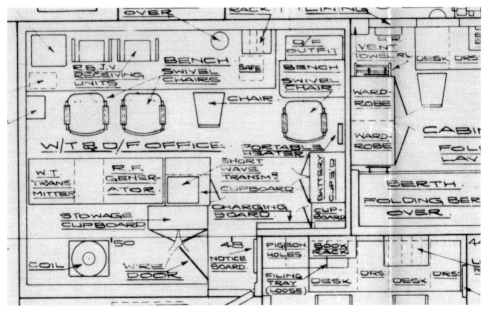

Details of the radio cabin of HMS *Barle*. Admiralty Collection, Box ADFB017, plan NPN0906 (NMM F5144)

HF/DF

U-boats relied on constant communication with their shore headquarters in order to find and track convoys and to form wolf-packs to act against them. For this they used high-frequency transmissions employing the Enigma code. British code-breakers at Bletchley Park, north of London, had great success in decrypting this code during certain periods in the war, but the ships at sea had another success in using the signals to find the positions of U-boats across the ocean. The German radio signals were in the high-frequency waveband, and they believed that they could not be traced. But the British and their allies developed a system known as high-frequency direction-finding, known as HF/DF or colloquially as 'Huff-Duff'. As its name implies, the direction of a U-boat's signal could be traced. This could be done from shore stations using sophisticated equipment, but only with an accuracy of 2000 to 200,000 square miles.[34] It was obviously far more accurate if it could be traced from a ship at sea in the vicinity of the U-boat. It was not easy to tell whether a signal was reflected off the Heaviside layer, and therefore some distance away, or being received directly on the ground wave, which meant it was within about 25 miles (40 km). Also, two HF/DF sets were needed some distance apart to give the position of the transmitting boat with any accuracy; a single set could only give a bearing.

The first practical HF/DF set was the FH3, developed in 1942 and installed in most of the early *River* class frigates. It used the 'aural-null' system. The operator trained a rotating aerial until the broadcast became louder, then reached a null point when it was pointing exactly at the target. A developed version of HF/DF, known as FH4, entered service in 1943. It had a cathode-ray display so that the operator could get a visual reference for a contact.

Another question was the type and siting of the HF/DF aerial. Masts of the time were not strong enough and the site aft on the bridge of the *Rivers* had been taken up by radar. Most of the *Rivers* had the HF/DF aerial on top of the shelter for the forward 4-in. gun crew, where it was only about 33ft (10m) above the water. In later ships it was situated at the masthead.

In March 1943, the head of an anti-submarine training school suggested that Asdic operators could relax until the ship received some kind of warning, either from aircraft, shore-based intelligence or HF/DF, which might indicate U-boats in the vicinity.[35] But in fact it took some time for HF/DF to become fully effective. One important stage was the appointment of specially trained officers, mainly in senior officers' ships.

In May 1943, the *Tay* was the only ship in Escort Group B7, escorting Convoy HX 231, to be fitted with HF/DF. She was also acting as the senior officers' ship, and Commander Peter Gretton gave a detailed account of the role of HF/DF in one of the most crucial convoy battles of the war. During the night of 4-5 April alone, the *Tay's* HF/DF allowed the detection of *U-530* on a bearing of 285 degrees. The destroyer *Vidette* was sent to investigate, and forced the submarine to dive. The corvette *Alisma* was then sent out on a bearing of 350 degrees and sighted *U-563*. Early in the morning, several ground-wave signals were received and showed that several boats were astern of the convoy, where they would not be able to attack that night. One more was detected ahead but driven off by escorts; another was heard soon afterwards, then found on *Alisma's* radar. Two merchant ships were lost during the night, but it was a small price to pay in an attack by a large number of U-boats.[36]

If HF/DF was so useful when fitted only to one ship, it was far more effective when two or more were available. Group B7's next convoy was ONS 5, and the leader, *Duncan*, also had HF/DF, until forced to leave due to fuel shortage. The next one, SC 130, was joined by the First Escort Group including *Wear*, *Jed* and *Spey*, and the total escort had five HF/DF sets at that stage. The three convoys represented the turning point in the Battle of the Atlantic, and HF/DF takes a large share of the credit. Combined with Type 144 Asdic and Type 271 radar, it gave the River-class ships an array of sensors which could detect U-boats in a wide range of circumstances.

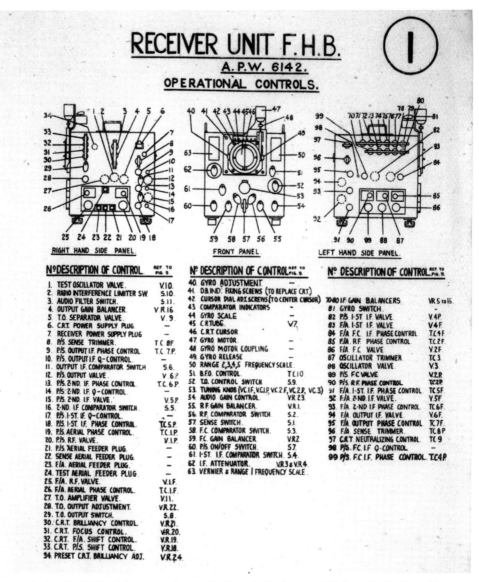

RECEIVER UNIT F.H.B.
A.P.W. 6142.
OPERATIONAL CONTROLS.

RIGHT HAND SIDE PANEL.

N°	DESCRIPTION OF CONTROL	REF. TO FIG. 2
1.	TEST OSCILLATOR VALVE.	V.10.
2.	RADIO INTERFERENCE LIMITER SW.	S.10.
3.	AUDIO FILTER SWITCH.	S.11.
4.	OUTPUT GAIN BALANCER.	V.R.16.
5.	T.O. SEPARATOR VALVE.	V.9.
6.	C.R.T. POWER SUPPLY PLUG.	-
7.	RECEIVER POWER SUPPLY PLUG.	-
8.	P/S. SENSE TRIMMER.	T.C.8F.
9.	P/S. OUTPUT I.F. PHASE CONTROL.	T.C.7.P.
10.	P/S. OUTPUT I.F. Q-CONTROL.	-
11.	OUTPUT I.F. COMPARATOR SWITCH.	5.6.
12.	P/S. OUTPUT VALVE.	V.6P.
13.	P/S. 2-ND. I.F. PHASE CONTROL.	T.C.6.P.
14.	P/S. 2-ND. I.F. Q-CONTROL.	-
15.	P/S. 2-ND. I.F. VALVE.	V.5.P.
16.	2-ND. I.F. COMPARATOR SWITCH.	S.5.
17.	P/S. I-ST. I.F. Q-CONTROL.	-
18.	P/S. I-ST. I.F. PHASE CONTROL.	T.C.5.P.
19.	P/S. AERIAL PHASE CONTROL.	T.C.I.P.
20.	P/S. R.F. VALVE.	V.I.P.
21.	P/S. AERIAL FEEDER PLUG.	-
22.	SENSE AERIAL FEEDER PLUG.	-
23.	F/A. AERIAL FEEDER PLUG.	-
24.	TEST AERIAL FEEDER PLUG.	-
25.	F/A. R.F. VALVE.	V.I.F.
26.	F/A. AERIAL PHASE CONTROL.	T.C.I.F.
27.	T.O. AMPLIFIER VALVE.	V.11.
28.	T.O. OUTPUT ADJUSTMENT.	V.R.22.
29.	T.O. OUTPUT SWITCH.	S.8.
30.	C.R.T. BRILLIANCY CONTROL.	V.R.21.
31.	C.R.T. FOCUS CONTROL.	V.R.20.
32.	C.R.T. F/A. SHIFT CONTROL.	V.R.19.
33.	C.R.T. P/S. SHIFT CONTROL.	V.R.18.
34.	PRESET C.R.T. BRILLIANCY ADJ.	V.R.24.

FRONT PANEL.

N°	DESCRIPTION OF CONTROL	REF. TO FIG. 2
40.	GYRO ADJUSTMENT.	-
41.	D.B.IND. FIXING SCREWS (TO REPLACE CRT.)	-
42.	CURSOR DIAL ADJ.SCREWS (TO CENTER CURSOR)	-
43.	COMPARATOR INDICATORS.	-
44.	GYRO SCALE.	-
45.	C.R.TUBE.	V.7.
46.	C.R.T. CURSOR.	-
47.	GYRO MOTOR.	-
48.	GYRO MOTOR COUPLING.	-
49.	GYRO RELEASE.	-
50.	RANGE 2,3,4,5 FREQUENCY SCALE.	-
51.	B.F.O. CONTROL.	T.C.10.
52.	T.O. CONTROL SWITCH.	S.9.
53.	TUNING KNOB (VC.I.F, VC.I.P, VC.2.F, VC.2.P, VC.3)	-
54.	AUDIO GAIN CONTROL.	V.R.23.
55.	R.F GAIN BALANCER.	V.R.1.
56.	R.F. COMPARATOR SWITCH.	S.2.
57.	SENSE SWITCH.	S.1.
58.	F.C COMPARATOR SWITCH.	S.3.
59.	F.C GAIN BALANCER.	V.R.2.
60.	P/S. ON/OFF SWITCH.	S.7.
61.	I-ST I.F. COMPARATOR SWITCH.	S.4.
62.	I.F. ATTENUATOR.	V.R.3 & V.R.4.
63.	VERNIER & RANGE I FREQUENCY SCALE.	-

LEFT HAND SIDE PANEL.

N°	DESCRIPTION OF CONTROL	REF. TO FIG. 2
70-80	I.F. GAIN BALANCERS.	V.R.5 to I5.
81.	GYRO SWITCH.	-
82.	P/S. I-ST I.F. VALVE.	V.4P.
83.	F/A. I-ST I.F. VALVE.	V.4F.
84.	F/A. F.C. I.F. PHASE CONTROL.	T.C.4.F.
85.	F/A. R.F. PHASE CONTROL.	T.C.2.F.
86.	F/A. F.C VALVE.	V.2F.
87.	OSCILLATOR TRIMMER.	T.C.3.
88.	OSCILLATOR VALVE.	V.3.
89.	P/S. F.C VALVE.	V.2.P.
90.	P/S. R.F. PHASE CONTROL.	T.C.2.P.
91.	F/A. I-ST. I.F. PHASE CONTROL.	T.C.5.F.
92.	F/A. 2-ND. I.F. VALVE.	V.5.F.
93.	F/A. 2-ND I.F. PHASE CONTROL.	T.C.6.F.
94.	F/A. OUTPUT I.F. VALVE.	V.6.F.
95.	F/A. OUTPUT PHASE CONTROL.	T.C.7.F.
96.	F/A. SENSE TRIMMER.	T.C.8.P.
97.	C.R.T. NEUTRALIZING CONTROL.	T.C.9.
98.	P/S. F.C. I.F. Q-CONTROL.	-
99.	P/S. F.C.I.F. PHASE CONTROL.	T.C.4.P.

The controls of the FHB high frequency direction finding set, also know as FH4. It was the standard set for River-class frigates. (TNA ADM 234/673)

Chapter 5: Officers and Crews

Officers

The River-class frigates were originally designed to carry seven officers each, including a commanding officer and a surgeon. By October 1942 it was decided that the chief engineer should be at least a warrant officer, with the same accommodation as a commissioned officer. As time went on, extra officers were added in individual cases. Out of forty-six ships in commission in early 1944, four had only seven officers apiece and a further five had eight, though some of these ships were working up and their full complement had not yet joined. More typically, fifteen ships had nine officers, five had ten officers and eleven had eleven. A few had larger numbers, including HMS *Rother* with sixteen; she was an escort group leader and carried extra officers for staff duties. *Exe* with fourteen officers and *Deveron* with thirteen were also group leaders. Other ships had extra officers for training.[1]

The Captains

The captain (or strictly, commanding officer) of a River-class frigate, like any of His Majesty's ships, was in a position of great power and authority, with total authority over the ship, its crew, ammunition and stores. According to the *King's Regulations and Admiralty Instructions*, the captain was to tour the ship on first appointment, to commission it by reading his orders to the assembled crew, and to take on provisions. He was to make arrangements of the quartering of all officers and men at their action stations, and to make sure that the armament was ready for use. At sea he was 'at all times to keep the ship in readiness for war'. The Admiralty advised him of his responsibilities:

> … once appointed in command, no matter what rank you hold, you are The Captain, which means that you are the ship – that when a fender is left over the side it is *your* fender left over by your O.O.D. [officer of the day], that when a confidential document is mislaid by a sub-lieutenant it is still *your* document, that when a seaman from your crew is seen wearing his cap flat-aback ashore, that seaman is reflecting a lack of pride in *your* ship; and that when you hit the tug and not the target with your first salvo it is *your* deflection that is wrong. [2]

Life was often difficult for River-class captains. Their ships went on long voyages in rough and dangerous seas, but with no specialist officers except the engineer and the surgeon, and many of the junior officers were very green indeed. However, the captains usually had some years' experience of the Battle of the Atlantic, often in command of a corvette in which the problems were far worse.

The commanding officer of a small warship only held the title of 'captain' by courtesy, as he did not usually have the full naval rank of captain. According to the Navy List of June 1944, frigates were usually commanded by officers of the rank of lieutenant-commander, two grades below captain. Five of the River-class, all group leaders, had full commanders, and occasionally a lieutenant might be put in command pending promotion, but the great majority were under lieutenant-commanders. Of these, the greater part (thirty-two out of forty-six) were officers of the Royal Naval Reserve. They were merchant-ship officers who had done some training with the Royal Navy in peacetime and been called up at the start of the war.

Richard Case was a typical RNR officer of the day. Born in 1904, he joined the merchant navy training ship *Worcester* in 1918 and entered the Royal Naval Reserve two years later. He got his merchant navy master's ticket in 1928 and served with Coast Lines just before the war. He took command of the Flower-class corvette *Campanula* in 1940, and his officers included Nicholas Monsarrat , who would gain distinction in different fields. But he was definitely *not* the model for Captain Ericson in Monsarrat's *The Cruel Sea*; according to Monsarrat, Case had a hectoring manner which made him closer to the bullying first lieutenant in the novel. In 1942, Case commissioned the first of the River-class frigates, the *Rother*. He kept diaries, which say almost nothing about his life at sea and describe a rather ordinary social life ashore.[3] He returned to Coast Lines after the war and also became an aide-de-camp to the Queen.

Humphrey Boys-Smith was the same age as Case. He trained in the merchant navy college at Pangbourne in Berkshire but left the merchant navy in 1935 to join the Colonial Service in Palestine. He was recalled to the RNR in 1940 and took command of the *Spey* during the convoy battles of 1943.

P.G.A. King was a year younger and was born in Dover. He did well in HMS *Worcester* and had his early RNR training in HMS *Argus*, the world's first true aircraft carrier, in the early 1920s. He had wide-ranging merchant navy experience between the wars, interspersed with naval exercises with the RNR. He served in armed merchant cruisers early in the war, after which he commanded the corvette *Anemone* and was appointed to the frigate *Avon* in 1943.[4]

R. E. Sherwood commanded the *Tay* during the crucial battles around convoys HX 231 and ONS 5 in 1943. He had had a long career in Irish cross-channel services before commanding a corvette early in the war.

Officers of the Royal Naval Volunteer Reserve (RNVR) were men from other professions. A few had trained part-time in peacetime, but the majority were temporary wartime officers who had known very little about the sea or the Navy when the war began. Nicholas Monsarrat joined the Navy in 1940 by answering an advertisement in *The Times* for experienced yachtsmen to train to become officers. The son of a surgeon, he had much yachting experience before he began training on the *King Alfred* in 1940. He took command of the *Ettrick* in 1944, the second RNVR officer to command a frigate, 'being beaten by a week or so' by his friend Maberley, who had served with him early in the war.

> If we had been told, as subs in HMS *Flower* [*Campanula*], that such a command would eventually come our way, it might have permanently affected our outlook – and with it our careers. It is perhaps just as well that at that stage we had no greater ambition than to earn our watch-keeping tickets and get the ciphers to come out right.[5]

Seaman Officers

The Navy was very careful to distinguish its temporary officers from the regulars. The officers of the regular Navy wore straight stripes. Most had trained for about six and a half years before being commissioned. The merchant seamen of the RNR wore a complex pattern of intertwined braid, and those of the RNVR, regarded as vastly inferior to 'real' officers of the regular Royal Navy, had wavy stripes. According to the popular saying, the RNR were sailors trying to be gentlemen, the RNVR were gentlemen trying to be sailors, and the RN were neither, or both, according to who was talking.

Petty officers' and leading seamen's rank badges.
Illustration from *The Navy and the Y-Scheme* (Admiralty, 1944). (NMM F5460-2)

By 1942, the great majority of officers in escort ships were members of the RNVR, who fell into three classes. A few had served as RNVR officers in peacetime. Some were experienced yachtsmen who had joined early in the war as members of the Royal Naval Supplementary Reserve. This was a scheme which had started in 1937, when the Admiralty began to compile a list of suitable men who had experience of navigation and seamanship. Erskine Childers published *The Riddle of the Sands*, suggesting that a German invasion might be foiled by amateur yachtsmen. This led to the formation of the Royal Naval Volunteer Reserve, but in fact it attracted few yachtsman. As one member of the interwar period wrote, 'To join the RNVR meant giving up so much leisure that it was almost impossible to combine the two.'[6] But now, at the start of the war in 1939, about 2000 yachtsmen were taken into the Navy in batches to train as officers of the Royal Naval Volunteer (Supplementary) Reserve.

The majority of frigate officers had joined the Navy as ordinary seamen for 'hostilities only' and were singled out at their basic-training schools, mainly for their superior education and strength of character. They went to sea for at least three months as commission and warrant (CW) candidates, where they were carefully observed. If successful they were interviewed and sent to the training establishment HMS *King Alfred* in Hove on the South Coast of England, where they had three months of intensive training in navigation, seamanship, weapons, naval discipline and law. They were usually commissioned with the rank of temporary sub-lieutenant, RNVR. They might reach the rank of lieutenant within a year with the right age and amount of sea service.

The first lieutenant was the executive officer and second-in-command of the ship under the captain. He was not normally expected to stand watch, but had a great deal of work in the administration of the ship, particularly in allocating the crew to its duties. According to Monsarrat,

> A good First Lieutenant should feel, all the time, a *personal* responsibility for the ship's organisation; there can be no collective authority to fall back on where he is concerned. If he had said: "*We* can't do it any other way," or shown anything except a conviction of direct personal control, I would have suspected that he was probably ready to share his job with other officers, or put his problems onto a vague impersonal basis which somehow excused their solution.[7]

The surgeon of HMS *Aire* credited the 'very able first lieutenant' with a 'strict supervision' over the messdecks, to the benefit of the ship's health.[8] The majority of first lieutenants of the frigates were RNR in 1943.

The first lieutenant was nearly always a full lieutenant, except in a senior officer's ship. The junior officers might be lieutenants, sub-lieutenants who would be promoted on reaching a certain age or seniority, or midshipmen if under the age of twenty. Out of forty-six River-class frigates in commission in autumn 1944, for example, there were fifteen midshipmen, 191 sub-lieutenants, and 169 lieutenants, including medical officers.[9]

The main duty of a junior officer was to keep watch, in charge of the ship for a period of four hours, once he had had enough experience to earn his watch-keeping certificate – until then, he would serve as junior officer of the watch. During his watch, an officer would have detailed instructions from the captain about when he was to be called – for example, on sighting land, hearing a suspicious echo, receiving an urgent signal or losing contact with the convoy. Apart from that he would keep the ship on course, avoiding collision and perhaps zigzagging to a prearranged pattern. He would take regular reports from Asdic and radar operators, lookouts and engine-room staff.

An important secondary duty was to take charge of a group of seaman to look after their discipline and welfare off watch. Nicholas Monsarrat describes the divisional system:

> … it is, to my mind, the Navy's most admirable organisation, and if the other services have no parallel to it, that is probably what is wrong with them… Briefly, a ship's company is divided into 'divisions', according to the various branches – seamen, stokers, communications, etc.: each group of men has an officer to look after it, an officer specially charted with its welfare and regulation. It is to him that they look in all their difficulties, whether concerned with promotion, training for a higher rate, doubts about their pay, internal quarrels and problems, domestic complications, compassionate leave, complaints of unfairness or favouritism. This division into small groups, if conscientiously applied, makes for a high degree of confidence between officers and men.[10]

One officer was chosen as the ship's navigating officer, responsible for the charts and compasses and for setting courses. Each frigate had an anti-submarine control officer, or ASCO, responsible for the asdic, the depth charges and hedgehog and their crews. Very few of these were completely trained in the pre-war sense, for only 235 officers had undertaken the full course by 1945 and most of these were on flotilla or headquarters staffs or on training duties. Ninety-seven officers had been trained 'in lieu of anti-submarine specialists', but the officers in the River-class ships were mostly from the 8000 who had done short courses in the anti-submarine training schools at the bases HMS *Osprey* and *Nimrod* on the Firth of Clyde.[11] The ASCO was the main authority on deciding whether a suspicious echo was 'sub' or 'non-sub'.

> The A/S C.O. should listen to the contact and see whether he agrees with the first operator's opinion of it. He should also consider the range recorder trace, and readings obtained from the depth recorder and any information received from the Plot on the Bridge. If he has been kept in the picture, his final opinion should, in many cases, be conclusive, as it is his duty to attain competence in this work. In some cases, however, the Captain may be in a position to form a better opinion for himself.[12]

Another was the gunnery officer. Short courses for RNVR officers were held mostly in the principal gunnery school, HMS *Excellent* at Whale Island, Portsmouth. RNVR officers did short courses using numerous simulators, learned the basic theory of gunnery and spent a good deal of time doing parade-ground drill.

There were no specialised administrative officers in frigates, so these duties tended to fall on the most junior seaman officers. Captains were warned that they would have to 'rely on young sub-lieutenants with no secretarial training, and plenty of other duties, who work in an office which no business man would tolerate'.[13]

Engineer Officers

The chief engineers of the Flower-class were normally only chief artificers, who were not commissioned and did not live in the wardroom. By an order of June 1942, the Admiralty recognised that the engineers of the new River-class should be at least warrant engineers or warrant mechanicians – in effect, having almost the same duties and status as junior commissioned officers.

The Admiralty was aware of the strengths and limitations of warrant officers as a class. 'The type of officer obtained from this source may be very much "set in his ways" and unsuitable for staff appointments, but within his limits he is an extremely valuable officer.'[14]

The naval warrant officer was rather a different figure from his namesake in the army, who usually served as a regimental or company sergeant-major and lived in the sergeant's mess. The army warrant officer was known for his military propriety and his parade-ground discipline rather than his technical skill. The naval warrant officers lived in the wardroom with the commissioned officers in a frigate.

The Admiralty took steps to create the new warrant engineers for the new ships, though it was not prepared to break down the class distinctions of the age. In October 1942, it invited commanding officers to recommend suitable chief engine-room artificers and chief mechanicians for warrant rank. They had to be within three years of their pension in normal circumstances, or recalled pensioners who would naturally return to civil life at the end of the war. The age limit of forty was to be disregarded.[15] The men thus promoted had already had a long and practical training in the Navy.

Another type of engineer officer relied on a short, intensive and mostly theoretical training. In October 1942, in view of the great expansion of the fleet, it was decided to expand greatly the number of engineer-officer candidates from the lower deck, and to train hostilities-only engine-room artificers (ERAs), enginemen and motor mechanics of reasonable intelligence and who were expected to have officer-like qualities; these were to be given training courses of about six months.

The training school was in King's Road, Chelsea. Up to a quarter of the men on each course had shore-based engineering qualifications and had never been to sea. It was difficult to organise courses for men of varying backgrounds, ranging from that of ERA or chief ERA in naval vessels to motor mechanics and service in the patrol service, for some had far more theoretical knowledge than others. The development of 'officer-like qualities' and their relationship to engineering skills was a perpetual problem with engineer officers.

The staff of the course aimed to give the trainees sufficient knowledge to enable them to carry out the duties of engineer officer in such ships as corvettes and frigate. The minimum standard, it was suggested, was the Board of Trade second-class certificate for merchant-navy engineers. They would not be able to sit the examination at that point due to lack of sea time, but it would provide an incentive for the future.[16] Graduates of the course were commissioned as sub-lieutenants (E) for engineering. By mid-1944, twenty of the River-class ships in commission had them in charge of the engine room, compared with twenty-six warrant officers.

There was no doubt that the status of an engineer officer in a frigate did not match his responsibilities. He had about a quarter of the crew under his control, but he was normally the most junior officer in the wardroom. In a slightly different context, the commander-in-chief of the Home Fleet recognised the problem in destroyers in May 1943: '…many of the other officers are young and inexperienced temporary officers and it is an anomaly that the Engineer Officer, if he be a Commissioned Engineer or Warrant Engineer, should be the most junior member of the wardroom mess'.[17]

The engineer officer had considerable responsibilities, according to Admiralty regulation:

> The Engineer Officer is to be regarded as the mechanical expert of the ship. Under the Captain's directions he may be empowered to inspect any of the mechanical fittings not in his charge and report to the Captain on their efficiency. The Engineer Officer is to have charge, and is responsible for the maintenance in a state of working order, and so far as may be, of readiness for immediate use, of all that is placed under his charge…[18]

That included the engines and boilers, engines of the ships' boats, auxiliary machinery such as capstans, pumps and generators, and a certain amount of the electrical machinery. In a passage which found its way into numerous forms of fiction, he was given instruction on 'Orders tending to injure machinery'.

> Whenever any order is received which, if executed, would, in the opinion of the Engineer Officer, tend to injure the machinery of boilers, or cause a useless expenditure of fuel, he is to make a representation to this effect to the Captain, but, unless the

order is countermanded after his representation, he is to execute it. [19]

On joining a new ship, the engineer officer would start a notebook in standard form, entering details of the machinery and any information which might be passed on to his successor. He had a good deal of paperwork to do, including regular reports to flotilla and fleet engineer officers, but he would also be expected to spend a good deal of time with the machines themselves.

Surgeons

In June 1942, the commander-in-chief, Western approaches, pointed out that most of the ships would be operating independently, and at the end of the month the Admiralty agreed that a medical officer would be appointed to each of the first twelve to complete. Temporary surgeon-lieutenants RNVR were taken from general practice ashore and given short courses on naval medicine before appointment to frigates.

A surgeon-lieutenant on a frigate had a very small practice: about 140 men, all young and fit, though very vulnerable to accident, war damage and various illnesses caused by exposure. In normal times he might find it difficult to fill his time. The lieutenant of the *Ness*, for example, spent much of August and September compiling statistics on the crew's accommodation and on weather observations, taking temperature readings every four hours and compiling weekly averages – matters which were on the periphery of his duties.[20] The surgeon of the *Towy* worried about an outbreak of twelve cases of enteritis, two of which were severe, and it was not confined to any particular mess.[21] Early in 1944 the surgeon of the *Spey* dealt with a twenty-one-year-old stoker who was injured by a plank while the ship was in dry dock; a forty-one-year old writer who was chronically seasick for several days, until he could be persuaded to eat some food and occupy his mind; and a leading stoker who was 'thoroughly drenched' on the forecastle and had to be sent to bed with giddiness, pains in the chest and a high temperature. The surgeon was quite happy about the health of the ship as it sailed south into warmer climates on the way to South Africa, and this was helped by the crew's participation in organised games.

Once there the ship was put into dry dock for fourteen weeks, and the problem was totally different. The crew continued to live on board, but the surgeon was more worried about other matters. He gave a standard lecture on 'The Dangers of Venereal Disease' but it did not help much, and ten per cent of the crew needed treatment by the end of the docking. Afloat again, the ship saw little action with the enemy, but on 29 November, while firing at a floating mine, a shell from the pom-pom gun exploded prematurely, killing one seaman and injuring four more.[22] The surgeon-lieutenant of the *Exe* gave a half-hour talk on venereal disease over the ship's loudspeaker early in 1943, and 'the men were told to have their sick-buckets handy'.[23]

Things were reasonably quiet on the *Nene* at the beginning of January 1944, as it escorted a convoy, and the surgeon-lieutenant was content:

> This lower incidence of throat infection may be partly attributed to the elimination of two suspected 'carriers', shorter periods at sea, three periods of leave during quarter, and improved weather conditions. General health of the ship's company has certainly improved since the last return.

This ended suddenly on the 7th, when the *Nene's* sister ship *Tweed* was struck by a torpedo. As the ship went down, one of its depth charges exploded, killing most of the men in the water and traumatising the rest. The *Ness's* whaler was sent out with two Carley floats and a system of 'rough selection' was used. The most severely injured men were hauled into the whaler, the rest onto the floats. Altogether, fifty-seven men were hauled out of the water, but one died in the whaler. Four more died on board the *Nene*.

The rest of the most seriously wounded were accommodated in the sick bay, the wardroom and the ERAs' mess. The rest were distributed among the messdecks and the surgeon and his sick-berth attendant visited them three times a day. Watches were arranged to give the two medical personnel some rest at night, and on the third day the ship's first-aid teams began to help. It was difficult to predict the future of individuals.

> For the first 48 hours or so, all the survivors suffered from shock … after which time it became clearer as to who would need continuous nursing care, and who was convalescent. A few, however, who appeared to be in fair shape on the third day relapsed and became seriously ill…

After five days the patients were landed at Londonderry.[24]

Surgeon-Lieutenant Hanratty of the *Cam* had to remove a leading seaman's appendix during action. Things were reasonably quiet when he started the operation, though he had to break the quarantine of a diptheria patient in the sick bay. The appendicitis patient was strapped to the operating table and the captains steered the ship into the sea and reduced speed. The surgeon was sewing up when the action-stations bell sounded. The officers assisting him had to go on deck, and the captain warned the surgeon to expect 'bouncing about,' but the operation was successful and the patient was transferred to the surgeon's own cabin until he could be landed the next day.[25]

Medical officers lived in the wardroom with the other officers, which could cause occasional difficulties. The surgeon of the *Exe*, against his better judgement, passed one of the officers as fit for full duty. 'It is not easy to be adamant with a person who faces you at every meal, particularly in a small ship where every officer counts.'[26] As predicted, the patient soon relapsed.

Petty Officers and Leading Seamen

The Higher Rates

Any military organisation relies strongly on experienced and competent people to form the link between the officers and the lower ranks, to advise the officers and supervise the troops or the crew. In armies they are known as non-commissioned officers, in navies as petty officers. The British petty officer was rather more senior than his American namesake. Officers universally saw petty officers as the backbone of the Navy and worried incessantly about finding suitable men, especially in wartime.

The petty officers lived in separate messes from the lower rates, with slightly more space per man. After one year in the rate they wore the 'fore and aft' rig uniform, a simplified version of that worn by the officers with peaked cap, jacket and collar and tie.

Even in overalls or duffel coat on board a frigate in the Battle of the Atlantic, his peaked cap would still pick him out. Their arm badge consisted of crossed anchors, worn on the left arm. They were freed from some of the more irksome restrictions of naval life, and allowed shore leave on easier terms, for example.

The petty officers of the gunnery and torpedo branches were known respectively as the gunner's and torpedo gunner's mates, though they did not necessarily serve under warrant officers with these titles. This was an interesting example of slightly less specialisation in the higher ranks. A gunnery rating, for example, would become highly specialised as an anti-aircraft gunner, control, quarters or layer rating. To become a gunner's mate, a petty officer with good prospects of promotion to chief, he would have to learn something of the other branches.

The chief petty officers were the most senior men of the lower deck. They, too, had their separate messes. They had no badge as such, but wore three brass buttons on each lower sleeve, with their specialist badge on the collars of their jacket. Their cap badge was slightly more elaborate than that of a petty officer, with a wreath around an anchor, under a crown.

Even in wartime, most petty officers were regulars, and they were needed more than ever to advise inexperienced officers. In 1943, Captain Pelly of the training school *King Alfred* advised newly commissioned officers:

> … you should bear in mind that the responsibilities of the higher rating are more important now than they have ever been. They should be made to feel that they are in your confidence, and they should be made to feel that they really are the men that matter. Bring them into any discussion of a job of work, drill, improvement or amenity. Not nearly enough is done by officers to encourage the status of Higher Ratings.

He warned junior officers to be aware of the problems of fast promotion. 'On the other hand, do not expect too much of your higher ratings. You cannot expect their standard to be a high level one, as large numbers are at present being made and many of them are of very limited experience.' [27]

By 1943, the problems of supply of suitable petty officers had attracted the notice of the First Lord of the Admiralty:

> There is increasing evidence that the number of higher and trained technical ratings is not keeping up with the rate at which the Navy has expanded and that a large proportion of men entered for 'Hostilities Only' lack the normal incentive for advancement. This may be partly due to the fact that the wages of many are being 'made up' by their civilian employers, and in any case they do not contemplate a career in the Navy with its attendant responsibilities.
>
> The shortages in the ratings concerned are chiefly in Seamen Petty Officers and Leading Seamen, Petty Officer and Leading Telegraphists, Yeomen and Leading Signalmen, Senior Artificers (Electrical and Engine Room, the latter with certificates qualifying them to take charge of watches) and in Supply and Writer Petty Officers. [28]

In August that year, the Navy was short of 2050 leading seamen and 940 petty officers. [29]

In October 1942 the Admiralty noted that the numbers of chief petty officers was not keeping up with the expansion of the fleet, for it tended to protect the rating – only petty officers of three years service were eligible in most branches, which meant that very few hostilities-only men would ever reach the rate. Many posts were filled by petty officers rather than chiefs. As a result, the *Barle* had only two chiefs in her crew in September 1943.[30] The chief petty officers' messes in many ships were 'comparatively empty' in many ships, while the petty officers' mess was overcrowded. Captains were urged to remedy this where possible, perhaps by allowing certain artificers and shipwrights to mess with the CPOs.[31]

The Coxswain

The coxswain, the senior chief petty officer, was a key man in any ship. According to Nicholas Monsarrat,

> A good coxswain is a jewel … The coxswain can make all the difference on board. As the senior rating in the ship, responsible for much of its discipline and administration, he has a profound effect on producing a happy and efficient ship's company. Usually he is a 'character', to use an overworked but explicit word: that is, a strong personality who would make himself felt in any surroundings, and who is, in his present world, a man of exceptional weight and influence. He keeps his eye on everything, from the rum issue to the cleanliness of hammocks, from the chocolate ration to the length of the side-whiskers of the second-class stokers. It is his duty to find things out, however obscure or camouflaged they may be – a case of bullying, a case of smuggled beer, a case of 'mechanised dandruff' in the seaman's mess – and either set them right or else report them forthwith to a higher authority. In the majority of cases, as might be expected, he is fully competent to set them right himself, and can be trusted to do so.
>
> He is the friend of everyone on board, and a good friend, too – if they want him to be, and if they deserve it; failing that, he makes a very bad enemy.[32]

The Admiralty urged new captains to recognise his importance.

> The Coxswain in particular has an especial position in the ship's company. There is no reason why he should not be a Second Officer of the Watch at sea. He should be a constant link between the Captain and the messdeck. He should know of any bad feeling in any mess; of any leading hand who is running his mess badly. If he can have an office of his own, his position is greatly enhanced. He must have the respect, but also the confidence of the ratings. He must be capable of reprimanding the other Petty Officers. He must have the welfare of the ship's company consistently at heart. If the junior ratings call him 'Sir', so much the better, and he should see that the other Petty Officers when on duty are addressed in a manner befitting their state.[33]

Other Petty Officers

The original scheme of complement for the River-class allowed only three chiefs and three petty officers in the seaman branch proper. These would normally include a gunner's mate, who took charge of the gunnery ratings and training in gunnery. The quartermaster was a petty officer or chief who supervised the steering of the ship at sea, took the helm himself during difficult manouevres, and assisted the navigator with the maintenance of his equipment such as sounding gear and patent logs. Though they were experienced men, quartermasters had no particular training for the job, and no navigational skill. Lt.-Cdr. Joseph Wellings of the US Navy noted that 'The navigator does not have a quartermaster to correct charts… The number of man hours required to keep even charts of the British Isles up to date is considerable…'[34] In a small ship such as a frigate, the duties of boatswain's mate and quartermaster's mate were often combined. This involved passing on orders to the crew and keeping a watch in harbour. They were there to 'assist the officer of the watch and to pipe any necessary orders'. They used the 'boatswain's call', or whistle, to transmit orders, and traditionally had loud voices to assist: for example, in rousing men from their hammocks, though this was less essential in the days of loudspeakers. The boatswain's mate had a strong disciplinary function. 'Whether at sea or in harbour he should keep his eyes open and at once report any irregularities and anything detrimental to the outside appearance of the ship.'[35]

Leading Seamen

The original scheme of complement for the River-class allowed for four leading seamen, two for each seaman's mess. The leading seaman had evolved in Victorian times as a highly skilled man rather than a petty officer, but there was tendency for the leading hand to be given more responsibility over the years, especially after the rating of petty officer second class was abolished. He was not recognised as a superior officer within the meaning of the Naval Discipline Act, and striking one was treated as 'an act to the prejudice of good order and Naval discipline' rather than an assault on a superior officer.[36] From its inception the rating was seen as a place for potential petty officers, and as late as 1943, Rear-Admiral Ford suggested that the rating was 'probationary' and intended to find out whether the man had 'Petty Officer-like qualities'.[37]

Captain Pelly of HMS *King Alfred* was well aware of the lack of authority of some leading hands and petty officers in 1943, and encouraged junior officers to support them:

> You must also bear in mind that the young higher ratings, and particularly the Leading Seamen, have a difficult job. They find themselves in charge of men older than themselves, some of whom endeavour to trip them up. If you spot any signs of insolence or disobedience do not wait for the Petty Officer to complain or run the man in.[38]

There were six main requirements to be considered for advancement in the seaman branch: total length of service; sea service; educational tests; health (no man with venereal disease was to be promoted); skill in seamanship or in a non-substantive rate; and the recommendation of one's captain after the prescribed period of sea service, intended to identify leadership qualities. The educational test for advancement to leading seaman, ET1, involved knowledge of simple arithmetic and vulgar and decimal fractions, and of English: 'Writing an ordinary passage of English to Dictation. Writing a simple essay. Meanings of words, technical and otherwise. Explanations in the candidate's own words of passages taken from the *King's Regulations and Admiralty Instructions*, the daily press, etc.'[39]

Seniority was also an important factor. The numbers of permanent leading seamen and petty officers were strictly controlled in peacetime: 400 chief petty officers, 800 petty officers and 1200 leading seaman in the seaman branch. In wartime this was increased to 1,000, 4,000 and 8,000[40], and the rest of the posts were filled by acting and temporary promotion. Accelerated advancement was available even in peacetime; men with special recommendations from their captains could be pushed forward by up to four months. Apart from that, everything depended on rising up the divisional rosters at the three home ports. These were maintained for each different rate within each branch, but essentially fell into two types. The highly skilled ratings, such as artificers, mechanicians and artisans, would be advanced when they fulfilled the conditions of service, education and recommendation, irrespective of vacancies. This was also true of the promotion of an ordinary seaman to able; but otherwise in the seaman branch, as with stokers, signalmen and 'miscellaneous' ratings, the man had to rise to the top of the roster by seniority or accelerated advancement before he was promoted to fill a vacancy.

The Seamen

Seamen's Entry and Training

The seamen of the Navy came from three main sources: the regulars, the reserves and those signed on for 'hostilities only.' The regular seamen were relatively rare on the River-class frigates for they tended to be big-ship men on battleships, cruisers and aircraft carriers. They had joined the Navy at the age of fifteen or sixteen, signing on for a period of twelve years after the age of eighteen. They spent a year of very tough training in the shore bases at HMS *Ganges* near Harwich or *St Vincent* near Portsmouth. After that, they did some time as boys in the fleet; then at the age of seventeen and a half or eighteen they were rated as ordinary seamen (OS). After a year they became able seamen (AB), and for some that was their last promotion. These men became the 'three-badge ABs' who had served at least thirteen years since the age of eighteen without becoming leading seamen or petty officers.

The reserve seamen came from several sources. Some were from the Royal Fleet Reserve, men who had already completed their twelve years (or more) and were recalled when the war started. They were already familiar with naval ways, though out of date on the latest technology. They were highly valued by the Admiralty. Next in order of value were the men of the Royal Naval Reserve. They were professional seamen who had done some naval training in peacetime and were called up at the beginning of the war. Their numbers were quite small – only 8397 ratings at the outbreak of war – and unlike RNR officers, they did not make much impression on the manning problem. Next came the men of the Royal Naval Volunteer Reserve. They were non-sailors who spent their peacetime leisure in naval training in static ships near the major port cities. Again, their numbers were quite small: 5371 ratings at the beginning of the war, apart from the patrol service which had different duties.

The crews of River-class frigates were overwhelmingly made up of hostilities-only men, or HOs, who had been recruited for the duration of the war. Again, there were two main categories: volunteers and conscripts. It was possible for a man who was not in a reserved occupation and was not already subject to conscription to volunteer for service in the Navy. The numbers available for this tended to reduce over the years, as more and more age groups became liable for conscription. By 1942, the only likely source of volunteers was from young men under the age of eighteen, who could volunteer for a particular service, and often a particular branch of the Navy, in advance of their call-up. The other HOs were men who been conscripted and then volunteered for the Navy. The regulations allowed a man to choose either the Navy or the Royal Air Force. If he failed to get into his chosen service, or made no choice, he was drafted into the Army. The Navy's prestige was much higher than that of the Army, and for much of the time it was above the RAF, so it had plenty of applicants. The Navy's selection standards were quite thorough, and for most of the war it only accepted about one in three of those who applied. It took on men of good physical health, including good teeth and eyesight in most circumstances, and gave priority to men who could offer skills such as engineering or radio experience.

HOs were given their initial training in converted holiday camps such as HMS *Royal Arthur* at Skegness, or in camps near the traditional naval bases, such as HMS *Raleigh* near Plymouth. They had ten or twelve weeks of 'disciplinary' training in which they did foot drill, learned how to wear naval uniform and absorbed a good deal of naval culture. They learned basic seamanship and elementary gunnery, rowing and personal survival. Stokers had their own schools, such as HMS *Duke* at Great Malvern and HMS Cabot at Bristol, and later in Yorkshire. By 1942, most signallers were trained at HMS *Scotia* at Ayr, and writers (clerks) went to *Demetrius* at Wetherby in Yorkshire.

During disciplinary training, men were assessed and selected for their eventual duties. Some were isolated as possible officer candidates. At the other end of the scale, some would go straight to ships as ordinary seamen, with no trade badge on their arms and limited promotion prospects. According to the July 1942 complement of the River- class, each ship would have fifty-eight members of the seamen branch, of whom twenty-seven would have no other skill. Other men would be selected, by means of medical and psychological tests, for training in one of the 'non-substantive' rates within the seaman branch. This was a system which had grown up over the last few decades. A man's substantive rate, as leading seaman, petty officer, etc., was partly independent of his skill at a particular activity within the seaman branch.

Gunners

Gunners had operated the main weapons of naval warfare for several centuries, but it was only in 1830 that the Navy set up a specialised training system for them. After that, the gunnery branch, both officers and lower deck, came to regard themselves as the elite of the Navy. Gunnery ratings were selected from among the able and ordinary seamen. In peacetime, a man would spend some time at sea before being put on the list for selection; in wartime, potential gunners were chosen at the initial training schools. There were schools at each of the three main bases: HMS *Excellent* at Portsmouth, *Cambridge* at Devonport and the strangely-named *Wildfire* near Chatham. As well as its skill in the operation of weapons, the gunnery branch was the custodian of naval drill and ceremonial, and the senior gunnery petty officer, the chief gunner's mate of a ship, was expected to be a strict disciplinarian.

Just before the war, the gunnery branch was reorganised and divided into four parts. First- and second-class members of the branch wore crossed gun barrels on the right arm, third-class members wore a single gun placed horizontally. Control ratings operated the rangefinders of destroyers and big ships and were not employed on the River-class.

Naval training at HMS *Raleigh*, Torpoint, Cornwall: new recruits learn to row a boat on dry land, in preperation for instruction on nearby water. (Imperial War Museum LADM A3141)

The quarters section included the men who operated the guns. A River-class ship was allocated two second-class ratings (QR2s) from this group, with the letter 'Q' under the gunnery badge. They were leading seamen, or at least able seamen passed for petty officer. They were trained to operate as captains of the ship's 4-in. guns. There was also a third-class quarters rating and four layer ratings third class: able or ordinary seamen who were trained to lay and train the 4-in. guns and wore the letter 'L'. The gunnery branch also supplied two anti-aircraft ratings second class, mostly leading seamen, and four third-class ratings who wore 'A' under the badge. This was presumably intended to provide one as the gunner on each of the Oerlikons, but was probably reduced on ships which had only four such weapons. Anti-aircraft gunners tended to be less intellectual than other members of the branch, selected for their practical skill in aiming rather than their ability to command or to make calculations. The final member of the gunnery branch in a River-class was the able seaman qualified in ordnance (QO), who was a QR3 trained in maintenance work.

Torpedomen

The torpedo branch was rather newer then the gunnery branch, and gained its first badge in 1885. In the early days, the torpedo was the main consumer of electricity aboard ship, and the torpedo branch took responsibility for it. Though there were now highly trained electrical artificers on board most ships, the torpedomen still had a good deal of general electrical work to do. This suited most of the ratings, as the experience might help them find work in the expanding electrical industry after they left the Navy.

Like gunners, torpedomen were trained in schools attached to the three main bases. Chatham ratings went to HMS *Marlborough*, Portsmouth men to HMS *Vernon* (mostly re-sited to Roedean School), and Devonport ratings to HMS *Defiance*. The main seaman torpedoman qualifying course consisted of seven days on high-power electrical, eight on low-power, four days on the study of mines, three days on schoolwork and fifteen days on the torpedo. A torpedoman would learn how to charge the weapon with air and electricity, to transport it and its warhead, to carry out various maintenance tasks including oiling, to operate torpedo tubes and deal with misfires, to fit and maintain the gyroscope and to make final adjustments before firing. He had an 'All-round knowledge of torpedo, inside and out.'[41]

The torpedo branch used the non-substantive system rather less than the gunners, and a man's technical skills were more closely related to his substantive rate as a leading seaman, for example. The River-class was allocated two leading torpedomen and four seamen torpedomen; of course, the ships carried no torpedoes, but the ratings were employed in servicing the hedgehog and depth charges, and in electrical repairs. A seaman torpedoman was able to undertake 'simple maintenance of ships' electrical motors, motor starters, dynamos and accumulators; fault-finding on 220-volt power and lighting circuits, on 220-volt bell, telephone, gun firing, etc., circuits'. The leading torpedoman was 'senior electrical rating of small ship and responsible for electrical and depth charge maintenance'.[42] In addition, a frigate was initially allowed a wireman (MS) to service the minesweeping gear. Since minesweeping was never carried out, it is doubtful if many of these were actually drafted.

Asdic

Asdic operators were rated as submarine detectors, with a higher non-substantive rate of higher submarine detector (HSD), and a yet higher one (mostly confined to shore bases) of submarine detector instructor. Many HSDs were leading seamen, but others were only able seamen, even if they were in charge of the asdic of the ship. A River-class frigate was allocated one HSD and six submarine detectors, enough to have two men on watch twenty-four hours a day with a three-watch system.

Because it had been neglected before the war, the Asdic branch had to expand rapidly in wartime, so it suffered more than most from the shortage of higher substantive rates. It had only 1200 trained men in 1939, compared with 7600 in 1945. The branch was based at Portland, on the south coast of England, until 1940, but this was a very exposed position after the fall of France, and the main training schools were both in the Firth of Clyde: HMS *Nimrod* at Campbeltown in the south of the Firth, with good access to the sea; and *Osprey* at Dunoon further up the Firth.

An Asdic operator might bear a great deal of responsibility in a lowly rate. Leading Seaman Woodward of the *Findhorn* was in charge of the Asdic when the ship sank *U-198* in August 1944 and he was commended as being 'untiringly zealous and conscientious in the upkeep of the Asdic gear'.[43] Sometimes an operator had to assert himself against his officers. According to Peter Gretton,

> *Tay* had taken station ahead of the Commodore and we were busy counting the ships when the Asdic operator reported 'echo right ahead'. We were rather sniffy about it, but he stuck to his guns, and the order to 'stand by' had just been passed to the depth-charge party when the U-boat had the cheek to lift his stern out of the water, just underneath our port bow.[44]

Conversely, an Asdic operator who got it wrong could cause great damage. Able Seaman James Hasty the HSD of the *Tweed*, was on watch in the Asdic cabinet with Ordinary Seaman Edward Millichope just after 4 o'clock in the afternoon of 7 January 1944. The operators had heard a number of fish and whale echoes over the previous twenty-four hours, and when they heard another one they quickly classified it as 'non-sub'. The junior officer of the watch quickly questioned this, saying, 'That is a good trace.' The operators then reported a hydrophone effect on the same bearing and the alarm was sounded only seconds before a torpedo exploded, breaking the ship in half and leading to the death of nearly two-thirds of her crew. A court of enquiry concluded:

> That blame for the torpedoing of H.M.S. *Tweed* must rest with the cabinet crew … in that they did fail to report the suspicious echo in time for the officer of the watch to take effective action. These ratings were fully trained and their fault was due to negligence. It was reasonable to entrust to them the duty which they were carrying out. They are both deceased.[45]

Radar Operators

Radar (known as RDF in the early stages of the war) was an even newer branch than anti-submarine, and as yet it had no real hierarchy on the lower deck. As an Admiralty fleet order put it early in 1942, 'Advancement to P.O. (R.D.F.) has not yet taken effect in sufficient numbers to allow these ratings in complements.' Radar operators were not included in the early versions of the River-class complement, and were additional to it. The standard scale of manning for ships equipped with Type 271 was based on the fact that a man could not concentrate on a set for more than half an hour without eye strain. One man would operate the set while another stood by to take over. Two operators were provided per set over three watches, making a total of six men in the ship, with a leading seaman in charge when available. Not all would be fully trained, due to the vast expansion in the use of radar in 1941-42. The training schools would provide three, and the rest were to be acting RDF ratings, trained up on board. Even the men from the training schools were not fully qualified. Captains were warned that there was only time to train men in the narrowest interpretation of their duties.

> Commanding officers must therefore appreciate that Ordinary Seamen (R.D.F.) newly drafted to sea cannot be considered fully trained either in practical operating or in sea sense. This training must be continued afloat and every help and encouragement must be given to operators to learn.[46]

The main training school for radar operators was at the training establishment HMS *Valkyrie* on the Isle of Man, where radar aerials could be set up with a good prospect over the Irish Sea. *Valkyrie* was a collection of hotels fenced off with barbed wire, and a formerly public road running through the middle, used as a parade ground. There was room for 1500 ratings in 1942 and they tended to enjoy the posting to the island, as rationing was lighter than on the mainland. There was a small base at Sherbrooke House in Glasgow for refresher training of officers and ratings attached to Clyde-based ships. Trainees were given some time afloat on the Clyde. Virtually all radar ratings were hostilities-only men. For security reasons they had no badge of their own, but they had high informal status, despite the absence of higher rates. It was quite common for a ship to be delayed in sailing because the key radar operator was absent.

Signallers

Nicholas Monsarrat liked working with the visual signallers:

> If you want an example of alert intelligence in the Navy, a young signalman, interested in his job and keen to get ahead, is probably the best specimen. From the very nature of his work, he knows more about the ship and her movements than any other rating, and he has the opportunity of learning much more besides. He sees almost every signal that comes in, on a very wide variety of subjects ranging from the First Lord's anniversary greetings to the provision of tropical underwear for Wrens. He spends long hours up on the bridge, in the centre of things, where he has the best opportunity of talking to his officers and of picking up fresh ideas.[47]

In contrast with Asdic and radar, the two main branches of signallers were well established and had a full complement of petty officers. The temporary war complement of April 1942 for the River-class allowed for a petty officer telegraphist, two telegraphists and three ordinary telegraphists. These were the men who operated the ship's radio systems. This was barely enough to allow two men on watch at once, and tended to increase over the years as more equipment was added. The telegraphists now had less responsibility for the maintenance of their equipment, for a new rating of radio mechanic had recently been created. These were selected from new entrants with a good technical education and trained in wireless colleges ashore. They held leading rate and were promoted to petty officer after a year; a River-class ship was allowed one of these. Coder was another new rate, often selected from men with good literacy yet poor eyesight. Three were appointed to each *River* in the Western Approaches command, to relieve the officers of the onerous task of deciphering numerous signals from the Admiralty.

In peacetime, visual signallers were selected from among the better-educated seaman boys in the training schools. In wartime, they were chosen from adult entrants. They learned to send and read visual signals by Morse code using flashing lights, by semaphore using flags, and by signal flags hoisted from the masthead. As well as speedy and accurate transmission and reading, they needed detailed knowledge of signal etiquette. In the original complement a River-class frigate was allowed a yeoman of signals or petty officer, a signaller and two ordinary signallers.

Engineers and Miscellaneous Ratings

Artificers

Artificers were highly skilled tradesmen and the elite of the lower deck. There were several types, including electrical and air artificers, but the main ones on the River-class frigates (and indeed, on most ocean-going ships) were the engine-room artificers, or ERAs. Each was trained, inside or outside the Navy, in the skilled metalworking craft of a fitter and turner, boilermaker, engine smith, coppersmith, moulder or patternmaker. In peacetime, the majority were recruited to the Navy at the age of fifteen or sixteen as apprentices after a stiff competitive examination. The Navy expected high standards of its artificers:

> The training and education of Artificer Apprentices is intended not only to make them good Workmen, but to give them a real understanding of the tools, materials and machines they will have to handle, and also to make them self-reliant, ready and resourceful.
>
> Accordingly, their knowledge should not be gained simply from books or taken on trust from their teacher; they should be trained to approach subjects from the standpoint of observation, and to reason out their own conclusions.[48]

By 1940, there were two establishments for the training of engine-room artificer apprentices. The mechanical training establishment at Rosyth had been completed just before the start of the war, and was purpose-built. The apprentice training establishment at Torpoint, near Plymouth, had been evacuated from Chatham on the outbreak of war and was largely improvised.

A hostilities-only rating who had completed at least two and a half years of apprenticeship in the relevant trades was eligible to become an ERA. After his basic training he would have at least a year's practical training in watch-keeping, but prospective employers after the war were warned that he had 'usually been employed in a limited range of duties' and that 'Efficiency as tradesmen varies widely and trade qualifications should be subject to close scrutiny before submission.'[49]

However he was recruited and trained, an ERA had a fast-track promotion. He would never wear the square rig of the ordinary seaman, but would start with a simplified version of the officers' 'fore and aft rig' with jacket, collar and tie. On qualification he would be rated as an ERA fifth class, equivalent to a leading seaman. From the start he would live in the ERA's mess, with conditions equivalent to a chief petty officer. He would learn the finer points of engine operation, spending time in engine-room watch-keeping and with the various types of machinery, including boilers and auxiliary motors, on board ship. After a year, and passing another examination, he would be rated fourth class, equivalent to petty officers. He would be promoted to chief petty officer rate after another year.[50]

Mechanicians were another means of making up the numbers of highly skilled engineers. An intelligent leading stoker could apply to become one. After an eighteen-month course in the mechanical training establishment at Devonport he would become the equivalent of a fully trained artificer, with the rank of chief petty officer. Mechanicians were quite a rare breed for there were only 398 of them in the Navy in 1937 and the numbers did not expand fast; eighty were under training in 1943, though the school had capacity for 140.

A River-class frigate had one chief ERA, who was the engineering officer's deputy, plus three ERAs (one for each watch). An ERA might be entrusted with great responsibility, especially on a small ship like a frigate. Engine-room Artificer Second Class Cyril Ford was in charge of the boiler room of HMS *Jed* during an attack on a U-boat:

> During D/C attacks on 28th August guage [*sic*] glasses were broken in Nos 1 & 2 Boilers, lights were extinguished and oil fuel suction was lost in No 2 boiler room. Ford obtained fuel supply almost immediately by opening valves on stand-by tanks, rigged up jury lights and fitted new glasses. His presence of mind and resourcefulness enabled attacks to be sustained without pause.[51]

ERA Third Class White was in charge of the engine-room department of HMS *Findhorn* during the illness of the engineer officer late in 1944. He kept the engines running despite major defects, and operated them during an attack which led to the sinking of *U-198*.[52]

Stokers

Stokers were the less skilled members of the engine-room team, equivalent to the able and ordinary seamen on deck. In peacetime, stokers were recruited at a later age than seamen: between eighteen and twenty-five. They never had the experience of being 'broken' at the training camps for boys, so they tended to be much more independent than the seamen, and less subject to formal discipline. In wartime there was no age difference between stokers and seamen, but traditions lingered and the engine room tended to have a freer atmosphere than the bridge or the deck. The title of stoker was misleading, as they did not have to tend coal fires as in the past. It was not attractive, and there was a suspicion that wartime members of the branch were less intelligent than seamen.

HMS *Cabot* was set up in July 1940 for part-one training of stokers under the command of the Plymouth Division, and moved to Yorkshire two years later. HMS *Duke* was commissioned at Great Malvern in 1941 to take 1000 stokers as well as miscellaneous ratings. Portsmouth men were trained at Stamshaw Camp near the city, where conditions were less than comfortable.

The stoker's duties were described in an official pamphlet:

> Under supervision, tends coal or oil-fired boilers, keeps watch on main and auxiliary machinery. Reads simple recording instruments, inspects self-lubricated bearings, oils open-type engines, runs fire and bilge pumps.[53]

A newly qualified stoker would probably be employed as a watch-keeper in the boiler room. If he showed himself 'capable and zealous' in the performance of his duties, he might be transferred to the engine room proper as a watch-keeper. After that he could be trained informally to look after the auxiliary machinery, after which he would be eligible for the leading stoker's course.[54] The temperature could become very high in the engine room. In the *Barle* it was recorded as 102°F (39°C). The boiler rooms were even worse; 104°F in the forward one and 111°F (40°C and 44°C) in the after.[55]

The stokers had slightly better promotion prospects than seamen for they had a larger hierarchy of petty officers and chiefs. A River-class frigate was allowed one chief stoker, six stoker petty officers and six leading stokers as well as twelve stokers. The stoker petty officers had their own mess.

The boiler room of HMS *Mourne* in Liverpool, with two stokers at work. (Imperial War Museum ADM A17875)

Miscellaneous Ratings

The third group of the ship's company comprised the 'miscellaneous' ratings who carried out clerical, domestic and medical duties. They were distinguished from the seamen and stokers by wearing 'fore and aft rig', an inferior version of the peaked cap and jacket worn by officers and petty officers. It was not a particularly popular uniform, having none of the glamour of the officer's gold braid or the seaman's cap, collar and bell-bottom trousers. One steward found it 'a cross between that of a taxi driver and a workhouse inmate'.[56] Clerical and domestic ratings wore a star on the right arm with a letter to indicate their branch.

Each ship of the River-class was allowed one leading supply assistant (S) to take charge of the stores under the first lieutenant. In domestic affairs, the class system of the age was observed carefully. There were two types of cook: the officers' cook (OC), who could produce a wide variety of food, and the ship's company cook (C), who specialised in plain bulk cooking for the crew. The original scheme of complement allowed a leading cook for the officers and a cook or assistant cook for the ship's company. The cooks studied the *Manual of Naval Cookery*, with chapters on cooking for a general mess as used in most ships, spices and condiments, invalid cookery, field cookery for landing parties, bread and cake-making and in miscellaneous subjects such as cleanliness, serving of meals and the dietary values of various foods. Cooking was still regarded as a menial trade rather than a high art in Britain at that time, and the status of naval cooks was low.

The sick-berth attendant (SBA) was the doctor's assistant. SBAs learned the trade in the three main naval hospitals at Chatham, Portsmouth (Haslar) and Plymouth (Stonehouse). At the start of the war the normal nine- to twelve-month course was reduced to ten weeks, largely by eliminating theoretical study. It was then increased to twenty, and later to ten yet again when there was great pressure to send men on to the fleet. An SBA wore a red cross on a white background inside a ring on his right arm.

One leading officer's steward (OS) and two stewards were allowed for the wardroom. They were trained in many duties which had little relevance in the stormy waters of the Atlantic, though they might have been more useful when the ship had a period of rest in port:

> A space of at least two feet should be allowed between the centres of each plate, but, wherever possible, this should be increased to 30 inches to allow more comfort to guests.
>
> In removing plates from the table, they should be taken with the left hand from the left-hand side of the diner. Dinner plates should be carefully lifted with both hands if necessary.
>
> Cabins should be tidied and dusted daily, bedding aired for as long as possible before the bed is made down, clothes thoroughly brushed, cleaned and folded before being put away, and boots and shoes cleaned daily. Cabins to be thoroughly cleaned out once a week.[57]

Of course, it was very different in wartime. According to Monsarrat, '…the allowance of three stewards for twelve officers seemed inadequate by any except hash-house standards: in harbour it meant one dishing up, one ashore on liberty and one to serve the meal on his own.'[58]

Chapter 6: Accommodation

Officers' Accommodation

Everyone was cramped on board a frigate, but officers lived in accommodation which was luxurious compared with that of the seamen. A Canadian report of November 1943 found that 435.75 out of the 1510.06 gross tonnage of the *Barle* was used for the accommodation of officers and men, or twenty-eight per cent. Out of that 435.75 tons, fifteen per cent was for the use of a dozen or so officers, fifty-eight per cent was for about 130 men, and the remaining twenty-eight per cent was for neutral spaces such as passages and the sick bay. Taken in these terms, the average officer took up nearly three times as much space as the average seaman.[1]

The Captain's Cabin

The captain was the only person on board whose cabin was big enough to live in privacy, though most chose not to do so and used the facilities of the wardroom for eating. The captain's accommodation was placed on the forecastle deck, under the forward end of the shelter deck, and took up nearly all the space on that deck between frames twenty-two and thirty-three. It was directly under the forward 4-in. gun and the cabin was interrupted by its support. The cabin was on the port side and took up about two-thirds of the space. It had to serve for sleeping as well as eating, recreation, entertaining and working, for there was no separate sleeping cabin as would be found on a larger ship.

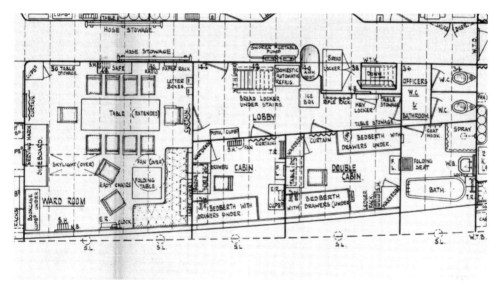

The Captain's cabin in the *Exe.* Admiralty Collection, Box ADFBI30, plan NPN8286. (NMM F5149)

According to Nicholas Monsarrat, the cabin was big but the furniture was spartan. 'My own cabin, with bathroom attached, was a big one, and adequately comfortable: though here again the wartime finish was apparent – it had none of *Winger*'s [a fictitious ship in *HM Frigate*] elegance in the form of polished woodwork or cushioned chairs.'[2]

On entering the captain's cabin through a sliding door on the after bulkhead, one would go through a short, narrow passage with the gun support on one side and a safe and drawers on the other. There was a circular table ahead, with three fixed chairs and a sofa against the port bulkhead. Forward of that was a small desk with chairs and racks for paperwork. Forward on the other side was the captain's bed with six drawers underneath. Aft, against the gun support, was his wardrobe. Between the two was the door to the captain's bathroom with toilet, seat, towel rail and hand washbasin – the captain was the only person on board with private facilities. The remainder of the space was taken up by the captain's pantry, where his steward would prepare food. It was entered through a door in the after bulkhead but had no direct communication with the cabin. It had benches and a sink for preparation but the steward would have to take the food to the galley to be cooked. In later ships, it was fitted as a small officer's cabin.

The captain rarely used his main cabin at sea, and its chief value was in allowing him space for entertaining visitors in port – something the Royal Navy set great store on. The captain also had a small sea cabin a deck above, just under the bridge. It had a bunk for snatching some sleep, a chair and table and a small cupboard. It was between the wheelhouse and the chart room, giving easy access to navigational information, but in action the captain would still have to go up a deck to the bridge where data from Asdic, radar and lookouts enabled him to make decisions.

The Wardroom

By long tradition, the officers used the wardroom as a common room for eating, recreation and often for working. In many destroyers and even in the recent Flower-and Black Swan-classes, it was still situated aft in the tradition of the sailing ship, making it difficult to get forward to relieve the watch in heavy seas. The *Rivers*, however, adopted the modern arrangement of putting all the officers' accommodation directly under the bridge.

According to Nicholas Monsarrat,

> The wardroom … was in much the same state of overcrowding as the messdecks: two subs had to eat at a separate table, and the competition for the sofa at the end of a meal recalled the after-dinner rush at a residential hotel … Wartime austerity was much in evidence as regards the furnishing – bleak iron radiators instead of a stove, and chairs of that modern tubular design which makes 'the shape of things to come' so morbid a prospect.[3]

The wardroom was on the starboard side of the upper deck, opposite the sick bay. It was entered from doors in the forward and after bulkheads, each with a curtain to maintain privacy. It was dominated by an extendable table with a chair at each end and four chairs on each side, giving room for ten officers. As Monsarrat mentions, there was a smaller table to the starboard side, with an L-shaped settee and two chairs. Intended mainly for recreation, it could also be used for meals. The after bulkhead had a bookcase and cupboards, and a sideboard for the use of the stewards. There was a safe, a radio, a paper rack and letter-boxes round the sides.

Aft of the wardroom was its pantry, L-shaped and fitted with ordinary and hot cupboards, racks, a bench and a sink. Communication with the wardroom was through a serving hatch over the sideboard.

New captains were warned of the dangers of spending too much time in the wardroom:

Another way of 'reverting to type' is to become too much of a wardroom officer. In the smallest ships the Captain is inevitably a member of the mess and its president, but in ships like a destroyer he is an honorary member, and has a comfortable day cabin of his own in which to sit. He should normally have lunch and dinner in the wardroom, as this will help him to know his officers, but his continued presence is bound to have a somewhat restricting influence, as is exemplified by the tradition that officers should stand when the Captain comes into the mess. A Captain should therefore not outstay his welcome.[4]

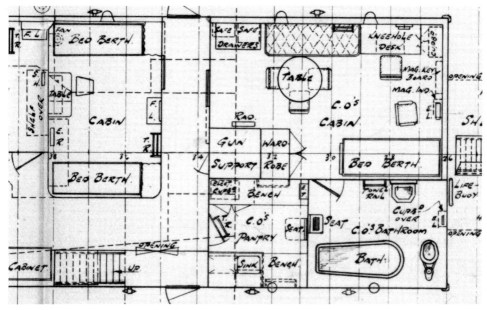

The wardroom and some of the officers' cabins in HMS *Exe*. Collection Box ADFB130, plan NPN8287. (NMM F5148)

Officers' Cabins

Junior officers lived in single and double cabins as far as possible, though sometimes it was necessary to put more men in a cabin. Officers normally expected to sleep in beds rather than hammocks (undermining the usual Admiralty defence of the hammock: that it was more comfortable than a bed at sea). However, when the complement of officers was large, the junior ones often had to sling hammocks.

The plans of the *Exe* show a single cabin just forward of the wardroom fitted with a bed-berth with six drawers underneath; a table or desk, with space for books and a chair; a cupboard; and an electric radiator. Forward of that was a double cabin with berths in each corner. The occupants, who were probably in different watches, had to share a single table. The other cabins were on the forecastle deck aft of the captain's cabin. There was quite a large double cabin with a berth on each side, then a single cabin, followed by another double with two-tier bunks.

As the war progressed, Admiralty fleet orders began to reflect the need for economy in fitting out cabins. In May 1942, for example, it was decreed,

> To economise in labour and material curtained hanging spaces, with wood tops, are to be fitted in lieu of wood corner wardrobes in officers' cabins. Wardrobe hooks and an overhead rod to take coat hangers are to be supplied for each hanging space.[5]

By a separate order, there was to be economy in the use of locks:

> *Chests of Drawers or Bed Berth* – Lock to be provided to one long drawer of the chest of drawers or alternatively to the sliding doors of the bed berth.
>
> *Writing Table or Secretaire* – Lock to be fitted only in the steel-lined drawer of the writing table or secretaire…[6]

Increases in Complement

At the end of April 1942, the Admiralty announced that it had decided to increase the complements of the ships, and more officers' cabins were needed. Though the engineer officer was usually only a warrant officer and therefore junior to all the other officers, he was to be given a cabin of his own on the upper deck. It was also to serve as his office and was to have direct voice-pipe communication with the engine room. Most other officers had to be prepared to share. Two of the three cabins on the forecastle deck were to be converted to doubles, one with a berth on each side, the other with bunks, one above the other. Two additional chairs were to be provided in the wardroom. A month later it was decided to convert the captain's pantry into a small cabin, also reducing the size of the captain's bathroom which had been described as 'enormous' by Constructor W. J. Holt.

In July 1943, after the ships had seen considerable active service, the captain (D) at Greenock reported on HMS *Towy* with a view to increasing officers' accommodation, which was a problem on ships belonging to the senior officers of escort groups who needed extra staff. Apart from the commanding officer's cabin there was a single berth for the first lieutenant, another single for the engineer officer (which also served as his office), and the cabin converted from the captain's pantry, which was very small. None of the single cabins, it was felt, were suitable for conversion to doubles. There were three double cabins and one, on the forecastle deck, was larger than the others and could perhaps be converted to three berths on senior officers' ships.

In the meantime, it was always possible for some of the junior officers to sleep in hammocks, despite the possibility of disruption to late-night wardroom life. The plan of the *Nadder* of 1944 shows spaces for up to four hammocks in the wardroom proper. In addition, the hammock berths in the wardroom lobby, though planned for ratings in the admiral superintending contract-built ships' (ASCBS) suggestions of September 1942, might have been given to officers instead. Using all of these, there was room for sixteen officers in some discomfort.

Messdecks

The Layout of the Messes

In the River-class frigates, as in all major British warships, the seamen and petty officers lived in messdecks in which sleeping, eating and recreation were all done in a single and rather crowded space. Each ship was subdivided into several messes and the men were allocated according to rank and cutstom. The standard messes in any ship were for chief petty officers, engine-room artificers, petty officers, stoker petty officers, seamen, stokers and domestic staff such as stewards. Apart from the obvious division by rank, stokers, seamen and stewards were all kept apart because of differences in culture and standards of cleanliness. Conforming to the general rule, the early River-class had a chief petty officers' mess designed for three men and was situated forward on the upper deck, opposite the lobby outside the officers' cabins. The engine-room artificers lived in a cabin just aft of that, designed for seven men, with the seven-man mess for the seaman petty officers forward. As designed, they were slightly more spacious and better fitted that the junior ratings messes, but on exactly the same principles. A seaman's mess was situated just forward of the petty officers on the upper deck. It was planned for twenty men. There were four tables, two on each side, each designed for four or six men.

The stewards and cooks were segregated on the upper deck aft of the wardroom, for there was a danger that they might pass on wardroom gossip if they got too close to the seamen. Also on the upper deck were the minesweeping messes, originally intended to be used while the ship was sweeping and the lower deck was sealed off. They would cause problems as time went on (see page 153). Well forward on the lower deck were two large messes. The main seaman's mess, the largest in the ship, was two decks under the officers and chief petty officers' area. It had room for forty men in the original plan. Forward of that was the stokers' mess, for they were kept separate from the seamen except in small ships. Traditionally, their culture was different because they had been recruited at a later age than the seamen, and their work with oil and grease meant that they could not adopt the seamen's standard of cleanliness.

The stokers' mess had a typical arrangement. It narrowed forward because of the shape of the bows, and the flare of the bows meant that it was far wider above than below. Seats were fitted against the sides of the ship, also doubling as lockers for the men's goods. Just inboard of them were four tables, two on each side of the ship, for four or six men each. The six-man tables were shorter but slightly wider and had a seat on the inboard side. There was quite a wide, empty space in the centre of the mess. Two steam radiators were fitted forward, and the forward bulkhead had racks for hammocks. The after bulkhead had racks for plates, cutlery, tea, sugar and kettles. Access to the mess was by a door in the after bulkhead from the seamen's mess, or by ladder form the upper deck.

The mess was at the centre of the seaman's social life. Able Seaman Tristan Jones describes one in a typical wartime destroyer, which was perhaps not very different from that in a frigate.

> My mess was the after seaman's mess … I didn't know it at the time, … that they were a crowd of the finest men I ever came across in my life, for all their personal peccadilloes. … I soon got to know all fifteen men in my mess very well, and sorted out the ones to cultivate and the ones to – not avoid – there was no such possibility on a crowded ship – *slide by*.[7]

Each mess had a leading hand in charge, but often he was in a difficult position.

> Due to their messing with the men the Leading Hands of a ship have a difficult job
> to maintain the extra dignity of their rate. Captains were urged to 'Render them
> all the help you can with advice and privileges in giving real meaning to the word
> "Leading."'[8]

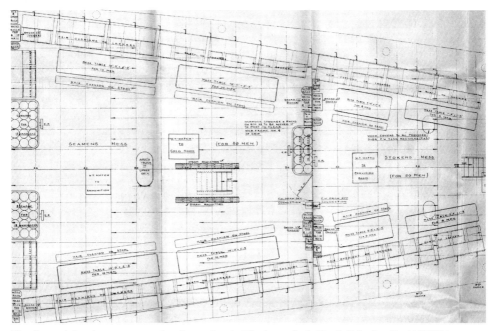

Messing and sleeping arrangement on forward part of the lower deck. Lloyd's Collection, Box LLDB0014, drawing 67. (NMM F5143)

Overcrowding

As with all ships in wartime, the complement tended to rise over the years. The River-class
was originally planned for a complement of 100 officers and men. The *Nith* is listed as
having 120 men in 1943, but that was quite moderate. Early in 1944 the *Cam* had 141,
including nine officers, four chief petty officers, five engine-room artificers, eight stoker
and eight seaman petty officers, five cooks and stewards and 102 seamen, signallers and
stokers.[9] Very little of this rise was recognised in Admiralty orders. These only allocated
three extra men for hedgehog duties in May 1942, a wireman for electrical duties a month
later, and four more torpedo and electrical ratings in July. However, it was recognised in
1941 that 'Apart from a few exceptional cases, R.D.F. [radar] personnel will not be shown
in complement schemes until experience has enabled the requirements to be determined.'[10]
Since part of the expansion came in that area, it is not surprising that it is not accounted
for in the records.

The surgeon-lieutenant of the *Ness* measured the mess spaces in the ship in the autumn of 1943, and found some anomalies. The ten officers had a floor area of 816 sq ft, or 82 sq ft per man – up to six times the space allocated to a rating. Accommodation was poorest in the stokers' minesweeping mess (as he persisted in calling it) where there was only 14 sq ft per man, and only nine of its sixteen members could sling their hammocks, the rest having to sleep on lockers. The remaining stokers were far better off with 24 sq ft each. The petty officers had no real advantage in this respect; the seamen petty officers also had 24 sq ft and the stoker petty officers had 23, slightly less than the ratings under them. The chief petty officers were well off with 42 sq ft each, because there were only three of them, but the ERAs, nominally equal in status, had only 27 sq ft. The stewards were quite well off with 23 sq ft, but the seamen were among the worst off, with 19 sq ft.[11]

Messdeck Fittings

According to the plans of the River-class, each seaman, stoker and steward was to have a steel locker 'lined with green Willesden canvas or other approved material'. The tops of the lockers were fitted with cushions stuffed with hair, for they would often serve as seats round the mess tables, or in some cases as sleeping berths, which must have caused some inconvenience. The lockers were fitted in rows, usually arranged around the sides of the ship. The shape of the space was often irregular in that area, with the hull sides sloping sharply outwards, and the space thus created was usually filled with racks for boots, cap boxes and attaché cases. The chiefs, petty officers and ERAs had separate lockers, each fixed against a bulkhead and allowing access at all times. According to the specification for the class, 'The mess tables in the C.P.O.'s and E.R.A.'s mess spaces are to be made longer than required for actual messing, so as to provide room for keeping engineer room accounts and for general writing purposes.'[12]

Each messdeck would also have racks for stowing hammocks, and 11 in. (28cm) was allowed for each when rolled up and lashed. There would be tables with seating room for all the men allocated to the mess – a minimum of 22in. (55cm) per man, and up to 24 in. (60 cm). As well as the seats on top of the lockers, there were separate benches on the inboard sides of the table, also with hair cushions. There were separate racks for gas masks, kettles, tea and sugar, with a bread locker close by. Messes were heated by steam radiators, along the sides or down the centre line in the case of large messes.

Everyone below the rank of warrant officer was expected to sleep in a hammock. This was a piece of rectangular canvas with sixteen eyelets in each end. Thin ropes known as nettles were attached to these, brought together at a ring and attached to a slightly thicker rope known as a lanyard. The lanyards at each end of the hammock were tied to a bar on the deck above, at a v-shaped indentation which marked each man's place; these were marked out on the builders' plans of the *Rivers'* messdecks. The standard allowance was 20in. (50cm) of width per man. Hammocks were lashed up in the daytime, and perhaps stowed in the racks provided in the messdecks. Despite constant night operations on convoy duty, British naval officers insisted on this; Captain Donald Macintyre of Escort Group B2 was horrified to visit a Canadian escort in which the men's hammocks were kept up in the daytime 'In case they got tired during the day.'[13] British seamen were, however, allowed to 'get their heads down' when off watch in the daytime. A man could find a quiet spot, or rest his head on a mess table, or lie on a seat, taking the risk that someone might disturb him to get to a locker underneath.

The Problems of the Minesweeping Messes

In May 1942, the constructor W. J. Holt found that the accommodation was generally very good, except that the

> …minesweeping mess is really too hot at present to be really suitable for accommodation and if there is to be a considerable increase of complement, necessitating the permanent use of these spaces for the crew of the ship, questions of ventilation and lagging of casing sides should be investigated.[14]

In June 1943, the minesweeping messes of the *Barle* were very little used. One was empty 'except for a few individuals who sling their hammocks there', presumably voluntarily.[15] By September, there were nine men in the starboard minesweeping mess, while the port one was used for storage of medical supplies and as a first-aid distributing station. The occupied mess reached a temperature of 94°F (34°C) in warm weather at night, and often the men slept in the gun shelters where it was cooler.[16] This was less of a problem in the turbine-powered ships, because the heat of the engine was situated much lower in the ship. In HMS *Tweed*, the surgeon found that the stewards' mess was much hotter because it was above the boiler rooms.[17]

By September 1942, the Navy was planning for a much larger complement for the River-class. According to the plan approved by the Admiralty, the messes themselves would stay, with approximately the number of men they had originally been designed for, except that in certain cases a few men would sleep on top of kit lockers, rather than hammocks – four in the seamen's mess on the lower deck (which already had thirty-three men in hammocks), two in the stoker's mess, which already had eighteen, and two more in the stewards' mess. The minesweeping mess was still so named, and it could hold twenty-nine men, though kit lockers were not fitted for them. Three more men could sleep in hammocks in the compartment on the lower deck around the gyrocompass, and two more in the passage outside the wardroom. In all, 136 men could be accommodated in hammocks and eight would sleep on lockers. The ASCBS wanted to fit in even more. He found other compartments fore and aft which could hold four men each, and he wanted four men in the wardroom passage and even two in the wardroom lobby, normally used only by officers. The biggest single change he suggested was to accommodate eleven men instead of six in the stoker petty officers' mess. This was technically possible as the mess was quite large, but it would conflict with Admiralty policy of keeping petty officers and stokers apart from seamen. Since there were only six stoker petty officers allowed in the complement, it was not easy to do anything about it.[18]

The deck plans of HMS *Nadder*, completed at Smith's Dock in January 1944, show how crowded a ship could become in practice. The most cramped space of all was the seamen's mess on the lower deck, with three rows of hammocks holding thirty-five men, while the stoker's mess just forward of it had eighteen hammocks, and the upper seamen's mess on the deck above had seventeen. There were indeed four hammocks in the gyrocompass room as ASCBS had suggested, with four in the corridor outside the wardroom and two inside in the lobby. However, the former minesweeping mess was less crowded than had been suggested. There were three hammocks in each of the two corridors leading to it on each side of the boiler uptake, with six on each side of the engine room and four more just aft of it. This made a total of twenty-two, whereas up to thirty-one had been suggested in the past.

In all, there were hammock spaces for 130 men, plus perhaps eight more on lockers. This was around the typical complement of a frigate at that time, so it seems that the *Nadder* reflected standard practice.

Health on the Messdecks

Overcrowding and severe meteorological conditions could make the messdecks very uncomfortable places in the Atlantic. The surgeon-lieutenant of the *Ness* complained in 1944:

> In general, on the messdecks there is insufficient space for stowage of personal gear… In certain of the messes the arrangements for the stowage of food are not satisfactory. Some of the containers are not large enough and many of them are not proof against vermin and insects.[19]

Ventilation of messdecks, in all conditions of sea and weather, was a matter of some concern to the surgeon-lieutenant of the *Towy*, who noted

> The long periods spent at sea in very bad weather made a healthy atmosphere difficult to maintain, but later the weather improved sufficiently to allow the vent intakes and outlets to be opened nearly all the time.

Later on, however, 'The weather was very good and full advantage was taken of this fact by the ship's company.'[20]

In the *Avon* the problem was clearly identified as condensation or 'sweating'. This was attributed to the inadequate lining of the bulkheads, which was intended to absorb moisture. The builder had been 'niggardly in the extreme in the application of cork'. This was solved by adding some more, but it was more difficult to alter the culture of the crew of the lower deck, who had an

> unhealthy disrespect, that seems to be traditional among seamen, for fresh air on the mess decks. Punkah louvres were often closed, flaps closed down over exhaust trunks although the latter was justified to some extent as some cases are on record where considerable quantities of ocean found their way to the mess decks via these passages.

Furthermore, the seamen were prone to an 'indiscreet use of electrical heaters', which made the situation even worse.[21]

> Even in port the ships could be unhealthy. According to the surgeon of the *Ness*, During the period of this journal, the ship has been in dock. Ventilation has therefore been by both artificial and natural methods and has been reasonably adequate. For a time the minesweepers' messdeck had been less efficiently ventilated but this had now been remedied by the installation of a fan and air trunking.[22]

Fitted for the East Indies, the *Teviot* had only minimal changes in the crew accommodation. The decks were lagged with asbestos against the heat, existing fans were renewed and twelve new table fans were provided for the messdecks.[23] At the other extreme, the surgeon of the *Lagan* found that 'in the cold climate of Newfoundland there was rather an excessive amount of condensation even to the point of rotting some of the ratings' hammocks'.[24]

The *Rivers* were no worse than other British ships of the period, and indeed better than the *Flowers*, for example. Their poor facilities reflected the neglect of interwar governments to raise standards of accommodation, followed by wartime emergencies in which they got even worse.

Other Areas

Space was always precious on a warship, especially a relatively small one which had to spend long periods at sea. Every possible area was adapted to living, fighting or storage space, even very awkward ones in the extreme bows, for example. Corridors were kept to a minimum, partly because first lieutenants disliked them – they were difficult to keep clean because it was difficult to establish who was responsible for them. More importantly, they were a waste of space. The only corridors on the River-class frigates were outside the officers' cabins, ship's office and wireless telegraph room on the forecastle deck; between the chief petty officers' messes and the wardroom on the upper deck and within the wardroom area itself; and on the lower deck, between the gyrocompass compartment and the various storerooms. All had a definite function: to maintain privacy for the officer; to ensure peace and quiet for the telegraphists and the ship's office, or to provide a space on the lower deck for the issue of provisions.

Galleys

By long tradition, the kitchen on a ship was known as the galley. R.B. Buckle, who joined the *Ribble* as a ship's company cook in 1945, described its cooking arrangements:

> Her galley situated on the port side of the upper deck was a fair size in comparison. It was larger than those in some Hunt-class destroyers. To starboard and separated by a wire mesh was the officers galley. At the back of the range was a steamer and against the for'ard bulkhead was the dough-mixing trough for the bread-making. No labour-saving electrical mixer here, it all had to be kneaded by hand.[25]

Each galley had an oil-fired pattern 25H firehearth for the officers and a pattern 5A firehearth for the crew, both with 'steadiflow' burners. They soon proved inadequate for increased crew sizes, as Commodore Stephenson of the *Western Isles* pointed out. This was supported by Surgeon-Lieutenant Tormond Macleod of the *Exe* in 1943; his ship had 128 men excluding officers, on a stove designed for 100.

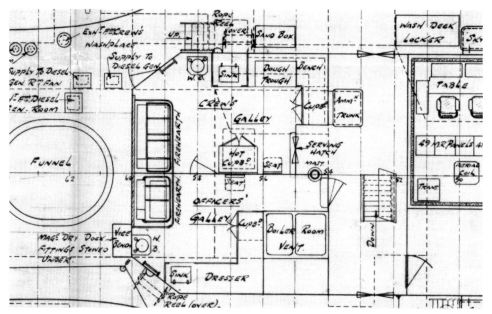

The Galley of _HMS Exe_ Admiralty Collection, Box ADFB130, plan NPN8286. (NMM F5148)

Macleod had contact with American destroyers during a visit to Guantanamo Bay in Cuba in 1943, and he returned 'completely ashamed' of the British system. The first problem was the antiquated type of stove. 'Our cooks work in a hot, oil-burning galley which cannot be kept clean properly for longer than an hour. They themselves are filthy, partly due to upbringing but chiefly due to the soot from the stove.'[26]

Macleod found ways to improve the crew's access to the galley of the _Exe_. As planned, the cooks of most of the messes had to come up the hatch from the lower deck, then out into the open to get the food from a grill aft of the galley. This caused unnecessary cooling in the air, congestion as the men moved to and from the hatch, and affected the ship's blackout arrangements. The grill was moved to the forward side of the galley, inside the superstructure and closer to the hatch, and the problem was solved.[27]

Heads and Washplaces

Naval toilets were known as heads, from the days of sailing ships when men had to sit in the open structure aft of the figurehead to relieve themselves. The distribution of heads reflected rank. With a complement of 141 officers and men, HMS _Cam_ had six seats for 107 ratings, or one per eighteen ratings; one for 12.5 chiefs and petty officers; one per four officers; while the captain had his own.[28]

Seats were of the 'horse-shoe' pattern. The crew's WCs had 'dwarf' bulkheads which did not go the full height, with dwarf doors in front. Urinals were provided for the petty officers and crew, while officers and chiefs had enough toilet cubicles not to need them.[29] Baths were allowed for the officers, and the captain had one of his own while the wardroom had one for up to a dozen officers. The crew was provided with showers.

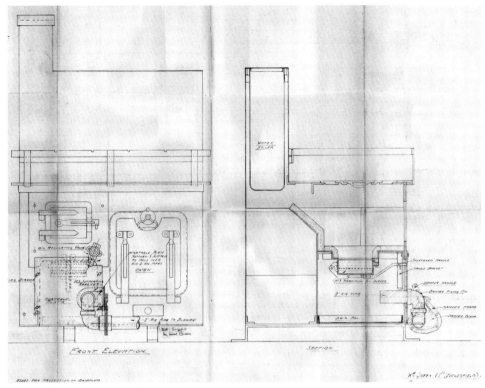

The Admiralty patent 25H galley range as fitted. Admiralty Collection, Box ADBB924, plan 768657/2, drawing 10163. (NMM F5150)

Two showers to be fitted in the crew's washplace. Each shower is to be provided with a spring-loaded valve. A mixing fitting and non-return valve is to be provided at the junction of the hot and cold freshwater systems for regulating the temperature of the supply. Non-return valves are to be provided to ensure that the hot water cannot enter the freshwater system.[30]

In the *Barle* it was found that the seamen's bathroom and latrines were uncomfortable at sea, because the deadlights were only opened for one hour each morning, and there was no other ventilation.[31]

The storerooms in the stern had their problems:

In frigates the quarterdeck has only about 5 ft clearance from the water, then even with a slight sea running this part of the ship is always very wet. Beneath this wet quarterdeck are the ship's food and clothing stores which are also damp – in fact we always have to dry the blankets and clothing … before giving them out. The food is also very damp and some has even been spoilt by seawater. During the last trip we had 6 inches of water in it all the time.[32]

The Sick Bay

In general, medical officers were very pleased with the sick-bay accommodation in the River-class. It consisted of a room near midships on the port side of the upper deck. The surgeon of the *Barle* found that three or four camp beds could be accommodated in addition to the two cots. His only complaint was that the taps were of the push type – not suitable for scrubbing up.[33] The surgeon-lieutenant was pleased with the equipment:

> This is satisfactory in every way. It is amidships on the upper deck. Measurements: 15ft x 12ft 6ins.
>
> Ventilation:- Supply form 5 [in.] with 6 louvres. Skylight. Four-bladed fan. Two portholes. Natural exhaust measuring 12[in.] x 24[in.].
>
> There is a separate ablution cabinet with one supply louvre and a 5-[in.] exhaust fan.
>
> The furniture consists of two very comfortable swinging cots, folding operating table, folding armchair, two ordinary chairs, desk, wooden cabinet for drugs and dressings, metal cabinet used for instruments, dressings, etc., and larger metal wall rack for stretchers and splints. In addition there are two wooden wall racks used for books and papers. The lighting is good, including shadowless lighting for the operating table, but the emergency floodlight and head light which should be available have not yet been fitted.
>
> A[n] electric instrument steriliser, electric kettle, and small electric high-pressure steam steriliser have been supplied. The last two have been particularly useful, enabling a supply of sterile dressings for minor cases to be available, while keeping sterile boxes sealed for major operations which may be necessary.[34]

The surgeon lieutenant of the *Aire* had the sick-bay doors removed and replaced with curtains, believing that it would aid ventilation.[35]

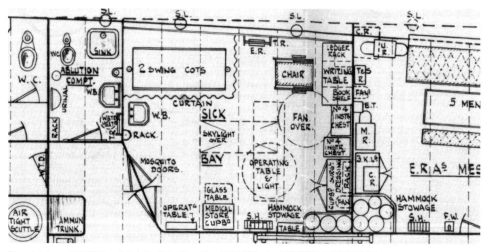

The sick bay of *HMS Exe.* Admiralty Collection, Box ADFB130, plan NPN8286. (NMM F5149)

Chapter 7: The Frigates in Service

The Battle of the Atlantic

The Origins of the Battle

The River-class frigates were designed specifically to fight in the long, drawn-out campaign that lasted for the whole of the war against Germany and became known as the Battle of the Atlantic. Conditions were almost as horrific as those on the Western Front of World War I, and the struggle lasted even longer, though few people would suggest that it was as futile. In terms of World War II, the Battle of the Atlantic had less publicity than Dunkirk, the Battle of Britain, the North African Campaign, the bombing of Germany and the invasion of Europe. The Battle of the Atlantic was long, with few clear-cut victories, and serious losses could not be revealed in wartime. Because it was largely fought by temporary officers, there was even a danger that the Royal Navy itself might forget it. In 1948, one admiral said, 'I know nothing about the Battle of the Atlantic! I was never involved in it! My war experience was in completely different theatres.'[1] This attitude caused D. W. Waters, later deputy director of the National Maritime Museum, to compile the staff history of the conflict.

Why was it called the Battle of the Atlantic? Usually a battle is taken to mean an affair lasting from a few hours to a few weeks; this one lasted five and a half years. A battle was traditionally fought in a single place, such as Trafalgar, Waterloo, the Somme or El Alamein. This one ranged even beyond the Atlantic into the Arctic Ocean, as the map of merchant-ship sinkings at the height of the battle shows. It involved sailors of the Royal and merchant navies, as well as many Allied fleets, airmen, shipbuilders, dockers, and famously, intelligence staff in the decoding of German signals.

It is no surprise to find that the extension of the meaning of 'battle' was created by Winston Churchill. At the fall of France, he claimed, 'We have lost a battle; we have not lost a war.' He said, 'The Battle of France is over; the Battle of Britain is about to begin.' This, it turned out, was not a full-scale invasion but a series of air fights over southern England in 1940, but the use of the term was established. In March 1941, Churchill was also the first to use the word 'battle' to describe the war with the U-boat. 'In view of various German statements,' he declared, 'we must assume that the Battle of the Atlantic has begun.' By extension it was used to describe the first U-boat war in 1915 – 18, so this became the Second Battle of the Atlantic. Later, the Navy would plan for a third Battle of the Atlantic against the Soviet Union.

Britain could only produce about half her own foodstuffs even in peacetime. In wartime she also needed vast quantities of oil for ships, tanks and aircraft; the traditional fuel of coal was useless for these. With most of the European continent occupied by the enemy, no supplies could come from there. Moreover, from June 1940 Britain's only hope of winning the war was with the support of the United States, at first in the form of supplies and munitions, and later with armies, ships and air forces. There was no doubt that closing the Atlantic route would mean the end of Britain, and of any American involvement in Europe for the foreseeable future.

Conditions in the Atlantic

The Atlantic is not the most hospitable of oceans. The Caribbean, Mediterranean and Pacific have all seen their share of conflict and tragedy, but still conjure up images of sun-drenched beaches and tropical or subtropical paradises. The Atlantic, with its great waves crashing against the rocks of North America and western Europe, tends to make one think of storm and hardship. It is much smaller than the Pacific and on the whole no more troubled by bad weather, but its islands are mostly situated around the edges rather than in the middle, so it usually has to be crossed in a single leg. Most crossings in the last 500 years have been across the North Atlantic, between northern Europe and North America. In the eighteenth century, they were achieved by slaves and convicts in conditions of great hardship. In the first half of the nineteenth century, poor emigrants, fleeing from, for example, the Irish famine, fared little better.

Early in the twentieth century, the great liners brought in a feeling of luxury for some, but that was undermined by the loss of the *Titanic*. For Europeans, the Atlantic was an ocean which their relatives had crossed at great peril to escape from the hardships of the Old World. For Americans, it was what their ancestors had crossed in fear and wonder. The great Battle of the Atlantic, from 1939 – 45, did much to reinforce this image of danger and hardship. The very title of Nicholas Monsarrat's novel, *The Cruel Sea*, sums up our fears about this ocean. But as one of his captains, Sam Lombard Hobson, points out, it was the U-boats, not the sea, which produced the cruelty.

The Atlantic Ocean proper consists of more than 31 million square miles, though most of the action took place in the north Atlantic, the main communication route between Britain and North America. Convoys from the United States and Canada were routed well to the north to avoid enemy air cover and the worst of the U-boat attacks. This took them through the notorious fogs of Newfoundland (present on sixty per cent of summer days) and close to the area where icebergs presented a danger. It took them through the depressions which form off Newfoundland where the tropical fronts meet. The depressions move westward in succession, creating circular patterns of strong winds accompanied by fronts and heavy rain. They are well known in Britain, where they are chiefly responsible for the unpredictable climate. The winds create strong waves and often a heavy swell many miles away, so the north Atlantic is one of the roughest sea areas in the world. Ships would often have to sail against heavy seas, and perhaps stop, or heave to, in the very worst weather. There was virtually no shelter from the winds between the ports of Newfoundland or Labrador and the coasts of Britain and Ireland. In the winter of 1941 – 42, there were eighty-eight occasions when winds were of force seven or more, almost at gale force, and seven when it reached storm force ten. The next winter, the first in which the River-class frigates were active, was even worse. There were 106 winds of force seven and upwards, and ten winds of force ten or more. It was a very inhospitable area in which to fight a major campaign.

The Course of the Battle

There never was a campaign of greater historical importance than the Battle of the Atlantic. Defeat would have starved Britain of oil, military supplies and food and would have prevented the country from continuing the war. The great Allied effort to re-invade Europe in 1944 would have been impossible, with an incalculable effect on world history. Either the Soviet Union – or, more likely, Nazi Germany – probably would have been left in total control of the European continent, and the victory of totalitarianism would have been complete. By the spring of 1942, when the first of the River-class entered service, the campaign had already gone through several stages. It began accidentally on the first day of the war, when *U-30*, against Hitler's orders, torpedoed the liner *Athenia*. It became far more serious after the fall of France opened up new bases for the U-boats, and Britain became Germany's main enemy. British shipping was routed around the north of Ireland, and the English Channel was virtually closed. The U-boats had their main success in a funnel extending west and north from the coasts of western Scotland and Northern Ireland.

By the spring of 1941, as neither invasion and bombing of Britain seemed likely to produce a result, the Battle of the Atlantic was seen as the main danger to the country. But the British were beginning to enjoy some success. Three of the great U-boat aces – Prien, Kretschmer and Schepke – were killed or captured in March. The U-boats began to move further out into the ocean, and the limits of convoy escort were moved with them. By June 1941, it was normal to have an escort all the way across the Atlantic. British success in decoding German Enigma signals meant that they were able to evade the worst attacks. When America entered the war in December 1941, the U-boat attack switched to the east coast of the United States. The American navy was sceptical about the need for convoy, suspicious of British advice, and in any case most of its resources were needed in the Pacific. The U-boats enjoyed another 'happy time' until the middle of 1942, when local escorts made the area much less easy for them.

The attack was now concentrated in the mid-Atlantic, in the 'air gap' where cover from aircraft based in Newfoundland, Iceland or Britain was not available. It continued through the winter of 1942 – 43. The Allies were winning the war on every other front. After the battles of Stalingrad and Kursk, the Germans were in retreat in Russia. After Midway and Guadalcanal, the Japanese had no hope of winning in the Pacific. After the Anglo-American North African invasions and the Battle of El Alamein, the Germans and Italians were on the defensive in the Mediterranean. But in the Atlantic, the U-boats were still inflicting intolerable losses on the most vital of the Allied supply lines.

Working Up

The crew of a newly built ship was selected by the drafting commander and his staff at one of the main naval bases at Portsmouth, Plymouth or Chatham. Men were sent there after they had completed their training, or had left an earlier ship for one reason or another. Some might spend weeks there, living in conditions of great squalor, and in February 1944 there were 75,000 men in the three barracks, with 500 moving in and out each day. Ratings whose skills were in short supply, such as anti-submarine and radar operators, would be drafted out in a few days. Men would be called out by tannoy or loudspeaker, assembled with their kit on the barrack square, then marched out to a train to take them to the ship. Since most of the River-class were built in Scotland or the north of England, they could expect a journey of many hours in slow and overcrowded wartime trains.

The captain, first lieutenant, engineering officer and some of the key ratings were already there and had made plans for the arrival for the rest of the crew. They were allocated berths and duties on board and the ship sailed out for the first time to carry out extensive trials. After that, the red ensign and the shipbuilder's flag were hauled down to be replaced by the white ensign of the Royal Navy as the captain signed for the ship. The frigate was now a fully commissioned ship of the Royal Navy, though there was much to do before it was ready for action.

Tobermory

HMS *Western Isles*, the main working-up base for escort vessels, was originally planned as a joint operation with the French at Quiberon Bay on the Atlantic coast of France, but events soon overtook that. The harbour at Tobermory on the island of Mull is one of the safest in Britain, sheltered from almost all winds. Since the ships would arrive complete with crews and most of their stores, the lack of a rail link was not important. The base began to operate in July 1940. It became overstretched, and there in December 1943 HMS *Mentor II* was commissioned at Stornaway on the Island of Lewis as an independent command.[2]

Vice-Admiral Sir Gilbert Stephenson RN (retired) commanded the Tobermory base. At the outbreak of war he was recalled as a commodore RNR: the highest rank available to a retired officer. He began as a commodore of convoys and took part in the Dunkirk evacuation in 1940.

From 1941, HMS *Western Isles* was located on a former Dutch ship of 1903, the *Batavier IV*. Sometimes it was suggested that a shore base would have been more appropriate than a training ship, against which it was argued that

> the fact that the ship is moored amongst the flotilla wearing the broad pendant of the Commodore has an important bearing on the success of the base. The psychological value of being afloat cannot be over-estimated… Power boats transport classes back and forward and many pulling boats – whalers and skiffs – are seen approaching the gangways, all under they eyes of the Commodore and his staff officers, who are on the look-out for slackness in observing the rig of the day, or for the errors of the inexperienced oarsman or coxswain. Human nature being what it is, it is safe to say that the first impression gained on arrival at Tobermory would be considerably lessened if the introductory interview took place in a shore establishment instead of the flag ship.[3]

Many stories were told about Stevenson. Richard Baker provides the 'authorised version' of a celebrated incident. The commodore came aboard a corvette one winter's morning:

> Without any preliminaries he flung his gold-braided cap on the deck and said abruptly to the Quartermaster - 'That is a small unexploded bomb dropped by an enemy plane. What are you going to do about it?' The sailor, who had evidently heard about these unconventional tests of initiative, promptly took a step forward and kicked the cap into the sea. Everyone waited for a great roar of protest from the Commodore. But not at all. He warmly commended the lad on his presence of mind, and then, pointing to the submerged cap said: 'That's a man overboard! Jump in and save him!'[4]

The Syllabus at *Western Isles*

The time at Tobermory varied according to the size of the ship. A frigate spent twenty days, and compared with a corvette it had extra training in gunnery, harbour drills and boat work, damage control and field training.[5] Though the personality of the commodore might have appeared to dominate the base, there was in fact a training syllabus, in its fifth edition by February 1944. Ideally, the newly commissioned frigate or corvette would arrive at 1630 and the commodore would meet the captain to explain the objects of *Western Isles*.

After that, the next few days were 'relatively calm'.[6] On the first full day a staff officer would come on board to discuss the fighting organisation of the ship with the officers and key ratings, while the *Western Isles* gunnery officer would inspect the armament, followed by inspections by the engineer, electrical and radar officers attached to the base – though, on the whole, the engineering department seems to have had it fairly easy during the course. Towards the end of the morning all men who were available would go to see the film *Escort Teams at Work*, followed by a short address by the commodore. He tended to assume no previous knowledge in the crew. He told one captain, 'You take it for granted that everyone knows nothing about his job and start from rock bottom.'[7]

That afternoon, as in the next few days, the crew would split into its separate departments. The signallers would be kept busy by incessant exercises, and one suspects that Stephenson did not trust the training done in the signal schools. Radar teams, including unqualified ratings, would have theoretical instruction, with practical work in a radar training yacht later in the course. Submarine detector ratings and their officers would see a film on attack procedures and then go on to the attack teacher. Gunners would carry out drill on the ship's own guns, plus practice on the dome teacher, and go to showings of the *Eyeshooting* film which instructed them on visual aiming against an aircraft. Seamen would practise boat drill, lookout duties by day and night, and study seamanship under the boatswain of *Western Isles*. Foot drill ashore, known as 'Field Training', would bring up to half the crew together at a time. Two periods of about two hours each were allotted to this. There were demonstrations of pyrotechnics, rifle practices and inspections of the ship's stores.

Eventually the ship would go to sea, carrying anti-submarine and gunnery officers from *Western Isles*, with a radar instructor rating. It would chase a motor launch acting as a U-boat on the surface, and carry out sub-calibre firing of the main armament. In the afternoon it would begin anti-submarine practices with a real submarine (the 'clockwork mouse'), and then anchor in Loch Lataich, in the south of Mull near Iona. Next morning, the ship would do more anti-submarine practice, then sea exercises such as taking a ship in tow, before returning to Tobermory to do two more days of departmental exercises; on the ninth day there was the possibility of a 'make and mend' or half-holiday 'at the commanding officer's discretion'.[8]

The second sea trip included another mock surface chase, intended to train the crew to detect and attack a U-boat on the surface. This was followed by eight rounds of full-calibre firing, and in the afternoon there were more exercises with the 'clockwork mouse'. This continued for two more days, with overnight stops in Loch Lataich, before return to Tobermory. The next day was a long one, starting at 0830 with buzzer exercises for signallers, rocket-flare drill for gunners and boat work for seamen. The ship sailed early in the afternoon and did an anti-aircraft firing practice with a towed target, followed by a second full-calibre practice with the main guns. After dark there was a night-firing exercise.

Over the last few days the group communications exercise to test the ship's communication and plotting organisation was discussed and planned in several periods. It took place near the end of the course and involved all the ship's executive officers, signallers, radar and anti-submarine operators and plotters. Still at anchor in Tobermory Bay, several ships would respond to a time-ball dropped by *Western Isles*, signalling the start of the exercise. The ships had already been briefed on the convoy they were supposed to be escorting, the state of the weather and the tactical situation. Signals flashed from the *Western Isles*, sending ships on mock chases of submarines identified by radar or asdic; if the latter, they opened a pack of prepared Asdic traces and followed the information given by them. They might be detailed to pick up survivors, which would take them out of the exercise for fifteen minutes and no more. They might be credited with sinking a submarine by gunfire. After two hours the officers and senior ratings would go on board *Western Isles* with their logs and plots, and compare them with the master plot prepared by the instructors, followed by a discussion on the lessons learnt.

This was followed by films, exercises, drills and a lecture on first aid. Finally, the ship was cleaned for a last inspection and the commodore came on board for a debrief. This could be a nerve-wracking moment for the captain and officers, for it was well known that Stephenson was harder on them than on the crew, and strictest of all with regular RN officers.

Boats crews training at Tobermory, rescuing survivors from a sunken ship. (Imperial War Museum D 20273)

Stornaway

Captain D. M. Cann commanded the Stornaway base. He did not have the sense of drama of Stephenson, but he seems to have been highly competent, and more thoughtful about the procedures. He outlined his principles in 1944: 'The thought in the mind of all instructors must be "We are here to help and advise these ships", *not* "We've got you now and you jolly well do as you're told." He gave a list of priorities:

- Fighting organisation is the first item.
- All instruction must be progressive.
- All radar instruction should be completed before the ship proceeds to sea.
- All gunnery instruction, except for Stores and Accounts, Shallow Diving
- Apparatus, Range and possibly one session of Field Training should be completed satisfactorily before proceeding for the Sea Gunnery Programme.
- The majority of A/S Attack Teacher and D.C. Training should be done before commencing A/S Exercises. A.T.W. [Ahead-throwing weapon] Training should be completed by this time to enable full value to be obtained from a second day's A.T.W. Attacks.
- Remaining subjects may be fitted in as convenient. It is desirable to keep a few harbour subjects in hand in case the sea programme has to be cancelled.
- In the case of a smaller ship, fewer subjects are required but it is not possible to programme so many subjects at one time. The total time required is therefore much the same in either case.

In most respects, Stornaway's procedure was not radically different from Tobermory's. On arrival, the officers and crew were addressed by the captain, who stressed the need for secrecy – secret weapons were 'not secret when talked about'. Working up consisted of individual and team training; speed was essential in modern warfare; instruction involved long hours, hard work and punctuality. Captain Cann concluded by hoping that 'efficiency will increase, confidence in self and shipmates will ensue, thus resulting in a happy ship, to the benefit of all'.

After that, the first day's work was 'always light' and frequently did not 'exceed checking the ship's organisation'.[9] All officers and men had at least one session on boat work, but the final number depended on the abilities of the crews. Two high-speed air-sea rescue launches were available for surface training when they were not needed for their normal work. The gunnery programme consisted of low-angle firing at targets, an anti-aircraft shoot at a smoke burst or balloon (in the early stages there was no towed target available for anti-aircraft practices, and these had to be done against smoke targets), starshell and rocket firing by night, simulated surface attacks by E-boats, a night shoot at two targets on both sides of the ship, and a night encounter exercises, which was not always possible in such northern latitudes in the summer.

Escort Group Training

A further stage in anti-submarine training, involving several ships of an escort group, was added in the second half of the war. Since there had been few realistic anti-submarine exercises before the war, each group had to evolve its own screen arrangements for convoys, its own tactics, and its own terms to describe them. When convoys were handed over from one group to another in mid-ocean, or a ship was transferred to another group, there was a great deal of confusion. In August 1941, for example, two groups united in defence of Convoy SL81. It was not possible to put one group on each side of the convoy so that they could employ their own group tactics in the allotted area, so one group, without its normal leader, was somewhat underused. 'It is probable… that many of them missed the old leader's voice and may on occasion have waited for an executive order which never came.'[10]

The first attempt to remedy this was in November 1942, when extensive shore exercises were carried out in the tactical school at Liverpool, allowing an analysis of techniques used by individual group commanders, after which Captain Gilbert Roberts compiled a common series of orders.[11] Meanwhile, Captain A. J. Baker-Creswell, in command of an escort group based in the Clyde, made contact with the submarines based there and gave his group half a day's practice before sailing with each convoy. Late in 1942, at the instigation of the First Sea Lord, he was given the chance to organise a group training school. He chose the yacht *Philante*, formerly belonging to the millionaire Sir Thomas Sopwith, as his flagship, and it was sent to Hull to be fitted out with staff offices. He settled for a submarine and two motor torpedo boats (MTB) to simulate U-boats at night. He was to operate from Londonderry, where a naval base had been improvised from nothing since the start of the war, and he would be in constant touch with ships on active service. This was not entirely successful. The river channel was badly marked, and ships under training often went aground; Baker-Cresswell had to lead them in and out in an MTB, doing his own navigation. He felt he was not getting enough cooperation from Captain Stewart at Londonderry, and the course moved to Larne for a time.[12]

Continuity Training

Though escort vessels in the Battle of the Atlantic were in constant danger while escorting convoys, they might go some time without any contact with the enemy. In 1943, for example, the frigate HMS *Itchen* escorted eight successive convoys without incident. It was important to maintain skills in weapons and sensors, and for that reason the shore bases were well equipped to train crews. The Londonderry base was equipped with an anti-submarine tactical school, two anti-submarine attack teachers, a depth charge, a hedgehog and a squid driller, gunnery, signal, and direction-finding schools and a mock-up of a U-boat interior to aid boarding parties to prevent scuttling and capture vital equipment.

By 1943, each group and ship had a sophisticated programme of continuity training between voyages, intended to practise skills which might not be used on each voyage, to teach new techniques and to aid teamwork within the group. On arrival at the home base for a relatively long period for boiler cleaning, half the crew was sent on leave, including all the Asdic team except one responsible rating, who was not the HSD. The next time, nearly all the Asdic team, including the ASCO, was available when the ship was out of action. They trained together in the many simulators that were available: for example, the night escort attack teacher and the anti-submarine attack teachers. Other members of the crew could drill in depth-charge loading on a special rig, or on hedgehog loading. There was a mock-up of the inside of a U-boat so that boarding parties could quickly find the sea cocks, the latest electronic gear, the confidential documents of a sinking submarine, and especially the Enigma machine. There were also gunnery, radar, signal and HF/DF schools for training other teams. At Liverpool, the captain (D) instituted anti-submarine attack tests (ASATs) for each ship on the attack teacher. These were intended to ensure that each crew had the correct procedure and skills to sink submarines, and were only passed when at least one hit was made on a target, with the ship still in contact afterwards.

Escort and Support Groups

Escort Groups

The escort group was the standard British unit in the Battle of the Atlantic. It was appreciated that it was best for the same ships to operate together over as long a period as possible, and indeed it was essential before 1942, as each group tended to evolve its own operating methods. The number of ships in an escort group tended to rise over the years. In the early stages of the war there was an average of two per convoy, though at the time U-boat attacks were not very intense. By September 1942, there was an average of 5.5 escorts per convoy; by the end of the year that had risen to 7.5.[13] A larger group could provide something approaching all-round protection to a convoy, and it could also afford to detach ships to bring the hunt of a U-boat to a conclusion. The status of an escort group was not clearly defined in the naval hierarchy, but it was obviously considered inferior to that of a destroyer flotilla, and well below a squadron of battleships or cruisers.

The Senior Officer

The leader of a group of escort ships normally held the rank of commander, though if he was promoted to captain during the course of his command, he might well remain in post with his new rank, as experienced group leaders were not easy to find. The responsibilities were great for an officer of middling rank: command of up to ten sea-going naval ships, responsibility for the 'safe and timely arrival' of a convoy of dozens of ships carrying millions of pounds worth of goods of immeasurable strategic value. The commodore of the merchant ship convoy was often a retired admiral who had once greatly outranked him, but the escort group commander was in charge in case of attack. The Navy was always reluctant to use acting rank, and it would have to do so on a grand scale to promote all the escort group commanders *en bloc*. They tended to be relatively young men, which was essential in view of the gruelling nature of the work. D. A. Rayner was 'burned out' and 'round the bend', in his own words, after five and a half years at sea and a few months in charge of an escort group.[14] The great majority of escort-group commanders were regular Royal Navy in contrast to the RNR and RNVR officers under them. This was perhaps the only level in the escort force, apart from the petty officers' messes, where the regular Navy predominated. The group commander had the rather prosaic title of 'senior officer' or SO, and these letters were often put after the name of his ship in reports on convoy proceedings.

    In the larger ships of the Navy, the command of the ship itself was carefully separated from the command of a fleet, even when the admiral was on board using the ship as his flagship. This was possible because in a battleship or large cruiser there was space for separate cabins, operations rooms and sometimes even bridges for both the admiral and the flag captain. Things were very different in the close confines of an escort vessel. Rayner was in command of the 30th Escort Group but had a captain under him. He found it very uncomfortable:

> I had a Captain in the ship in which I was living as Senior Officer.... it could never be made to work. It was not fair to either side, if only because the ships themselves were not big enough to house the two in comfort. After years of having my own steward, sea cabin and chart table, I would now lose the Captain's pencil, or find that he had carried off my rubber in his pocket. To make matters even more difficult there was the ship's navigator as well as my own staff navigator. All four of us who had an interest in the ship's position had to use the same chart table.[15]

Transferring temporarily to the *Tay* just before the crucial convoy HX 231, Peter Gretton took a small staff with him:

> …An Asdic specialist (a bosun), a navigator as operations officer, a H/F D/F specialist whom I made communications officer, a radar specialist and a few communications ratings – were accommodated in the *Tay*. The ship was horrified at the thought, but the arrangement worked well on the whole, due mainly to the tolerance of all concerned and especially the Captain, who always tried to make life as smooth as possible.[16]

The *Rivers* as Senior Officers' Ships

Monsarrat suggested that the River-class ships were intended mainly as the headquarters ships of escort groups 'designed to be the tough nucleus of an escort group rather than a rank-and-file member of it'.[17] This is not borne out by the papers on the design process, which make it quite clear that they were intended for mass production to replace the Flower-class as the standard ocean escorts as soon as possible. Admiral Sir Max Horton, commander-in-chief of Western Approaches from November 1942, tended to favour the frigate as a senior officer's ship. A fast ship like a destroyer was likely to be in chase and away from the convoy at vital moments. 'The frigate is thought to be the ideal ship for the Senior Officer Escort which gives him sufficient speed to manoeuvre round the convoy while allowing his high speed destroyers to be free for hunting,' he wrote in June 1943. The senior officer of B3 group was about to transfer to a frigate to test this.[18]

A list of the senior officers' ships of the escort groups in July 1943, when about eighteen *Rivers* were in service, suggests that they were rarely used by senior officers. Out of twenty-three groups in operation, three were led by *Rivers*: B3 with *Towy*, as part of the experiment mentioned by Horton; C1 by *Itchen*, but only temporarily while a destroyer was out of action; and C5 by *Nene*. Six more were led by sloops, including two of the Black Swan-class. Destroyers were the most popular with escort-group leaders. Despite the problems of short range and difficulties of movement in bad weather, their speed and gun armament were apparently valued. They were the senior officers' ships of ten groups. One was an old S-class ship from the last war, thirteen (including three taken over from the Brazilian navy at the outbreak of war and three operated by the Canadians) were interwar designs, and two, on loan from the Home Fleet, were to the latest design. One group was led from an escort aircraft carrier.[19]

By the middle of 1944, more *Rivers* were being used as senior officers' ships. Nine ships – the *Dart, Deveron, Exe, Helsmdale, Rother, Swale, Taff, Teviot* and *Towy* – had a commander in charge and a small team of specialist officers on board. All the commanders were regular RN except for T. Cleeves of the *Rother*, who was a long-standing member of the RNR.

The *Rivers* in the Escort Groups

In the early stages of their service, the *Rivers* tended to be concentrated in small groups. Early in September 1942, the *Exe, Rother, Spey* and *Tay* formed the 45th Escort Group based at Londonderry but later sent to the Clyde for minesweeping training. By early 1943, the 1st Escort Group included the *Jed, Rother, Spey* and *Wear*, and it was about to begin its service as a support rather than an escort group. The 44th Escort Group included the *Test, Teviot* and *Trent*, and the 40th Escort Group included the *Moyola, Nith* and *Waveney*. Two other groups – B4 and B7 – had one River-class ship each.

By mid-1943, the new frigates were spread mostly round the various escort groups. A typical group now consisted of nine or ten vessels. Some of these might be out of action at any particular moment, so there was an average of about eight in service – enough to give all-round cover to a convoy. The typical group had two or three destroyers, one (or, occasionally, two) frigates, and four or five corvettes. There were advantages in having a mixed group like this. The corvettes provided the numbers, and could maintain the ring while faster ships chased the U-boats. The destroyers provided speed and gun-power. The frigate brought a number of assets. Each had Type 271 radar, which was becoming essential. Each had an HF/DF set, which was vital in providing an early warning of attack. Each had a doctor and a well-equipped sick bay. A River-class frigate had better sea-keeping than most ships, and occasionally was able to keep the seas when a destroyer had to turn back. It had better speed and stability than a corvette. With scarce resources, it was natural to spread the *Rivers* thinly among the escort groups. Only the 1st Escort Group, now confirmed as a support group, had a large number of *Rivers*.

Support Groups

By law and regulation, the first duty of an escort group was the safe and timely arrival of the convoy. This, and tactical considerations, meant that a promising hunt of a U-boat often had to be abandoned to maintain the ring around the convoy. Special hunting groups had been tried in World War I and found wanting. Simply roaming around the ocean in search of submarines was known to be a waste of time, as they were only likely to show their heads in the vicinity of a convoy. The answer was the use of groups of relatively fast ships which would move in support of one convoy or another as it came under threat from a pack of U-boats. This was likely to take place in the air gap in the mid-Atlantic, where most attacks were concentrated in early 1943.

This had been known for some time, but it was March 1943 before enough ships were available to form the first five support groups, with the loan of some modern destroyers from the Home Fleet. Unlike an escort group, it was best that a support group was homogeneous, with reasonably fast ships, well-trained crews and the latest possible armament. Only one, however – the 1st Support Group – was made up mainly of River-class ships. It was led by the pre-war sloop *Pelican*, supported by the ex-US Coast Guard cutter *Sennen*. The last ship was large and seaworthy and had a good crew, but was only just acceptable with a speed of 16 knots, which slowed the rest of the group down. The main bulk of the force was provided by the River-class frigates *Rother*, *Spey*, *Wear* and *Jed*, later joined by *Evenlode*.

The First Support Group began its initial voyage in that role when it left Londonderry at 07.00 on 18 April 1943. The group headed out for the air gap for a few hours, until an Admiralty signal diverted it to the support of Convoy SC 126, heading in from the south and approaching the west of Ireland. That was changed at 20.30, and the group headed northeast again towards the air gap. Two days later, as the group approached the mid-Atlantic, more specific orders were given to support Convoy ONS 4, then heading east towards North America at a speed of 5 knots. This changed yet again at noon the following day as the group came close to ONS 4. It was now to head east to make contact with HX 234, heading northwest off Greenland at a speed of 9 knots. But at 13.15 on the 22nd, the orders were changed yet again – this time, to go southeast. The group commander was moved to protest in his official report:

> I was reluctant to comply… At this time HX 234 was nine hours steaming away and could have been contacted by nightfall. Up to 12 U-boats were reported in its vicinity, and in fact its escorts reported sighting two U-boats during the night 22/23. It was clear to me at the time that the First Support Group could arrive at just the most effective time to achieve results.

Nevertheless, he had to obey, and by daylight on the morning of the 24th, the group was supporting Convoy SC 127 as it headed northwest away from Newfoundland. The support group acted as an extended screen to the convoy. A few HF/DF contacts were obtained and it was thought they might be ground waves, so single-ship, two- and three-ship sweeps were carried out in pursuit of them, with no results. After a day and a half of this, the group was diverted east to make contact with Convoy ONS 4, which was heading for Halifax. The group spent another day and a half with this convoy, then went into St. John's, Newfoundland. It had been a frustrating time and the group commander believed that neither SC 127 nor ONS 4 was ever seriously threatened while the support group was in the area. 'No points of major tactical interest occurred during the cruise.'[20] The First Support Group had its finest hour the next month (May) in support of Convoy ONS 5.

Bases

As the Battle of the Atlantic developed in the summer and autumn of 1940, it was clear that the traditional naval bases in the south of England would be no use in the conflict. Portsmouth, Chatham and Plymouth had all been founded in the days of the sailing ship for wars against France. They were subject to a great deal of bombing during the war, and they were too far from the convoy routes to be useful. Of Plymouth, Captain Donald Macintyre wrote, 'We were intruders there and made to feel ourselves nuisances. Our demands for dockyard assistance were invariably questioned and grudgingly granted… they served to illustrate what a backwater the great port of Plymouth and Devonport had become, with the shifting of the nerve centre of the Atlantic war to Liverpool and its satellite ports.'[21] Furthermore, merchant shipping would not be able to use the southern ports of London, Southampton and Bristol. The ships would be heavily bombed on the way there, and also while they were in port. It was necessary to route shipping round the north of Ireland to the ports of the Clyde and Mersey.

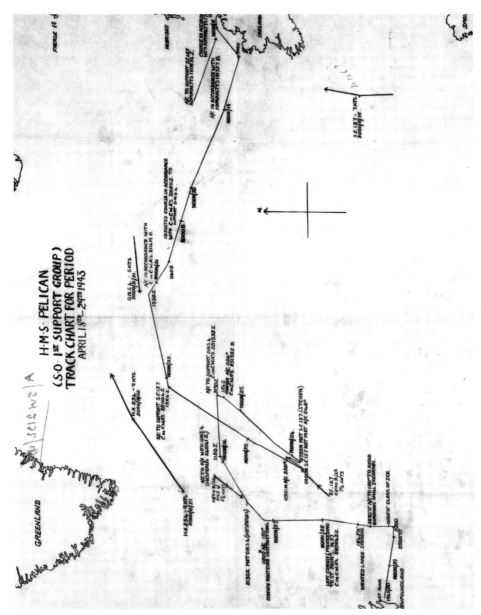

The track of the First Support Group in its first voyage in April 1943. (TNA 199/579)

The bases used by escorts in the Battle of the Atlantic were all to some extent improvised. They included huge ports, like Liverpool, which were already well-established commercial harbours but had little naval activity in peacetime, as well as great natural harbours such as Argentia in Newfoundland, which had been almost uninhabited before the war.

The escort groups based in a particular port were under the command of the captain (D). Originally, this meant the officer with the rank of captain who was in charge of a destroyer flotilla, usually with eight or nine ships under him. By 1939, the local captain (D) was in charge of the escort forces, though the job soon outgrew the rank. This was partly recognised by promoting the senior officer at Londonderry, with more escorts than any other port under him, to commodore. But in September 1943, captain (D) in Liverpool had thirteen destroyers and forty-one other escort vessels under him – far more than a mere commander of a destroyer flotilla. His job, however, was largely administrative, and he had little role in the operational command, as orders were passed directly from Western Approaches headquarters to the escort groups at sea. To assist him, commodore (D) in Londonderry had a staff of forty-seven officers in January 1944.

Liverpool and the Clyde

Liverpool was perhaps the best known of the escort bases. It was the only one that was close to a large city, and it gave a welcome to visiting seamen. Escorts in Liverpool usually moored alongside in Gladstone dock, which made going ashore much easier. Liverpool was also the headquarters of Western Approaches Command, and the British side of the Battle of the Atlantic was run from Derby House in the city. For all its great advantages, it was better as a merchant ship port than a naval port. It had much better dock and transport facilities than the other west-coast ports, so naturally merchant shipping had to be given priority. This, in turn, naturally attracted the attention of the Luftwaffe, which bombed the city in the early months of 1941, though this was largely over by the time the River-class arrived in service. Liverpool was also further from the Atlantic Ocean than other ports – a voyage of more than 150 miles (241km) was needed to reach the Mull of Kintyre where convoys assembled. This was a waste of precious fuel which might have been more useful in getting the ship across the Atlantic. Relatively few *Rivers* were based at Liverpool. In September 1943, there were only six: the *Mourne*, *Swale* and *Deveron* in different escort groups, the *Balinderry*, *Odzani* and *Waveney* together in the 41st.

Before the war, the Clyde ports been relatively small compared with London and Liverpool, accounting for less than four per cent of British trade. Glasgow had dealt mainly with liner traffic, with cargoes of 2,000 to 5,000 tons, whereas in wartime it had to handle ships carrying 10,000 tons each. It had mainly handled exports, whereas imports were now the priority. There were only 3,600 dockers in Glasgow, compared with 27,000 in Liverpool and 28,000 on the Thames, but 5,000 to 6,000 would be needed.[22] The road and rail links at Glasgow Docks were adequate for the pre-war local trade, but not for the new demands.

The Clyde was second to Liverpool in the Battle of the Atlantic, but it also had many other functions. Its wide, deep and sheltered waters and its distance from enemy bases made it ideal for training of aircraft-carrier pilots, submarine crews and in amphibious warfare. It produced a large proportion of the naval and merchant ships built during the war, and these underwent their trials in the area. It was a base for submarine operations and hosted great fleets on occasion: for example, the launching of Operation Torch, the invasion of North Africa, in November 1942. As a result, its waters became very crowded in wartime.

The escort forces based in the Clyde tended to be smaller than those in Liverpool and Londonderry, with only thirty-seven escorts based there at the beginning of 1942.[23] When in port, they anchored on the Tail of the Bank (the sandbar separating the firth from the estuary in the Clyde) off Greenock, because there was no room for them in the crowded docks. This did not please Nicholas Monsarrat:

> The corvette and destroyer anchorage was about half a mile off-shore, at the Tail-of-the-Bank, and here we lay in isolation, swinging to our own anchor cable, served by supply and liberty boats which, being converted herring drifters built like wooden tanks and crewed by stalwart Scots fishermen who like to signal their arrival with a good solid thump, were a constant menace to paintwork and plating.[24]

The Clyde was also little used by the *Rivers*. In September 1943, there were only three based there: the *Towy* in the 3rd Escort Group, the *Exe* and *Moyola* in the 40th.

Londonderry

The idea of using the Northern Irish port of Londonderry as an escort base originated in September 1940. It had been a prominent shipping port until the partition of Ireland in 1922, when much of its hinterland was cut off. The port was 4 miles (6.4km) up the River Foyle, in a narrow river with rather run-down facilities such as jetties and a graving dock. But Londonderry's greatest advantage was its situation. Apart from Campbeltown, near the end of the Kintyre Peninsula, it was the closest British port to the area in which the Battle of the Atlantic was fought. Yet Campbeltown was isolated and in a very sparsely populated area; Londonderry was close to industrial Belfast and had a large civilian labour force, for Northern Ireland was not subject to conscription.

Captain Phillip Ruck-Keene, an experienced submarine officer, took charge and began to build up the base with great energy. Unlike the Mersey and the Clyde, the base was not expected to deal with merchant shipping and could concentrate on the servicing of escort ships. The plans were expanded by February 1942, when it was agreed that the base was needed 'to relieve the Clyde and give greater endurance to the escort forces'.[25] The river was deepened using the harbour commissioner's ancient dredger *Hercules*, which broke down so often that the work was not finished until late 1944. A large repair workshop, 250ft long and 110ft wide (76 x 34m), was constructed. Berths were built on the east side of the river where destroyers and corvettes could come alongside several deep. The old graving dock was lengthened by 45ft (13.7m), initially to take the ex-American Town-class destroyers, but this also made it suitable for the River-class when they came along. Cranes were fitted to its sides. Another jetty was planned further downriver for American use at Lishally, but it took some time to complete. An armament depot was begun at Kilnappy in September 1941 and completed in January 1943.[26]

Maintenance was carried out at Londonderry, where the most important thing was to keep the ships ready for sea:

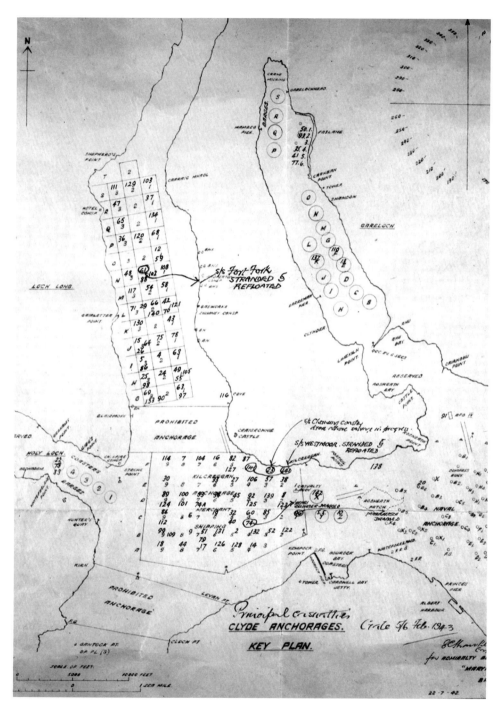

The Clyde anchorages in 1943. The handwritten comments refer to ships that broke loose in a storm in February. The naval anchorage is to the bottom right. (TNA ADM 1/3430)

The aim of the maintenance and repair base is to service the vessels so that they continue running efficiently. Approved alterations and additions are only progressed or carried out when such action is possible within the turn-round periods.

However, new gear was fitted where possible, and Canadian ships found it useful to get the latest British equipment. Much of the work was done under contract by the great Belfast shipbuilders, Harland and Wolff.

By February 1941, there were thirty-six ships based at Londonderry. The base had a staff of 555 in early 1942, rising to 1455 by the beginning of 1944. It was headed by a commodore (D) with a staff of nearly fifty, plus small teams for port defence, minesweeping and naval control of merchant shipping. There was a large base of accounting staff, including many Wrens under a paymaster-commander, and an engineering team under an engineer rear admiral. Civilian labour was also employed on tasks such as boiler cleaning. Gunnery and torpedo staffs concentrated on maintenance of weapons and training of crews. The instructional and training crews included petty officer instructors and Wren cinema operators. There was a pool of ratings to replace those taken sick in escorts, though circumstances prevented it from reaching its planned total of 200 men. There was a supply and victualling organisation, although it was complained that its storehouses and refrigerated plants were 'well dispersed in town and country'.[27]

Commander Rayner describes the approach to Londonderry:

Leaving the dispassionate sea behind you as you go up the River Foyle, the friendly, green land enfolds you. Further and further your ship noses her way up the tortuous channel, until an S-bend at Lishally entirely shuts out all sign of the sea. Your ship steams on between the walls of woodland, so that her salt-encrusted sides are almost brushed by the overhanging branches; and your bow wave and wash, which for weeks have been lost among the immensity of the ocean, now slip-slop amongst the tree roots, and stir the long tendrils of seaweed on half-tide ledges. Another S-turn, and there before you lies the enchanted city, silhouetted against the light of the noon-day sun. In the shadow of the wharf would be lying a long single line of escorts.... In later years the line became four or five deep, and ninety per cent of them were ready for sea.[28]

Londonderry became the main base for River-class ships in the Battle of the Atlantic. There were fifteen British and Canadian escort groups based there, eleven of which used *Rivers*. Most were spread singly around the groups, but the 5th Canadian Group had the *Findhorn* and *Inver* while the First Support Group used five *Rivers*. Belfast was also used as an escort base, but mainly by American-built Captain-class frigates.

North American Bases

Several bases were used in the other side of the Atlantic, mostly operated by the Royal Canadian Navy. Halifax in Nova Scotia is a very fine natural harbour in an inlet four miles (6.4 km) long and nearly a mile wide, with a narrow passage leading up to Bedford Basin. A small dockyard had already been built there, and it was much expanded after 1939. Halifax's main role was as an assembly point for westbound convoys, especially before the American entry to the war allowed the use of New York. It was largely ice-free, so it could continue to operate through the winter. Many warships were also based there, and some came in for repairs from damage sustained in the Atlantic. Sydney Cove in Cape Breton Island also served as the assembly point for slow convoys, though it was further north and was icebound in winter. It, too, had facilities for servicing warships, though these were mostly destroyers and corvettes of the Royal Canadian Navy. Argentia in Newfoundland was developed by the United States Navy. Captain Donald Macintyre was the liaison officer there as it was built:

> So out of nothing a base was to be created. The dock facilities, the repair ships, the supply organisation and the refuelling arrangements of old-established ports like Liverpool or Greenock, as well as a full-sized air station, had to be provided in a few months. It was a project to daunt the heart of anyone accustomed to the orderly and deliberate progress of peace-time civil engineering. But to the Americans, with their tireless New World enthusiasm and utter disregard of the cost, it was just another job.[29]

Though Argentia was often used by British ships, the most important western escort base for them was St. John's, slightly further east in Newfoundland. Its greatest advantage was that it was the nearest point to Britain, though as one naval song put it, 'From Newfy to Derry's a bloody long way'. The port was very small: less than 700 yards wide and 2100 yards long (640 x 1920m). It was difficult to protect, but it was used for several functions: as a port of refuge for merchant ships damaged by weather or enemy action in the Atlantic, as an assembly point for vessel heading for Greenland and various other places, and as the base for a number of escort craft. Though Newfoundland was not then part of Canada, the Canadian government spent 10 million dollars on improving it up to September 1942. During that year it expended more than 9000 man-days repairing 834 ships.[30] The first two frigates were based there in June 1943, and there were twenty-seven operating from the port at the beginning of 1945, along with eight destroyers and thirty-nine corvettes.[31]

Other Bases

River-class frigates do not seem to have used the British bases in Iceland much. Possibly this was because they had sufficient range to cross the Atlantic without stopping, unlike many destroyers and corvettes. Also, *Rivers* had relatively weak anti-aircraft armament and were not normally used in Russian convoys, which often started from Iceland. However, they did go some way to the south, using the base at Freetown in Sierra Leone. This, too, had a good geographical position, the only natural harbour on the Atlantic 'narrows' where the ocean was 'only' 1500 miles (2414km) wide. There was an ambitious programme of construction which included a corvette jetty, a barracks, oil depot, workshops, recreational facilities and even a barracks for Italian prisoners of war used as labour. Little of this had been completed by the beginning of 1944, and visiting ships relied largely on depot ships for support.[32] The Freetown Escort Force included several *Rivers*, as it protected ships heading for South Africa, or around the Cape when the Suez Canal was unavailable. The *Dovey*, for example, arrived in Freetown in May 1944 and helped escort convoys between there and Gibraltar, with occasional trips to Takoradi, Lagos and Cape Town.

Convoy Escort

Convoy Routes

The River-class frigates were designed mainly for the Atlantic convoy routes, including the principal lifeline between Britain and North America. The convoy system developed into a worldwide network in the Mediterranean, Arctic Ocean, Caribbean, Pacific and Indian oceans, but the *Rivers* were less use in areas such as the Mediterranean and Arctic, where serious surface-ship and air opposition might be encountered. Their long range meant that they were at their best in the long distances of the North Atlantic, and later in the Pacific and Indian Oceans. Their moderate speed meant that they were very suitable for escorting merchant ships (except the very fast liners, which could sail independently). They were too slow to escort warships such as battleships and aircraft carriers, which might travel at 25 or 30 knots.

Convoys were denominated by code letters (which gave some indication of destination) and numbers within that series. The most prolific of all was the HX series, which started on 16 September 1939 and continued until the end of the war in Europe. Altogether there were 377 convoys in the series, containing nearly 18,000 ships. Originally they started at Halifax, Nova Scotia, for Britain, but after HX 208 in September 1942, they sailed from New York. They included relatively fast ships by merchant standards, capable of at least 9 knots. A series for slower ships, of at least 7½ knots, started from Sydney, Cape Breton Island, in August 1940. It ran to 177 convoys of more than 6800 ships and it, too, shifted to New York in September 1942. Ships making the return voyage to North America were put into the ON convoys after July 1941. By the middle of 1942, they usually went to ports such as Halifax, Boston and Cape Cod; after August 1942, they ended at New York. Alternate convoys were designated fast and slow until March 1943, when a new series, ONS, was formed for the slower ships.

For southbound ships, from 1941 the OS series took ships to Sierra Leone, where they sailed onwards to their ultimate destinations. For the return voyage, ships joined the SL, supplemented by the MKS convoys from North African ports from the end of 1942. Ships for Malta and the Mediterranean formed the OG convoys, which started at the beginning of the war, while the return voyage was done by the HG convoys. Convoys in support of the North African landings were designated KMF.

Convoy Organisation

British merchant ships, plus many ships from neutral states or occupied countries such as Norway and Greece, were chartered by the Ministry of War Transport, which arranged their cargoes and destinations. The actual routing was planned by the trade division of the Admiralty or by the equivalent American or Canadian authorities. While on the eastern side of the Atlantic, the convoys and their escorts were under the tactical control of Western Approaches Command, based in Liverpool.

The convoy itself – that is, the merchant ships under escort – was headed by the commodore. He held the rank of commodore in the Royal Naval Reserve, and he was often a retired regular naval officer who had held much higher rank in his day. The ocean-convoy commodores included several quite famous admirals such as Sir Frederick Dreyer and Sir Reginald Plunkett-Ernle-Erle-Drax (best known for having the longest name in the Navy). A few had been captains in the RNR before the war, many were captains in the Royal Navy, and others were retired rear-, vice- and full admirals. Among those who served in the post were Vice-Admiral Stephenson (*see* page 163), who soon became the head of the training school at Tobermory, but his abrasive manner was not suitable for the more diplomatic task of convoy commodore. Even the current rank of commodore was two grades above that of the escort-group commander, who was likely to be a commander, or at most a captain; occasionally a mere lieutenant commander might find himself in charge of an escort group.

Yet there was no doubt that the escort-group commander was in charge of the operation, subject to orders from the headquarters on either side of the Atlantic. The commodore's orders stated clearly that he was to 'take charge of the convoy as a whole, subject to the orders of the Senior Officer of the Escort'.[33]

The convoy conference was a major event, held ashore just before departure and attended by all the Royal Navy and merchant navy captains. It was the last time captains could meet with their peer group before leaving on a long, gruelling and dangerous voyage, and the last chance to ask questions about their duties. The conference might be addressed by the local harbourmaster on procedures for leaving the port. The convoy commodore would speak about the order of the convoy, speed, the need to stay in position and the danger of straggling; darkening ship and concealing the convoy's position; the disposal of rubbish, which might give clues to the enemy; and the reduction of smoke. He would talk about the radio frequencies to be used in an emergency and what to do in the event of attack by surface ships, aircraft or submarines. The escort-group commander would also speak, perhaps on the need to avoid straggling and the likely dangers from the enemy. Each captain would be given a pack with details of route, arrangements and emergency procedures. If a convoy was leaving from several places – for example, Greenock, Liverpool, Milford Haven and Loch Ewe for outbound transatlantic convoys – there would be a separate briefing in each port.

Convoy Arrangement

Atlantic Convoy Instructions (CB 04234), the bible of convoy escort, was a large volume bound together with screws. It was subject to constant amendment, particularly around 1943, when the dynamism of Admiral Horton combined with the innovation of the tactical school under Captain Roberts. A well-used copy would have deletions, in pen, of short sentences or whole passages; short slips pasted in at one edge, or larger ones pasted over a whole paragraph or page; pages removed; and pages inserted. There were eight major amendments during 1943 alone, usually coming from a new Admiralty fleet order or an order from Western Approaches Command.[34]

A convoy was arranged in columns abreast of one another, and it was much wider than it was long. In June 1943, ON 190 had ninety-six ships in fourteen columns of six or seven ships each. The columns were to be 3 cables (400 yards/366m) apart until west of 7 degrees, then 5 cables (1000 yards/915m). The ships in each column would be 3 cables apart. This was a relatively fast convoy, with an intended speed of 9½ knots. Slower convoys were sometimes hard-pushed to make 7 knots. Of ONS 7, escorted by B5 group, including the *Nene* and *Swale* in May 1943, it was said, 'This was a very slow convoy, and although no ships were listed as less than 8 knots anything over 7 produced stragglers.'[35] The commodore's ship was at the head of the centre column, with the vice- and rear-commodore, who would deputise for him at the heads of other columns. A convoy might be several miles wide and 2 or 3 miles deep.

A westbound convoy such as ON 190 formed up in an area known as Oversay, between the Mull of Kintyre and Northern Ireland. The main portion, from Liverpool, was there by 09.50 on the 25 June and was joined by ships from other ports. In all, the convoy included eighty-nine ships when it started, the series' largest so far. Numbers were soon reduced as the *Bangkok II* had to turn back at midday on 26 June. The commodore, A. M. Hekking of the RNR, was in the *Glenbeg* of 12,000 tons, built in 1922, but the ship soon had to turn back due to engine trouble. With some difficulty the commodore's extensive possessions and his staff were loaded into the *Itchen's* motor cutter and transferred to the *Triona* of the Bank Line under Captain C. H. Beaton.

The escort, C1 Canadian Group, was led by the British-manned *Itchen* under Lt.-Cdr. Bridgeman RNR. It was soon joined by the 5th Escort Group in support, including the *Tweed* and *Nene*, allowing enough ships to form an extended screen with ships in extended-screen positions AA, NN and DD as well as the usual close escort positions for nine ships. For much of the voyage the convoy was north of 56 degrees, and there was little need for night stations – at that time of the year there were only about three and a half hours of semi-darkness as the sun dipped below the horizon.

Near midnight on 25 June, *Itchen's* HF/DF picked up some puzzling signals. At first it was thought to be a U-boat transmitting off-frequency, but it was later concluded that it was a shore station, and no threat. Again on the night of 28 – 29 June, five bearings were taken by ships in the convoy but later identified as shore stations.

Between 5 and 8 in the afternoon of 30 June, a U-boat transmission was detected, but only a single bearing was found. It was not clear whether it came from the port or starboard of the convoy, so *Nene* and *Tweed* were detached to search 25 miles (40 km) on either side. They found nothing, for it was later estimated that the boat was about 60 miles (96.5 km) away. In the early hours of the next morning, the two ships were sent out to form part of a distant escort 12,000 yards (11km) astern of the convoy to prevent shadowing. Meanwhile, the American merchant ship *Cyrus H. McCormick* reported seeing a periscope, but this proved to be a floating mast, presumably from a lost ship. As there was no evidence of any real threat to Convoy ON 190 and at 07.00 on 1 July, the 5th Escort Group left for other duties. Group C2, left on its own, formed a standard daytime close screen, with ships ahead of the convoy and on each side, and one astern. There was plenty of air support by planes from Iceland and Newfoundland, and communication with them was good, marred only by a tendency for the ships to talk too much over the radio in the latter stages of the voyages.

The *Triona* proved not to be a very suitable commodore's ship. It had been fuelled with cheap Durham coal which gave off heavy smoke and threatened to betray the convoy's position. At 21.25 on 2 June, the convoy was at its most northerly point in the route. The weather was foggy and there was known to be ice in the vicinity. The *Itchen* came close to the *Triona* showing red and white steaming lights. It signalled with lamp and foghorn and pointed its searchlight at two small icebergs through the fog. The commodore was below at the time, but the captain of the *Triona* thought it his duty to warn the convoy right away, by making a sound signal and turning 40 degrees to port. The commodore, summoned by the noise, was furious and cancelled the course alteration, claiming that there was no real danger and that the captain had no right to signal the convoy without his authority. The signal caused a collision between an American and a Norwegian ship. Both were damaged above the waterline and were unable to continue with the voyage.

Stragglers and ships which did not obey convoy discipline were a constant problem for every escort commander. The Oban section of Convoy HX 315, escorted by HMS *Towy* in October to November 1944, became known as 'the five unruly Yanks' and lived up to the name. It was 'hardly a convoy at all, but five ships proceeding independently to their destination, and they paid little or no attention to either their commodore or to their escort'.[36]

ON 190 suffered more damage on 8 July, in the last stage of the voyage. The American *Harrison Smith* approached the Norwegian *Polartank* 'at great speed' and collided with her starboard quarter. But Norwegian ships were not entirely innocent, and the *Brajara* under Captain Skaar made 'two exceedingly bad and dangerous manoeuvres' as the convoy formed into two columns for the final stages of the voyage. He was fortunate to avoid a collision, according to Commodore Hekking. But the convoy had arrived without any real interference from the enemy, as most did at that period of the war.[37]

Escort Dispositions

The *Convoy Instructions* manual contained a grid with eighteen possible positions for the escorting ships, though of course, no convoy had that number of escorts. In September 1943, for example, the average escort group in the North Atlantic had eight ships, although it might have as few as four or as many as eleven. Often two or three were away for repairs at any given moment, so that a typical convoy might expect six to eight ships, and more if it was joined by a support group. ON 190, for example, was escorted by seven warships, a rescue tug and a trawler. Very few convoys had enough ships to form a tight Asdic screen round the convoy. Every escort distribution was 'the best compromise between the requirement of defensive screening and that of offensive action against the U-boat which has penetrated the firing position within the limits of the torpedo danger zone of the convoy'.[38]

Position A was in front of the convoy, B and L were a similar distance in front of the merchant ships furthest to port and starboard. M was 60 degrees off the starboard forward corner of the convoy, N was 30 degrees off it, while C, D, G, H, Q and R had similar positions in relation to the other corners. O, P, E and F were on the wings. S was an important position directly astern of the convoy and the ship occupying it might well be the first to take action in the event of a surprise attack. It was to 'act as "whipper in" to prevent straggling, and also to act as "watchdog" over the convoy to observe incidents and to be in a position to take action immediately in an emergency'.[39] Escorts were usually 4000 yards (3.6km) from the nearest merchant ship when sweeping ahead of the convoy, 3 or 4,000 yards away when on the sides, and the ship in position S was 2000 yards (1.8km) away. No arrangement was permanent, for ships had to be called away to chase contacts, hunt attackers or rescue survivors, and every escort commander had to remember to close the gap when that happened.

If a convoy had an adequate number of escorts, perhaps with a support group in company – more than six for a small convoy and eight for a large one – then a line could be formed far ahead with positions lettered according to those in the close screen, but with double letters. MM, for example, was 12,000 yards (11km) ahead of the port side of the convoy, at 30 degrees from its course.

Attack from astern was unlikely in daytime, for a submerged U-boat could not keep up with a convoy, and a surfaced one was likely to be detected. The main bulk of the escort was therefore placed ahead and on the sides. A six-ship escort, for example, would have one in position A 4000 yards dead ahead, one each at M and C 3000 yards (2.7km) and 30 degrees from the leading corners, two more at P and F 4000 yards to port and starboard and the inevitable S 2000 yards aft. An eight-ship escort would have three ships at L, A and B 4000 yards ahead of the convoy, two at N and D 3000 yards and 60 degrees off the forward corners, and two at P and F 4000 yards on each side. Together they formed something like a flattened semi-circle ahead and on each side. Again, there was a ship in position S 2000 yards astern. By 1943, it was presumed that all escorts could operate radar, and of course the gap had to be closed around any whose sets were defective.

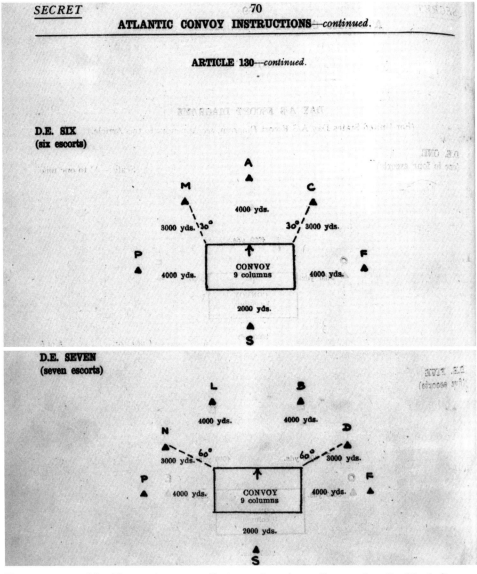

The arrangement of the ships round a convoy with six escorts, and one with seven, from the *Atlantic Convoy Instructions* (TNA ADM 239/344)

An extreme case of placing all the escorts ahead in daytime was used when intelligence showed that the enemy was laying in wait ahead of the convoy. All the escorts except one could be put in a line up to 3000 yards apart, with only the ship in position S astern of the convoy to protect the rear and deal with any casualties. It was recognised that the screen could not cover all possible areas in which a U-boat might approach.[40]

By night, it was likely that a U-boat might use its surface speed to attack a convoy from behind, and stronger escorts were needed astern. A six-escort convoy would have them disposed evenly around, with A ahead and the usual S astern, N and D 60 degrees forward and R and H 30 degrees off the stern. With eight escorts, the two extra ships would be at P and F, abreast the centre of the convoy.

In either day or night formation, any extra escorts might be disposed in the area of greatest danger. In good weather that was ahead, as U-boats might lie in wait. In strong winds, commanders were advised, 'In rough weather consideration should be given to strengthening the weather bow of the convoy at the expense of the lee beam.'[41] With a strong wind on the port bow, for example, escorts might be stationed in positions PP to port, MM ahead and to port and BB ahead, while position F in the close escort might be left vacant. Gretton adopted these principles for HX 231:

> Placing the field was easy. There was a strong wind and sea from the port quarter, so that the starboard bow was left unprotected and the main strength concentrated to port with the *Duncan* on the port quarter. The placing had been right. The first attack was dealt with by the *Sunflower* on the port bow; then followed by no less than four attacks on the port quarter, all of which were driven off by the *Duncan*.[42]

Intelligence

Before setting off, each captain of an escort vessel was fully briefed on the latest situation in the Atlantic before and during the convoy conference. For more general but up-to-date background he was given the latest edition of the *Monthly Anti-Submarine Report*. This was a magazine produced by a former Welsh solicitor at the Admiralty, based on the latest reports from Admiralty intelligence, and containing many other features. The issue of March 1943, for example, contained the usual review of the U-boat offensive and the counter-measures, with detailed articles on the attacks on HX 229 and SC 122. There were accounts of the maritime activities of Coastal Command of the RAF, of the stories of individual U-boats which had been captured, and of successful U-boat hunts. There was a serious attempt to get inside the mind of the enemy with interrogations of prisoners of war and analyses of his technology. New Allied technology such as the range recorder for the Asdic or the PPI for radar was often described in detail, so the magazine was highly secret. There were numerous maps and diagrams of convoy actions, and pictures of the latest equipment.

Meanwhile, the tracking room at the Admiralty, under Commander Rodger Winn, continued to use its sources to plot the position of every known U-boat and its relation to the convoys at sea. There is little evidence of effective espionage at the U-boat bases, though they were mostly in occupied countries. There were many attempts to get information from prisoners of war, with varied results. If nothing else, they presented a very bleak picture of life in the U-boats, which was transmitted to the escorts via the *Monthly Anti-Submarine Reports*.

A prisoner stated that, having had experience of U-boats, and being most unwilling to serve in one again, he applied to be sent to a petty officers' training course for destroyers. His application was refused, and it seems that transfers from the U-boat service are not permitted.

Another prisoner stated that the majority of U-boat crews now operating had been drafted without option, particularly those with special qualifications.[43]

At their best, these interrogations produced useful background information, though of course they could say very little about the most urgent matter, the future movements of the enemy. They seemed to say that, however harsh life was in the escort force, it was far worse for those under the sea.

The tracking room's most dramatic source was Ultra, the decoding of the German Enigma system. By the middle of 1941, the code-breakers at Bletchley Park were able to read most signals and to send them on quickly enough for them to be operationally useful. There was a setback in February 1942, when the Germans introduced a fourth rotor to the Enigma coding machine, and this was not resolved until after a new example was recovered from a captured U–boat that autumn. The codebook was changed in March 1943, which led to a short blackout during a crucial period of the Battle of the Atlantic, but apart from that, the tracking room based its analyses on profuse and reliable information. When working well, this was a gold mine of information that revealed the enemy intentions in some detail. It could, for example, uncover German plans to form lines of U-boats in order to find a convoy. In theory, this allowed the convoys to be routed round the lines, except in times such as the spring of 1943, when there were just too many U-boats at sea to do that effectively.

Other sources included radio direction finding, both from the escort's own HF/DF sets, and from shore-based stations spread around the ocean. This allowed the fairly accurate plotting of the actual positions of many of the boats. There were other devices, such as recognising the Morse touch of an individual radio operator so that his boat could be identified. The escorts themselves were not equipped to decode German signals, but they could identify a sighting report or an intention to attack, for example, by its length and certain key letters. Even the volume of traffic might well indicate that something was about to happen. The Germans remained unaware of the Allied capabilities and did very little to restrain the chatter among the U-boats or to send misleading signals. The Admiralty tracking room also sent constant signals to the convoy escorts about the movements of U-boats. When a U-boat attack did develop on a convoy, it was not usually unexpected, though the precise time and direction was not always known.

Searching

Despite the increasing use of Asdic and radar, visual searches were still important in all forms of sea warfare. *Atlantic Convoy Instructions* advised captains, 'An essential factor is a good look-out at the masthead, so as to sight the U-boat before being sighted.'[44] Lookouts were also placed on the bridge wings, and in the bows in poor visibility. If enough men were available, they were relieved every twenty minutes in order to avoid eye strain, and did only one 'trick' per hour; in a three-watch system that meant nine men for each lookout position, and therefore thirty-six to maintain four positions: enough to strain the resources of a ship with a complement of 140. Compartments used by lookouts and officers of the watch were lighted in red so as not to spoil their night vision. Each lookout was given a specific area of sea to search, and taught how to scan it in the most efficient manner. One of the greatest challenges in the Battle of the Atlantic was for every member of the crew to give the task his full attention during long, uneventful watches after many days of short and interrupted sleep. Officers were warned,

> Interest in the task is of supreme importance. Nobody is very good at a task which does not interest him, and this applies as much to watching for U-boats as to anything else. Keeping a watch for U-boats over an endless expanse of water for hours on end calls for a conscious attempt to overcome boredom and fatigue and maintain interest.

Some 'mental aids' were recommended:

> A proper understanding of the relationship of the individual task which is being performed to the total effort of anti-submarine warfare.
>
> A thorough knowledge of the methods employed to carry out the visual side of the task.
> A realisation that, however good the eyesight, it is the brain which ultimately determines what is seen, and that look-out duties call for an active concentration of attention and expenditure of mental energy.[45]

Most of these principles could apply just as well to the Asdic and radar watch-keepers, who were just as vital in the safety and efficiency of the ship. During ordinary escort duties, each Asdic searched an arc of 80 degrees on each side of the ship's course. At night or in low visibility, the senior officer had to consider whether to rely on the passive system, hydrophone effect, to try to hear the enemy's own noises. This had some chance of detecting a U-boat on the surface as well as under the sea, but that was less necessary as the use of radar increased. Different types of asdic sets used different frequencies, and group commanders were recommended to intersperse them in the escort so that they did not interfere with one another.

Radar searches were to be carried out at night and in low visibility, and by late 1943, barring accidents and losses, it was generally possible to maintain a tight ring round a convoy. Ships with the common Type 271 radar found it difficult to search astern if they were stationed in the rear of the convoy, for the aerial could only rotate through 400 degrees before it had to be reversed. If possible, a ship with the later Type 286 set should be stationed in the rear, as it could revolve continuously.

Escorts were faster than the ships of the convoy, and were able to follow a zigzag course that gave two advantages. Firstly, it could confuse the enemy as to the position and movements of the escort. According to orders of 1943,

> U-boats must by now be aware of the escort diagrams in use and may be influenced by this knowledge in planning their approach. Escorts should, therefore, keep on the move within their beats by carrying out broad zig-zags; these zig-zags should not, however, take any escort on the close screen more than 1 mile from his appointed station.[46]

Secondly, zigzagging allowed an escort to increase the area covered by its asdic and by its physical presence. According to the *Atlantic Convoy Instructions*,

> The area of the convoy torpedo danger zone is too large for the number of escorts normally available to ocean convoys to provide complete Asdic cover. In practice only a small proportion of this area can be effectively swept out. Escorts, by their movements within this area, can seriously embarrass a U-boat closing to a firing position at periscope depth, and zigzags should be so designed and co-ordinated in order to provide the maximum degree of protection by obstruction which speed and endurance allow. [47]

The *Rivers* had an advantage here with their relatively long range. The destroyer *Duncan*, in contrast, sometimes had to conserve fuel by staying in the centre of the convoy and keeping a straight course.

At some stages in the Battle of the Atlantic it was common for the convoy as a whole to zigzag, but this was less normal by 1942. Standard patterns were devised for this. Zigzag Number 8, for example, was 'For use in open waters where submarines have not previously been operating, but where they may appear.' It was 'Suitable for ships of all speeds.' A ship or convoy would begin it by altering course 25 degrees to starboard. After four minutes it would then go 50 degrees to port of the set course, then 25 degrees to starboard again after twelve minutes, and so on until a two-hour cycle was completed. Zigzags like these tended to waste fuel and prolong the journey; this meant that the ship only progressed 93 percent of the distance it had run by log. [48] Such tactics were used less later in the war. Instead, convoys relied on evasive routing to avoid known U-boats. This was used to great effect in the defence of SC 130 in 1943. The first turn was made just before dawn in the morning of 19 May, when the convoy was ordered to alter course by 90 degrees to starboard to avoid an anticipated attack. It was done many more times during the voyage, and Commander Gretton considered that 'They were manoeuvring beautifully now, and never before could one convoy have made so many alterations of course. The result would not have shamed a battlefleet.' [49]

On arrival in British, Canadian or American waters, a transatlantic convoy would be reasonably safe from U-boat attack as they did not operate inshore between 1940 and the introduction of the snorkel in 1944. The convoy would disperse to its various destinations, perhaps Liverpool, Greenock, Milford Haven, Loch Ewe or Oban in the case of an HX or SC convoy. The safe arrival of a convoy was a matter of great relief for all concerned. Captain Donald Macintyre describes his reaction in the destroyer *Hesperus*, but it was probably similar when he crossed in the frigate *Mourne*, even if the captain's cabin was in a different place:

> The first night in harbour after these voyages will always be highlighted in my memory. After the long, anxious days at sea in all weathers it was an unforgettable joy to be able to come aft to one's harbour cabin, to slough off one's clothes for the first time in many days and lie wallowing in a hot bath…
>
> The enemy we knew we could cope with, but the vindictive savagery of the Atlantic gales and the mountainous waves they raised, which came snoring down the wind at us, towering high above our heads, many a time put the fear of God into

me. It was almost a tangible joy, therefore, to be snug in harbour in a secure berth, with a westerly gale moaning through the rigging, and knowing that an undisturbed night in one's bunk and between sheets lay ahead.[50]

Anti-Submarine Defence and Attack

The U-Boats

The Battle of the Atlantic was an unusual campaign, in that practically all the effort on one side was centred on a single weapons system, the U-boat. The Western Allies used many types of aircraft and an equal variety of types of ship: corvettes, destroyers, sloops, escort destroyers, frigates, cutters and escort aircraft carriers. The Germans used only the U-boat, apart from occasional forays by great ships like the *Bismarck*. If German aircraft were involved, it was to direct U-boats to convoys or to protect their routes through the Bay of Biscay. Even then, they only operated on the fringes and not in the mid-Atlantic. The Allied campaign involved shipbuilders, naval and merchant seamen, airmen, code-breakers, dockers, scientists, engineers, operational researchers and almost every kind of transport. The German attack used only shipbuilders, naval seamen and a limited number of airmen. If the U-boat campaign can ultimately be considered a failure, it was also highly successful in the short term in diverting a huge amount of Allied resources. This went right to the top of the British war machine. Winston Churchill, who famously stated that, 'The only thing that ever really frightened me during the war was the U-boat peril'[51], chaired the anti-U-boat committee of the War Cabinet for several hours every second week for the middle years of the war. The Allies were forced to adopt a multifaceted response to a rather one-dimensional threat.

Among the U-boats, the Type VII, developed just before the war, was by far the most common. More than 700 out of more than a thousand U-boats built were of that class, mostly the Type VIIC. It was 67.1m (73 yards) long and displaced with a tonnage of 761 on the surface and 865 submerged. Its diesel engines could drive at 17 knots on the surface, and it could achieve a maximum range of 6500 nautical miles at a speed of 12 knots. Underwater, its electric motors could drive it at 7.6 knots, but only for a limited period before its batteries ran out. It could do 80 miles (129km) at 4 knots but this was far too slow to chase any convoy. It had a crew of forty-four and carried four torpedoes firing forward and one aft, with nine reloads. It could defend itself on the surface with a variety of guns over the years, including the highly effective 88mm. Early German torpedoes had problems, but they soon proved deadly enough and had sunk nearly 1700 Allied and neutral merchant ships in the north Atlantic by the end of 1942. Most were straightforward in their aiming system, but later types included the *FaT* of 1943, which would follow a zigzag or 'ladder' course in the vicinity of a convoy until it hit something, and the *Zaunkönig* or 'wren' which would home in on the propellers of an escort vessel.

Under their leader, Gross-Admiral Karl Dönitz, the U-boats evolved very effective tactics for attack convoys. The first task was to find them in the broad Atlantic. For this they broke the British Naval Cipher No. 3, which gave them a good deal of information on routes. Then they placed a line of boats across the convoy route. The one which sighted the convoy first would shadow it in the daytime and direct the others to it for a night attack.

All this required a great deal of signalling – a weak point in the German system.

With his experience in U-boats in World War I, Dönitz soon found that a 'wolf-pack' attack of large numbers of boats was necessary to saturate the defences. The pack had no leader as such, but was controlled from U-boat headquarters in France. The attack was not precisely coordinated, but could take place over many hours and several nights. The boats would attack mainly on the surface at night, in order to keep up their speed and defeat the Asdic. These were the tactics the River-class frigates were specifically designed to defeat.

Finding a U-Boat

Escorts were given detailed instructions on what to do on evidence of a U-boat in the vicinity. If it had an Asdic contact which was regarded as 'submarine', the escort would hoist a warning signal and contact its consort and aircraft by radio telephone. If the contact was doubtful, it would drop a depth charge on the spot before leaving. On hearing a suspicious noise by hydrophone effect, it would steer towards it, report it by RT and try to find other evidence of what it was. With a radar contact, it would also alter course towards it, institute 'anti-wren' tactics, estimate its course and speed and make every effort to establish its identity. On sighting a U-boat, the escort would open fire and perhaps attempt to ram. It would set depth charges to shallow, on the presumption that the sub would dive soon, and warn the rest of the convoy and escort. By night it would fire snowflake and tracer shots with the Oerlikon gun to point out the position, and at any time it would sound six blasts on its siren and report by RT to consorts and aircraft, and by wireless telegraphy to the headquarters. If the U-boat dived, the escort would mark the position by danbuoy or smoke float.

U-boats could also be detected some distance away by various means. If it was sighted by an aircraft in the vicinity of the convoy, the plane would stay over the site as long as possible. The senior officer of the escort had to use his discretion in ordering an attack, bearing in mind the weakness of his screen if he detached ships for the hunt, and the time consumed in getting back. If the target was 5 miles (8km) away, two ships might stand a reasonable chance of finding it; if 15 miles (24km) away, he would need to detach at least five ships. If there was only one boat known to be in the area, the convoy would be protected by sinking it; if more than one, then the convoy was placed in danger.

If a U-boat was believed to be shadowing the convoy, an escort might be sent to force it to submerge and prevent it from following. Again, the group commander had to consider his strength if an attack developed, and decide how soon to recall his ship.

Illumination

If a ship in the convoy was torpedoed before the submarine was detected, the common practice early in the war was for all the ships to fire flares, starshells and snowflake rockets and to turn night into day. The escorts would turn outwards and look for the attacker, hoping either to sight a U-boat on the surface or to force it to dive, when it would either be detected by Asdic or at least forced to lie still and abandon the chase. By 1943, there were reasons to modify this. In the first place, it did not take into account the possibility that the U-boat was inside the convoy. Secondly, the increasing use of radar made the lighting less valuable. If enough of the escorts had radar, then it was better to detect the U-boat with it, for illuminants could ruin the night vision of the hunters and indicate the position of the convoy to submarines still seeking it. Group commanders used them far more sparingly. Merchant ships were not to be ordered to use them as a matter of course, and escorts would use them with more control and direction according to policies drawn up by the group leaders.

Raspberry

The problem of the U-boat inside the convoy was first tackled by the tactical school in Liverpool. They devised a system 'to sweep out an area by Asdic in which the U-boat may be forced to dive by the illuminants, whilst making as much use as possible of R.D.F. and illuminants in case the U-boat is still on the surface'.[52] On being alerted of the attack, the ship in position S would zigzag towards the convoy. The other escorts would head towards the convoy for about ten minutes and fire starshells in prescribed 90-degree arcs for maximum cover. They would turn away and complete a triangular course to eventually take them back on station. This was known as a raspberry. A 'half-raspberry' was a shorter version of the same operation.

The raspberry took its name from the rude noise which, it was suggested, the manoeuvre was blowing at Hitler. It started a fashion for other types of attacks named after fruits and vegetables, all developed in the tactical school and tested at sea. Escort captains were well drilled in the techniques at the school, then the ships trained thoroughly in them under the command of HMS *Philante* between operations, so in general they were able to operate them promptly and effectively in battle.

Artichoke

Operation Artichoke was devised for use when a ship was torpedoed in the daytime. The codeword 'artichoke' was issued by radio telephone and the ship in position S moved up to the victim to try to get information about the direction of the attack from survivors, or by looking at the wreckage. Meanwhile, the escorts ahead of the convoy – in positions A, B and L, for example – turned outward through 180 degrees and headed in the opposite direction to the convoy at 15 knots: the fastest speed at which an Asdic would work. The other ships on the sides and rear of the convoy would wait until the van ships were level with them, then turn to join the sweep, any ships on the outer wings turning in diagonally towards the convoy and the others turning through 180 degrees. Once they were all 6000 yards (5.5km) astern of the convoy, they would turn through 180 degrees again and sweep in the opposite direction. If there was not clear information on the U-boat's position, they went back on the same course as the convoy. If there was information, they might go up to 30 degrees to one side or the other for up to thirty minutes. The sweeps were designed to cover as far as possible the area in which the U-boat was 'likely to be, paying particular attention to the quarters of the convoy on the sweep astern, and to the convoy's wake on the return sweep by which time the wakes should have faded away'.[53]

Artichoke was a very common tactic during 1943 and was sometimes used at night. Most operations failed to detect a U-boat, and of course it is far more difficult to measure its success in keeping their heads down and deterring attack. One of the more successful operations was in the early hours of 17 May, while escorting Convoy ONS 7. After two hits on a single merchant ship, Artichoke was signalled and *Swale* was ordered to pass at 15 knots among the convoy between the second and third columns, where it was believed the attack had come from. Nothing was found on that pass and it turned through 180 degrees to go back to position. An Asdic contact was obtained and *Swale* made a depth-charge and hedgehog attack. A probable kill was claimed, but it was later confirmed that *U-640* had been sunk.[54]

Banana and Pineapple

Operation Banana was used at night when a pack attack was not expected and only one U-boat was believed to be involved. On hearing the codeword, the escorts would fire starshells in prescribed arcs and make wide zigzags and loops for twenty minutes, to increase the coverage of their Asdics. One of the rear escorts would enter the convoy and carry out an Observant search (*see* below) around the torpedoed ship.

Pineapple was used if more than one boat was believed to be attacking. It was intended to force a second U-boat to dive before it could attack, to give a chance of detecting the boat which had already attacked, to prevent any other boats from sighting the convoy, and to 'form a greater physical obstruction in the submarine attacking area'. On hearing the codeword, only selected escorts were to use starshells, firing them towards the expected direction of attack and never towards the convoy. All escorts would go into a pattern of wide, 1-mile (1.6-km) zigzags for thirty minutes, or until countermanded.[55]

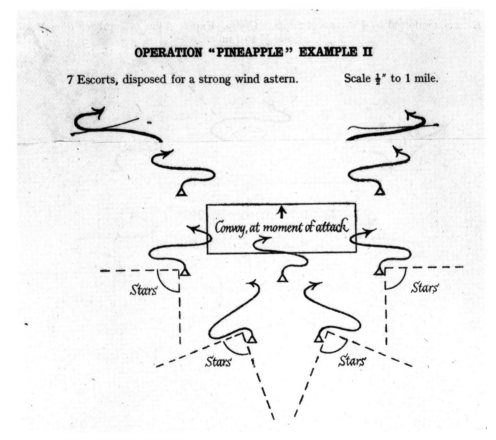

Operation 'Pineapple'. (TNA ADM 239/344)

Searches

Several methods were devised for searching for U-boats known to be in a specific area, either by single escort or by small groups. The code word 'Observant' was used to initiate a search round a specific point, either the wreck of a torpedoed ship or the position of a contact which had been lost. It was based on a datum point, either the wreck or the last point of contact of the boat. The first escort to arrive on the scene dropped a flare to indicate the point, then followed what it thought would be the most likely course of the submarine. If it was not found, the ship searched around a square 2 miles (3.2km) on each side, relying on the slow underwater speed of the U-boat. If a second escort was allocated to the search, it went to the datum point, then joined the square at a point opposite to the first. If a third, it should protect the datum point or act as the senior officer ordered.[56] *Swale* and the sloop *Wren* carried out an Observant on the night of May 12 1943, in support of ONS 7. *Swale* dropped a ten-charge pattern on a doubtful contact, while the convoy altered course by 90 degrees.[57]

An Alpha search began when a U-boat was sighted on the surface. The nearest escort would head directly for it, forcing it to dive. It would then alter course 20 degrees away from the direction the U-boat was most likely to go. When within a mile of the boat's expected position it would reduce speed to 15 knots for Asdic operating. It would then begin the Observant procedure.

The Beta search was slightly more sophisticated, and designed for ships with superior plotting equipment. On sighting a U-boat on the surface, the escort would alter course towards it, but not directly towards it, and increase to full speed. When the sub dived, the escort would head for the position where it was likely to be when an interception was made. At a speed of 15 knots, which was the maximum Asdic speed, the escort should aim 15 degrees off the U-boat's diving position if it was expected to head across the course, but some complicated plotting might be needed at this stage. On reaching the estimated position, the escort should begin Operation Observant.[58]

The Chase and the Attack

After training with HMS *Philante* was instituted at the end of 1942, the escort groups tended to use the same methods of defence and attack, though there was still room for details to be settled with the group. The members of the 40th Escort Group for example, including HMS ships *Exe* and *Moyola*, were instructed never to get directly astern of a U-boat in a chase:

> Keep about 500 yards away from his track. If he alters course away from you bring him on the other bow. Aim to get 4-500 yards on his beam. He is unlikely to let you do so but is even more unlikely to alter course across your bow either on the surface or after diving. You have therefore confined him to one side of the line of chase.
>
> If close enough to consider ramming, a position on the quarter will help you prevent him turning inside your turning circle, and at night you will be able to maintain constant snowflake illumination with safety.
>
> You will never be able to ram from right astern or know for certain which way he has altered course on diving.[59]

Ramming was considered a very effective tactic early in the war, but by 1943 there were serious doubts about it. Escort commanders were told:

> Whilst it is not desired to prohibit ramming when the opportunity arises, it is pointed out that instances have occurred recently where severe damage has been sustained by the ramming vessel without a kill being effected on the U-boat. An analysis made of U-boats rammed shows that ramming is in the majority of cases quite unnecessary to ensure destruction of the U-boat.[60]

The River-class had strengthened bows for ramming, for they were designed in 1940 when it seemed a viable tactic. The *Tay* did try to ram *U-306*, which appeared suddenly in front of the frigate while it was escorting Convoy HX 231, but it got inside this ship's turning circle and escaped.[61] There is a suspicion that the turning circle of the *Rivers* was too large for effective ramming. Because of this, because their speed was less than that of a destroyer, and because new orders tended to discourage the practice, no River-class frigate is recorded as having damaged a U-boat by ramming.[62] If ships did decide to ram, they were advised that they should use a speed of more than 15 knots in order to penetrate the U-boat's pressure hull, and to be careful in attacking a half-submerged boat, for that would do far more underwater damage to the attacking ship. On the whole, it was far better for an escort to rely on its guns to attack a U-boat on the surface, and its hedgehog and depth charges if it was underwater.

Plaster and Creeping Attacks

Apart from the simple attack by the hedgehog or depth charges of a single escort, several new forms of attack came into use during 1942–43. Most were developed by Captain F. J. Walker's Second Support Group of Black Swan-class sloops, and relied on the fact that increasing numbers of escorts were becoming available for more intensive hunts. With the advent of support groups, escort commanders did not always have to worry about leaving gaps in the convoy screen.

The plaster attack was used to saturate an area round an indistinct contact with a U-boat hiding in the depths. Three ships in line abreast dropped charges at five-second intervals, set at the maximum depth of 550ft. It was used several times and in different forms by *Sennen*, *Jed*, *Wear* and *Spey* of the First Support Group as they came to the relief of Convoy SC 130 in May 1943:

> *Spey* arranged a modified 'Plaster' with [*Wear*]. Ships were to be abeam, one cable [200 yards/183m] apart, *Spey* directing and carrying out the attack. Sixteen charges were to be dropped by each ship, twelve from the rails at six second interval, and one pair of throwers (one port and one starboard) fired with the third rail charge and the other pair with the ninth.

It had no result, but *Wear* and *Spey* were also pioneering another technique. *Wear's* Asdic was not operating as *Spey* directed it to a target, and a pattern of twelve charges set at 500 to 550ft was dropped as *Spey* dipped a flag. Again there was no result, but it partly anticipated tactics developed by Walker a month later.[63]

Walker realised that a U-boat could anticipate an attack by listening both to the propeller sounds of the escort and to the noise of its Asdic, and could choose the best moment for evasive action. Walker developed the creeping attack, in which one escort would turn its Asdic off and move at about 5 knots to the target, directed by another escort. To find when the attacker was directly over the target, it was necessary to measure the range between the two ships. Radar was not accurate enough for that, and the *Rivers* were at a disadvantage compared with the *Black Swans*, in that they did not have accurate gunnery rangefinders. They were obliged to use less accurate navigational rangefinders. Even with the best equipment, the attack was not particularly accurate and relied on a massive pattern of twenty-two or twenty-six charges, dropped with a certain amount of trepidation because of the ship's low speed. The attacking ship then moved clear, and the directing ship moved in. It was unlikely that it would regain Asdic contact in water disturbed by depth charges, but it dropped another twenty-two or twenty-six-charge pattern in the general area. Success depended on:

> The slow and undetected approach of the attacking vessel to the U-boat so that the latter will not be scared into taking avoiding action.
> Careful and accurate conning of the attacking vessel by the directing vessel. This must be practised whenever opportunity offers.[64]

The creeping-barrage attack involved three attacking escorts and one to direct them. The directing vessel controlled the centre of the three ships, while the others kept half a cable (100 yards/91.5m) on each side. On approaching the target, the centre ship dropped eighteen charges form its rails at 25 or 50-yard (18- to 46-m) intervals. As the fifth charge was dropped, all three ships doubled their speed to 10 knots and the outer two began to fire eighteen charges form their rails, plus four more each at specified intervals for their outer throwers.

There is no sign that the *Rivers* used the creeping attack very much, and it was largely a trademark of the Second Support Group with its sloops. As Walker's group reached its height by sinking six U-boats early in 1944, the 10th Escort Group led by the *Spey* sank two. Walker's feat made him a naval hero, but the *Monthly Anti-Submarine Report* was more complimentary to *Spey's* group:

> The contrast in the methods employed by these two highly efficient groups is interesting. The Second Support Group took an average of four hours and 106 depth charges to sink each of its six U-boats. "Spey" … destroyed both her boats in a matter of minutes … On the other hand the Second Support Group's methods require exceedingly close co-operation between ships and almost unlimited time and depth-charges; to force the U-boat deep is essential to a creeping attack.
> It is obviously tactically advantageous to kill the quarry as quickly as possible … The danger of the creeping attack lies in the fact that it tends to develop into a long drawn-out struggle during which Asdic conditions may deteriorate, thereby causing the hunting vessels to lose contact and giving the U-boat an opportunity to escape.[65]

Daily Routine

Daily life in the escort force was one of the most gruelling areas of the armed forces in wartime. Aircrew usually had time to rest between missions, and were taken off operations after specific periods or a number of missions. The bulk of the British Army was not in contact with the enemy for the middle four years of the war. In the Navy, battleships could act as a deterrent and often spent long periods in harbours such as Scapa Flow. Motor torpedo boats and other coastal forces pursued short, intense operations and were usually in port after a day or two. Landing-craft crews had short periods of danger after long periods of training. But escort vessels could only earn their keep at sea, escorting a convoy or chasing U-boats. They often spent several weeks at a time at sea, with a minimal turn-around time in port before the process was repeated. Despite the increased size and seaworthiness introduced by the River-class, by peacetime naval standards they were small, overcrowded and in constant danger. It was essential that the life of each ship was carefully organised to protect it and the convoy at all times, to make living in such a small space tolerable and to make sure that every man pulled his weight.

Watches

The essence of this was the watch system, which ensured that a part of the crew was on duty at any given moment when at sea. The *Seaman's Pocket-Book* of 1943 implied that the two-watch system, with men having four hours on and four hours off, was used on all but the largest ships, but this was almost certainly not the case in the escorts, with their long days at sea. Monsarrat was adamant that a three-watch system, with four hours on and eight hours off, was 'the only possible method except for very short trips'.[66]

There were five four-hour watches in a day, with two two-hour 'dog watches' between 16.00 and 20.00. These allowed some variation in the system so that men were not in the same watch every day. The first watch began at 20.00 and lasted until midnight. In theory it represented the time when the day's routine was over and the watch took over for the first part of the night. The middle watch followed – perhaps the worst watch, with no daylight and the greatest danger of U-boat attack. The morning watch began at 04.00, and at least its men had the chance of seeing the dawn, except in the depth of winter. The rest of the men were roused during that watch and the hammocks were brought down and stowed. The ship's working day began, though that often had little relevance in the middle of the Atlantic, when routine maintenance was impossible in rough weather and the men needed all their strength to maintain a good lookout. The forenoon watch lasted until midday, the afternoon watch from 12.00 to 16.00, and then the cycle began again.

The captain and first lieutenant kept no watch, but were constantly available if needed. The captain was rarely in his cabin on the upper deck at sea, but spent any spare time in his sea cabin under the bridge. Often he would be on deck for long hours as the ship passed through a dangerous area, perhaps staying up all night and snatching a few hours of sleep in the daytime when attack was less likely. The first lieutenant was occupied in administration, while the navigating officer might well be excused watches but was available to take a fix or calculate a course at any hour of the day and night. The rest of the officers were in watches, perhaps with two on duty at any given moment if numbers allowed.

During normal cruising, according to Nicholas Monsarrat, the bridge was manned by the officer of the watch and probably his deputy, a signalman, two lookouts, a bridge messenger and a spare Asdic operator, resting between half-hour or twenty-minute spells on the machine. Down below in the wheelhouse were the quartermaster, responsible for steering, a man to operate the telegraph and the boatswain's mate in charge, while the petty officer of the watch, responsible for events on deck, spent most of his time there, too.[67]

Several different types of lookout might be needed according to the conditions. Far lookouts were posted in good visibility, including one in the crow's nest. They used their binoculars on and above the horizon. Near lookouts were posted on the bridge, keeping the horizon in the top of their binocular field. In bad visibility, fog lookouts were posted as far forward as possible to give warning of collision. Lookouts worked in twenty-minute periods to save eye strain, provided numbers were available. At night they were trained to scan a sector making small movements of head and binoculars, pausing regularly. If something was sighted, they would report it in the form 'Red six oh, near, ship steaming left.'[68]

Asdic and radar sets were operated by two men per watch if they were available. One man would take a spell at watching or listening for half an hour while the other rested or was available for other duties. Thus concentration was maintained, and a second operator was instantly available if a suspicious contact was made.

The engine room of practically every ship maintained a three-watch system. Again, the chief engineer, the chief ERA and the chief stoker were likely to be excused watches but spent just as much time on duty setting standards and dealing with problems. The complement of a River-class frigate allowed each watch one ERA, two stoker petty officers, two leading stokers and four stokers. Some were employed on the boilers, some in the engine room itself, and some on the auxiliary machinery such as heating, electrical and steering equipment.

Defence and Action Stations

In a danger area, the basic watch was not enough to cope. Ships could be held in various states of readiness against aircraft, submarine and surface ship attack. Commander Peter Gretton describes the situation when the ships expected attack:

> In the *Tay* the ship's company was at defence stations, with only half the officers and men closed up, but every man off watch was lying fully dressed ready to rush to his action station whenever the alarm bells rang. No less aware of the situation were the men in the boiler and engine rooms, well below the water-line, whose chances of survival if a torpedo struck were remote. There were indeed men who, unable to stand the thought of being trapped below when off duty, were trying to get some rest in corners of the wet, cold upper decks....
>
> For those on watch above decks, exposure to the weather was unending. On the bridge, at the guns, and on the quarter-deck aft, where the depth charge crews waited for action, the men were faceless ghouls, wrapped in duffel coats, the hoods drawn over their heads … As the spray came sweeping, rattling over them, each man ducked, then waited calmly until the arrival of the next wave's onslaught.[69]

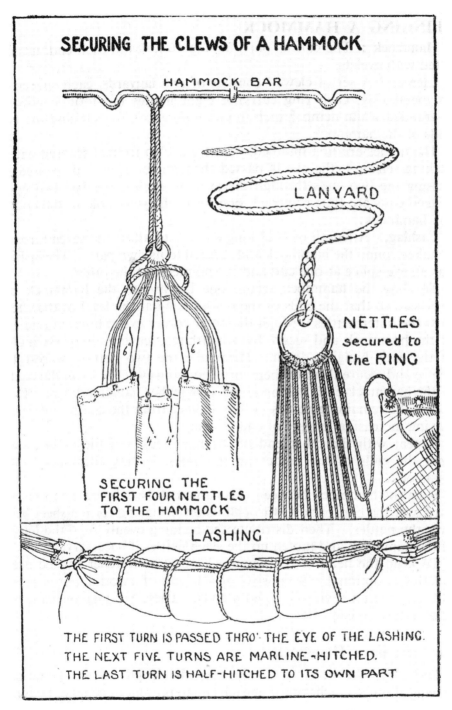

Securing the clews of a hammock. Illustration from *A Seaman's Pocket-book*, HMSO (Admiralty) June 1943. (NMM F5129)

Food

Large ships (cruisers and above) used the system of general messing, by which 'The Admiralty provides the complete messing, i.e. breakfast, dinner, tea and supper.' Frigates, like destroyers and sloops, used the standard ration and messing system.

> The Admiralty supplies a portion of food in the form of a Standard Ration, and pays a Messing Allowance, with which messes supplement the Standard Ration by purchase of food from the canteen. Each mess manages its own messing, prepares the ingredients, and takes the food to the galley to be cooked.[70]

It was also known as the canteen messing system. Some men in each mess took it in turns to act as 'cook of the mess' for a week, with varying results. Trainees at HMS *Ganges* were warned that

> The mess caterer will decide what the mess will have to eat. *You*, when cook of the mess, will prepare the food – on the mess table – and take it to the galley to be cooked – after which you will hear what your messmates think about it as a *meal*.[71]

It was quite difficult to find recipes that could be prepared in one go without several trips to the galley, but seamen were recommended to learn how to make pastry and dumplings, and to prepare different kinds of vegetables: beetroot should not be skinned or its value would be lost, beans and dried peas should soak overnight, parsnips should be washed well before eating. Simple recipes were suggested, such as cottage pie, 'poor man's goose', apple dumplings and a variety of suet puddings. The most exotic was beef curry with rice. The effect of this is described by Buckle of the *Ribble*:

> The less spent on food, the more money they received at the end of each month as rebate. This led to some very strange dishes being brought to the galley to be cooked. Some of the 'clacker' (pastry) was beyond the wit of man to render eatable. One forenoon the stokers' mess brought up a fanny of stew for dinner, and it was placed on top of the range among a galaxy of various shaped pots and pans. About an hour later I detected a slight smell of burning which was soon traced to the stokers' fanny. Pulling it to one side, I ladled the liquid into another container to discover at the bottom of the fanny and stuck there, a dozen small white blobs. These were supposed to be the dumplings, but the 'cook of the mess' had simply mixed flour and water together and dropped them into the stew without saying a word about them. ... I spoke to the cook and asked him to tell the messes to tell us in future what ingredients they had put into their lash ups....
>
> One big difference was breakfast, or rather the lack of it. When 'call the hands' was sounded the men always turned out at the last moment and had what was called 'a destroyer breakfast'. This was a cup of tea and a tickler [cigarette].'[72]

Medical officers were often critical of the cooking arrangements. The surgeon of the *Cam* commented in 1944, 'I noticed that for ease of preparation, cooking, etc., an undue amount of tinned food was being consumed. I reported this to the First Lieutenant and instructions were given that fresh vegetables and fruit were to be obtained whenever possible.'[73] Tormond Macleod of the *Exe* considered that the cook of the mess system was a problem in itself. He was often appointed 'not because he has any knowledge but because he is forced to'. As a result, 'the cook of the mess having all the scrubbing out to do is invariably indescribably dirty particularly about the hands. I have yet to see one trouble to go aft to wash his hands before preparing the food.' As for the system of 'mess savings' by which the men were supposed to save money on the food bill towards their private consumption with the NAAFI, in practice this was hardly ever paid, and was 'mainly a racket'. The food itself was often of good quality, but 'frequently spoiled by bad cooking'. 'Breakfast on that ship usually consisted of a cup of tea, and all too often dinner was roast beef and potatoes. Macleod complained that "What was good enough for Nelson is good enough for me" seems to be the general attitude.' He advocated a rearrangement of accommodation to allow the cafeteria system as used by the Americans.[74]

The Return to Harbour

Arrival back in port was always welcome, as described by Monsarrat:

> The arrival in port was a time of great relief, as it was the prelude to a whole range of delights about to be showered on us; sliding through the dock gates towards our berth, getting the first heaving-line ashore, then the head-rope, then the stern-wire; ringing off the engines – their first respite for perhaps four hundred hours: the curious warm silence which fell on the ship as the mail came on board and was doled out: the first guaranteed night in port, first drink, first undressing for a fortnight, first bath, first good sleep. [75]

After that, it was usual to send half the crew on a short leave, including all but one of the Asdic operators. They returned and the other half left, leaving an almost complete asdic team to practice together on simulators. The routine was usually based on the needs of the ship and the convoy cycle rather than the individuals, so longer leaves were mostly granted when the ship was in dry dock for underwater repair, or undergoing a routine boiler cleaning.

First Actions

The U-boats were returning to the mid-Atlantic by July 1942, after their successes on the east coast of the USA, and the *Rivers* began their main work of helping to defeat them. The recently commissioned *Spey* and *Rother* joined the 45th Escort Group in Londonderry, to take Convoy OS 33 to Freetown. There were three eventful days on the 11 – 14 July, when two or three U-boats were in contact. *Spey* shared in the sinking of *U-136* by depth charge and hedgehog, though it was not recognised as a kill at the time (*see* page 86). All forty merchant ships arrived safely.[76] *Exe* and *Swale* were part of the escort of NKF 1(Y) to the Mediterranean in November. Both detected U-boats by radar but failed to attack them. Things were relatively quiet in the bad weather of January and February 1943, but intelligence reports showed that the number of U-boats in the mid-Atlantic was building up to record figures.

The Defeats of March 1943

By the beginning of 1943, there were fifteen River-class frigates in service, all except two attached to the Londonderry command. They played an increasing part in the crucial convoy battles of the spring of 1943. Their role was rather slight and inglorious during the disasters of March when two convoys – SC 122 and HX 229, both from New York to Liverpool – were attacked with the loss of twenty ships out of eighty-nine. *Swale* was part of the escort of SC 122, replacing an old destroyer which was a regular member of the group. Being faster than the corvettes which made up the bulk of the escort, the frigate ranged out 4 miles (6.4km) to starboard from where attack was expected. It did not detect *U-305* when the sub came in from roughly that direction to begin the second wave of the attack. Later, early in the morning of 19 March, *Swale* detected a vague contact at 4000 yards on radar, but the officer of the watch hesitated briefly before bringing the crew to action stations, until a cargo ship was torpedoed a minute later. The U-boat submerged and *Swale* attacked with a pattern of fourteen depth charges with no result. Meanwhile, *Moyola* and *Waveney* escorted Convoy HX 229a as part of a more modern escort group. Diverted north to avoid the U-boats, *Waveney* collided with some ice, fortunately forward of the collision bulkhead. Later the lookout failed to report a huge, flat-topped iceberg only 500 yards (457m) away but the captain gave it a wide berth anyway; the man was carefully watched for the rest of the voyage. The convoy arrived without loss.[77]

Convoy HX 231

Three successive convoys that spring, all escorted by Escort Group 7 including the frigate *Tay*, represented the final turning point in the battle. Convoy HX 231 left New York on 25 March, two days after the battered survivors of HX 229 reached Liverpool. With sixty-two ships and a planned speed of 9 knots, it was considered a fast convoy. Four days later, its local escort left and it was joined by Escort Group B7 under Commander Peter Gretton. His usual ship, the destroyer *Duncan*, was refitting, so he and his staff transferred, with some discomfort, to the frigate *Tay*. After finding the convoy and putting it back in order after several misadventures in fog and ice, they set sail into the Atlantic. The crews were fearful after recent losses, while the U-boats expected another victory. The escort, consisting of one frigate, four corvettes (one inefficiently commanded) and the old destroyer the *Vidette*, was weak and *Tay* was the only ship with HF/DF, so it would be impossible to get cross-bearing on an enemy transmission. However, all the escorts had radar.

The next three days were quiet, but after that there were HF/DF contacts. The 4th Escort Group of four destroyers was ordered in support, but would not arrive for some time. Meanwhile, the U-boat attack began on the night of 4 – 5 April, and showed up deficiencies in both the convoy and the escort. An accidental flare helped give away the position and there were delays in reporting sightings. Two merchant ships were torpedoed that night and several more were separated from the convoy to be sunk later. The *Tay* chased several contacts but failed to sink any.

As time went on and the urgency of the situation sank in, communications got better. An aircraft from Iceland arrived in the afternoon of the 5th. It reported seeing a U-boat and *Tay* chased it. Unfortunately, this left a gap in the escort screen which allowed a U-boat to torpedo a tanker. But an escorting aircraft attacked two U-boats and sank

U-632. As night closed in, Gretton talked to imaginary aircraft by radio in the hope that the U-boats were listening, and pretended to have ten escorts rather than five under his command. In the dark, *Tay* suddenly found a U-boat ahead of her bows, heading towards the convoy, the radar having failed to spot it. It crash-dived and *Tay* dropped an accurate pattern of depth charges. *U-635* was destroyed.

At dawn *Tay* took station ahead of the convoy and the asdic operator quickly announced a submarine contact right ahead. Gretton conducted the attack himself without calling up *Tay's* captain, but the target was within the ship's turning circle and there were faults in procedure – only five depth charges were dropped instead of ten. The ship found herself between two columns of the advancing convoy but continued the attack. A smoke marker was mistaken for a U-boat by the merchant ship gunners, who opened fire dangerously but ineffectively.

Things improved later in the day as another aircraft arrived to give cover, while the destroyers of the 4th Escort Group finally caught up with the convoy. By custom they were placed under the convoy escort commander, who had knowledge of the situation, though their senior officer was senior to Gretton. They provided another HF/DF set to give fixes, and there were now enough ships to provide a much more secure screen around the convoy. There were no attacks during the night of 6 – 7 April, and on 7 April a few were beaten off in the mist. After that, it was clear that the U-boats had been left behind and the convoy approached the north coast of Ireland. In all, seventeen U-boats had been involved in the attack. Two were sunk for the loss of three merchant ships with the convoy and three more which were straggling from the convoy.

ONS 5

Duncan was back in service for B7's next convoy, the eastbound ONS 5, so *Tay* was reduced to an ordinary escort again. The convoy of forty-two ships was a slow one, which could barely reach its planned speed of 7 ½ knots. But EG7 had carried out intensive training at Londonderry, and was in far better shape.

Attacks began in the afternoon of 28 April between Iceland and Greenland. The weather was bad and no air cover was possible. Numerous U-boats were driven off, with the loss of some merchant ships. At dawn on the 29th, *Tay* was sent to sweep astern of the convoy and found a submarine while protecting a rescue ship picking up survivors. The frigate did not sink the sub but forced it to abandon its attack on the convoy.

As the convoy headed south from the coast of Greenland on 3 May, the great disadvantage of destroyers in convoy escort became apparent. The *Duncan* was now short of fuel and it was impossible to refuel at sea in the present conditions. It had to retreat to Iceland. The weather was too rough to transfer personnel, so Gretton, to his permanent regret, had to leave the convoy. It was left under the command of Lt.-Cdr. Sherwood in the *Tay*.

Again the omens were not good. A line of no fewer than thirty U-boats was stretched ahead of the convoy, with eleven more ahead of that. There was some hope when the 3rd Escort Group, led by the destroyer *Oribi*, joined on 30 April, though they had to leave again on 6 May. Thick fog made it difficult for the U-boats to operate – unlike the escorts, they had no radar. There were ten losses on 5 May.

The 1st Escort Group, resting in St. John's after a series of frustrating chases across the Atlantic, was ordered out in support of ONS 5. In included three *Rivers* – the *Jed*, *Wear* and *Spey* – as well as the sloop *Pelican* and the ex-American coast-guard cutter *Sennen*, which was slower than the others and was left some way behind. The group, spread out at 4-mile intervals, came up ahead of the beleaguered convoy early in the morning of 6 May. At 03.50, *Wear* reported a radar echo ahead and ten minutes later a U-boat was sighted at a range of 2 cables (366m). The enemy was taken by surprise and forced to dive, breaking off the attack. The senior officer reported,

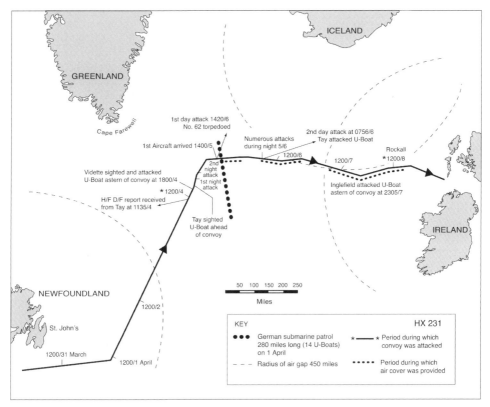

The battle of Convoy HX 231 in March to April 1943. Redrawn from an Admiralty track chart.

> This is a good example of a support group arriving at just the right moment to achieve complete surprise. The U-boat proceeding at about 9 knots probably thought herself clear of immediate danger and it is considered that she had been either driven off after an attempt to attack or was proceeding ahead to take a day attack position.[78]

By this time, 7th Escort Group was in need of help. By 06.15,

> … it was clear from *Tay's* signals that due to ramming, expenditure of depth charges, rounding up of scattered ships and departure of the 3rd Support Group there were at that time only two effective ships on the close screen.[79]

EG1's ship took up position around the convoy, and at 07.40 *Spey* picked up a contact on radar, closing rapidly. It sighted its target at 800 or 900 yards (732-823 m) and opened fire, scoring several hits, but not enough to prevent the submarine from crash-diving. Joined by *Wear*, *Spey* carried out three attacks with depth charges but the submarine had gone deep. Yet the tables had been turned and the U-boats were now on the defensive.

The *Pelican* sank *U-438*, one of five U-boats sunk in the vicinity of ONS 5 on 5-6 May. The intervention of the 1st Escort Group had forced the remainder to break off the attack. In all, Convoy ONS 5 lost eleven ships out of forty-one, but avoided complete disaster against a strong attack.

ONS 5, as much as any other convoy, marks the turning point of the Battle of the Atlantic. Captain S. W. Roskill, the official British historian of the naval war, later wrote,

> The seven-day battle fought against thirty U-boats is marked only by latitude and longitude and has no name by which it will be remembered; but it was, in its own way, as decisive as Quiberon Bay or the Nile.[80]

SC 130

For the return voyage with Convoy SC 130, Gretton was determined that *Duncan* would not have to miss the action yet again. He made great efforts to reduce topweight while at St. John's, and while at sea he kept the ship in the middle of the convoy where it did not have to zigzag and could save fuel. However, it was restricted in its ability to chase contacts, and the advantage of speed would be lost. This time, *Tay* would remain as an ordinary escort and would not be called on to take command. The frigate did carry out an attack on a U-boat which had been sighted by an aircraft on 19 May, 11 miles (18km) from the convoy. The submarine dived and *Tay* dropped a ten-charge pattern. One of the explosions threw the Asdic repeater on the bridge out of alignment and the *Tay* rejoined the convoy, claiming only to have 'shaken' the enemy.

However, the River-class was to help in another way. Again Escort Group 1 was ordered in support. The sloop *Pelican* was absent, and the group consisted of the *Rivers Wear* (carrying the senior officer, Commander Wheeler), *Jed* and *Spey*, with the ex-American coast-guard cutter *Sennen*. They were ordered to help SC 130, and in the afternoon of 19 May, they approached the convoy from the starboard quarter. They were in their usual formation four miles apart, and again the cutter *Sennen* was lagging behind – there were doubts about whether, with a top speed 4 knots less than the *Rivers*, it was suitable for work with a support group.

Fifteen miles (24km) from the convoy on the morning of 19 May, the lookout in *Wear's* crow's nest sighted a U-boat on the surface, and *Jed* sighted another. Both ships pursued their targets, and *Jed*, later joined by *Sennen*, dropped depth charges which produced oil and wooden wreckage. They had sunk *U-209*. *Wear* and *Spey* hunted the other contact with less success.

EG1 joined the convoy escort, and Gretton allocated them as part of the screen. He commented, 'The Senior Officer of the group [EG1] was most helpful and after the first incident suggested that, to save time, I should give his ships their orders direct instead of passing requests to him. The two groups worked splendidly together.'[81] *Jed* and *Spey* both chased contacts on the night of 19-20 May and *Spey's* hedgehog attack at 03.46 was frustrated by premature explosions. Up to twenty U-boats were attacking the convoy but they were driven off by ships and aircraft. It was clear that the enemy attack had failed, and at 11.00 on 22 May, the 1st Escort Group was able to leave the convoy. No merchant ships were lost, but five U-boats were sunk by ships and aircraft. Success was attributed to four factors:

> Heavy air support during the time the U-Boats were in contact.
> The arrival of the First Support Group p.m. on 19 May.
> The accurate appreciation of the state of affairs by the Senior Officer.
> The very successful evasive steering of the convoy.[82]

At last the experience of two and a half years of war, the intensive training programmes, the use of air power and the introduction of new ships and weapons was beginning to tell.

After this battle, and HX 239 in which one of the new escort carriers played a prominent role, Gross-Admiral Dönitz had to recognise defeat – at least for the moment:

> The overwhelming superiority achieved by the enemy defence was finally proved beyond dispute in operations against convoys SC 130 and HX 239. The convoy escorts worked in exemplary harmony with the specially trained support groups… Operations could only be resumed if we succeeded in radically increasing the fighting power of the U-boats.
>
>> This was the logical conclusion to which I came, and accordingly I withdrew the boats from the North Atlantic. On 24th May I ordered them to proceed, using the utmost caution, to the area south-west of the Azores. We had lost the Battle of the Atlantic.[83]

It was not the end of the U-boats, but for the moment the way was clear for the great quantities of munitions, stores, fuel and vehicles that would be transported across the Atlantic. In June, the Allies finally decided that the invasion would take place in Normandy in the middle of 1944, knowing that they would be able to get all the troops and equipment they needed to the launching point in southern England. From July to August 1944, HXS 300, the largest convoy to date, reached Britain with 156 ships carrying 300,000 tons of oil, about the same weight of military vehicles, and 400,000 tons of food, timber, iron and steel and other cargo. The escort was led by the Canadian River-class frigate *Dunver*.

The *Rivers* in the Bay Offensive

After the withdrawal of the U-boats from the mid-Atlantic, it was decided to seek them out as they left their bases in the Bay of Biscay. This policy had long been pursued by the aircraft of Coastal Command, and from June 1944 they were joined by all available ships from the support groups. Early patrols were carried out by Captain F. J. Walker's Second Support Group of sloops. *Waveney*, part of the 40th Escort Group, had to withdraw from patrols in August due to engine trouble. The group, still including *Waveney*, was back on station off the northwest corner of Spain from 19 to 25 August but had no sightings. Nightly radar sweeps were made difficult by the large numbers of fishing boats. The 5th Support Group, including *Nene* and *Tweed*, joined them on 21 August and they were attacked by seventeen enemy aircraft on the 25th – a relatively rare experience for the *Rivers*, which usually operated further from enemy shores. None of the *Rivers* was damaged by the attack but the cutter *Landguard* was hit by a radio-controlled glider bomb. The 1st Support Group relieved the 40th after that, including the *Rother* and *Jed*. *Rother* made a radar contact on the night of 26 August and attacked with depth charges and hedgehog, with no success. Next day there was an attack by eighteen enemy aircraft; *Rother* had two near misses by bombs and some fragments came on board. The sloop *Egret* was sunk by a glider bomb and *Jed* helped pick up survivors.

The next morning *Jed* had a radar contact at 4500 yards (4km) followed by an asdic contact ten minutes later as the submarine dived. The frigate dropped 104 depth charges and made two hedgehog attacks, while *Rother* and the destroyer *Grenville* dropped thirty depth charges each. A large bubble of oil rose 10ft (3m) above the water, and *Jed's* whaler collected 'two bales of sheet rubber' and 'an odd assortment of wood'. This was probably a decoy, as no U-boat was sunk.

The 5th Support Group, including *Wear*, *Nene* and *Tweed*, arrived on 2 September. They followed up various contacts obtained by aircraft and HF/DF but found nothing worthy of an attack. By the middle of the month, the U-boats were returning to the mid-Atlantic, having been re-equipped for a new offensive. It never became as dangerous as the earlier ones, but the support groups were withdrawn from the Bay Offensive to deal with it. The offensive had only limited success. During three months, only four U-boats were sunk by surface ship, for the loss of the *Egret* and damage to two other surface ships.[84]

Other Campaigns

The *Rivers* took little part in the Russian convoys, or the campaign in the Mediterranean, where a strong anti-aircraft armament was essential. Some, however, were sent to join the Freetown Escort Force which escorted convoys between West Africa and Britain. The *Fal* spent a short time at Londonderry after completing working up at Tobermory in the summer of 1943, but was sent to Freetown in August as part of the 57th Escort Group. The *Dovey* arrived there in May immediately after Tobermory.

The *Rivers* played a relatively small role in the landings in France on D-Day. *Chelmer*, *Deveron* and *Tavy* joined the escorts for convoys supplying the armies in France, but the bulk of this work was carried out by the American-built Captain-class frigates, which had better anti-aircraft armament for operations close to an enemy-held shore. *Cam*, *Teme* and *Mourne* formed part of the groups covering the approaches to the English Channel against a concerted U-boat attack. *Mourne* was torpedoed on 15 June 1944 and *Teme* was in collision with an escort carrier on the 10th. But again, the Captain-class formed the bulk of the groups, while most of the *Rivers* remained in their designed role in the mid-Atlantic.

Two of the *Rivers* (*Nith* and *Waveney*) served as landing ships (headquarters) in the Normandy invasion, acting as the HQ for the landing and support of a brigade group each. The *Nith* carried the senior officer of Assault Group G1 on Gold Beach and controlled a very accurate landing of the 231st Infantry Brigade on Jig Green Beach, east of Asnelles. The *Rivers* proved highly successful in this role and were just the right size compared with the Captain-and Hunt-classes. It was planned to convert more for the war in the Far East.

The *Rivers* in the Far East

By 1944, even in the Atlantic, the *Rivers* were being superseded by the Loch-class frigates. These were improved, mass-produced versions of the *Rivers* with the highly effective squid as their main anti-submarine armament. The *Rivers* were now earmarked for the war in the Far East, and British participation was expected to increase after the war in Europe ended. They were too slow to work with the carrier task groups which were intended as the main British contribution in the Pacific, but were useful against submarine attack on the long supply lines. German and Japanese submarines both operated in the Indian Ocean and in the first quarter of 1944, and more than 75,000 tons of shipping were sunk – more than any other theatre at that time. By November 1944, only five Royal Naval *Rivers*, all escort group leaders, were still in home waters. Most of the rest had been sent to the Indian Ocean.

One of the first to go east was the *Bann*, which sailed for India in August 1943, three months after its completion. The ship escorted convoys KMF 22 and WS 33 around the Cape, then joined the Aden Escort Force. It participated in the sinking of a German tanker which had been refuelling U-boats in the Indian Ocean. The *Helford* joined the Aden Force at about the same time and took part in an unsuccessful operation to intercept a Japanese submarine carrying officials from Germany to Singapore. By August 1945, twenty *Rivers* were on station with the East Indies fleet, and nine more with the British Pacific fleet.

The *Avon* went east soon after its commissioning in 1943 and spent some months as in independent command escorting single troopships from Gibraltar. Later it was escorting a convoy to the Persian Gulf when it took over the attack on a suspected U-boat from a corvette with engine trouble. The *Avon* was having difficulty with its own propellers and was moving too slowly when it dropped a pattern of depth charges, almost damaging its own stern. There was a great release of oil, but not of the kind used by submarines; in fact, the frigate had attacked a sunken oil tanker. Later, it steamed eighteen hours on the report of an aircraft that some survivors were in a lifeboat. It picked up 194 men from a sunken troopship. At the end of May 1944, The *Avon* formed part of a hunter-killer group around an aircraft carrier, as had originally been intended for the frigate. In January 1945, it transferred to the Pacific Fleet, escorting the fleet train. But in six months of this duty, the frigate never saw anything of the enemy except floating mines.

In August 1944, the *Taff, Findhorn, Nadder* and *Parret* formed a hunting group, Force 66, with the escort carriers *Begum* and *Shah*. Two U-boats had sunk several merchant ships in the area. On 10 August, an aircraft from *Shah* sighted a U-boat on the surface and forced it to dive. Group 66 steamed 55 miles (88.5km) towards the position but failed to find it until another aircraft sighting reported it 80 miles northwest of the Seychelles. On 12 August, it was found by the Asdic of the Indian ship *Godavari*, but it had no hedgehog and awaited the arrival of the *Findhorn* and *Parret*. *Findhorn* destroyed *U-198* with its first hedgehog salvo. The frigate was not a raider, but was carrying a cargo to Japan. The German U-boats surrendered in May 1945, and the threat to shipping was much reduced. The *Rivers* were diverted to supporting army operations along the coast of Burma.

After participation in the Battle of the Atlantic, the *Jed* was refitted from December 1943 to April 1944, then sailed east to join the 61st Escort Group to protect convoys around India. It was refitted again at Cape Town and sent to Colombo, but did not arrive until the war was almost over. The *Barle* left Britain on 1 January 1945 for Sydney to join the British Pacific Fleet. By the end of August, it had steamed more than 33,000 miles

(53,108km) escorting, among others, a floating dock being towed by tugs. The *Avon* sailed east in February 1945 and arrived at Manus on 5 March to join the British Pacific Fleet. It escorted the ships of the fleet train, which kept the main fleet supplied. By now, however, the River-class frigates were far from the centre of the action, unlike their role in the Battle of the Atlantic.

Chapter 8: Conclusion

An Assessment

In all, 133 River-class frigates were built, fifty-seven in Britain and eight in Canada for the Royal Navy. Sixty more were built in Canada for its own navy, and the Australians built eight for themselves. They were quickly succeeded in the shipyards by new ships known as the Loch-and Bay-classes. In fact, these were not very different from the *Rivers*, for they used the same hull design, widened by nearly 2ft (0.6m) to increase stability yet more. The main difference was that they were adapted for mass production. Sir Stanley Goodall had eliminated many of the curves in the cross sections of the *Rivers* early in the design. Now the curves in the sheer plan or side view were eliminated as well, so that there were two points where the deck line visibly altered. As part of a programme for 200 new escorts, *Lochs* and *Bays* were built in sections, often by steel manufacturers and bridge builders, and assembled in shipyards. Electrical installation was a major bottleneck due to increased complexity and shortage of labour, so ships built on the Clyde were towed to a basin at Dalmuir, while those on Tyneside went to Hendon Dock, where teams of electricians moved rapidly from ship to ship. The armaments were also changed. The *Bays* were designed as anti-aircraft ships, mostly for use in the Pacific. They had four 4-inch guns on high-angle mountings, and four 40 mm Bofors, which were proving to be the most effective anti-aircraft guns of the war. The first one, *Bigbury Bay*, was launched in December 1944.

The *Lochs* retained the anti-submarine function, and built on the experience of the *Rivers*. The after 4-in. gun was abandoned and its place taken by anti-aircraft weapons. The new mounting, Mark V, was more suitable for anti-aircraft use. The depth-charge armament was largely unchanged, but twin squids replaced their old rival hedgehog. This time there was no problem about training crews, and no problem with morale, as the squid's depth charges made very satisfactory bangs whether they hit the target or not. Squid proved to be at least as effective as hedgehog in its single mounting, and twin mountings as used in the *Lochs* had a success rate of more than 40 percent once a U-boat was detected. The new frigates would have made a powerful contribution to the Battle of the Atlantic – except that they did not enter service until the middle of 1944, when the deep-sea campaign was over.

How successful were the *Rivers*? They were not perfect ships in that they were built within tight limits of cost, length and engine power. They were a little slower than their captains might have wanted, but they had a very effective hull design which used their resources well. They were unlucky in their weapons, for the hedgehog was forced into service too soon. Their power plant was old-fashioned but effective, and they were the last riveted ships to be built in large numbers for the Royal Navy. But they were the first economical ocean-going anti-submarine ships to be built in large numbers. They were important in the line of development of the frigate, and they were there when they were needed: at the crisis of the Battle of the Atlantic.

It has been asked, not unreasonably, if the River-class ships were good value for money. Each cost about twice as much as a Flower-class, took up two valuable engines instead of one, and needed a larger crew at a time when men were extremely scarce. Yet they did not have twice the success rate of the Flower-class. This view is tenable if one sees the River-class only in terms of replacements for the Flower-class. This was how they were originally conceived, but by the time the *Rivers* came into service, the *Flowers* had been improved by the lengthening of the forecastle and the addition of bilge keels to become adequate escorts in a purely defensive role, perfectly capable of filling the gaps in an escort screen. But an escort made up entirely of *Flowers* would not have been very successful; the ships were too slow to pursue submarines on the surface, nor could they carry out a prolonged attack and then have the speed to catch up with the convoy afterwards. A few faster ships, at least, were needed in each escort group.

The *Rivers* were just fast enough to serve in support groups, as they did in the 1st Support Group in 1943. But they were slower than sloops, destroyer escorts and destroyers, which were perhaps better in that role. It might be argued that the main effort of the *Rivers* was to form an economical replacement for such faster ships in the escort groups, freeing them to join support groups. Taken in these terms, the *Rivers* and their successors, the *Lochs*, were a highly successful and vital contribution to winning the Battle of the Atlantic – one of the most important campaigns in world history.

After the War

The *Rivers* came home from the Far East at the end of the war to find that there was little need for them. The Navy was reduced from 865,000 men in 1945 to 140,000 in 1950. Ships were not necessarily scrapped, but some were transferred to Commonwealth and Allied navies; *Avon* was handed over to the Portuguese in 1949, *Bann* to the Indians late in 1945, and the *Nadder* became the Pakistani *Shamsher*. Several *Rivers*, including some built for the US Navy in the first place, were transferred to the Americans in 1946. Three of these supported the American landings at Inchon in Korea in 1950. Of those that remained in British service, few were sent to sea. The Navy still needed frigates, but it had the newer *Loch* class ships to exercise and patrol with, and the *Rivers* were reduced to the reserve fleet. Thus HMS *Helford* came home from the Japanese War in 1946 to be laid up with a nucleus crew at Devonport, and the *Dovey* came back from the South Atlantic to be laid up at Harwich. Only the *Rivers* converted to headquarters ships for amphibious landings, such as the *Waveney* and *Meon*, found an active role after the war. Ironically, the *Nith*, the first ship used for these purposes, was sold to the Egyptian government in 1948. A change of regime led to conflict, and as *Domiat* it was sunk by HMS *Newfoundland* during the Suez campaign of 1956, after a hard-fought battle against great odds.

For the remaining *Rivers*, life in the reserve fleet was not exciting. Fearing another Battle of the Atlantic, the Admiralty was determined to be ready this time, and in 1948 – 58, there were always at least a hundred frigates in reserve, compared with about half that number of destroyers, ten to fifteen cruisers, an average of five carriers and one to five battleships, according to operational needs. The *Rivers* were usually to be found in commercial ports such as Cardiff and Hartlepool, moored three or four abreast. Their internal parts were preserved by dehumidification. The hull was sealed and the humidity was reduced by twenty-five to thirty per cent, slowing down the process of deterioration. External fittings such as guns, funnels and hatches were preserved by 'Kooncoting', popularly known as 'mothballing'. This involved covering them with netting and then spraying plastic on top. But according to the regulations of 1952, ships in Category A still had most of their stores and ammunition and were to be made ready for service for up to three months at thirty days' notice. Category B ships would be called up after that, while Category C ships had no stores on board.[1]

The *Rivers* did not escape national attention completely. Nicholas Monsarrat's novel *The Cruel Sea* was published in 1951 and became a bestseller on both sides of the Atlantic. The last third of the book was set on board a fictitious River-class frigate, HMS *Saltash*. Monsarrat was not entirely accurate in his description of it. It was given three main guns instead of two, and its hedgehog 'threw a positive spray of small depth charges over the side', rather than 'contact charges over the bows'. But it is clear that, in replacing the sunk and equally fictitious corvette *Compass Rose*, it represented a break with the past, a new and much more successful phase in the war against the U-boat. To its new captain and first lieutenant, *Saltash* appeared enormous, and 'a formidable ship'. Strangely enough, this was not carried over to the film which came out in 1952. An old corvette, *Coreopsis*, was retrieved from the Greek Navy and used for filming, but no frigate was available. A Castle- class corvette was lent by the Navy, but the visual impact was much reduced. The Castle- class ships were larger than the *Flowers*, but considerably smaller than the *Rivers*. The ship was erroneously referred to as a frigate throughout and given the name *Saltash Castle*. The River-class had missed its chance of fame.

The frigates *Ribble*, *Chelmer* and *Tay* laid up at West Hartlepool after the war. (By kind permission of Ian Buxton.)

In April 1950, it was proposed to scrap nine of the *Rivers* in the reserve fleet, along with some of the Hunt-class destroyers. The new Parliamentary Secretary to the Admiralty, James Callaghan, argued against this from his own wartime experience as an RNVR lieutenant. Though slow by modern standards, they might still be useful to keep up the numbers of escorts. He went down to Plymouth to look at the ships himself, and proved that their condition was not as bad as was thought. He referred to the ex-American Town-class of 1940, which had proved useful despite grave faults. That was not a happy example, but Callaghan had his way, and with the outbreak of the Korean War a few weeks later, they were reprieved, and even considered for modernisation.[2]

This could not last for ever. A third battle of the Atlantic seemed possible even in the days of the atom bomb, but by the mid-1950s, the much more powerful hydrogen bomb was linked with the unstoppable intercontinental ballistic missile, or ICBM. What was the point of running a convoy system if the ports themselves were to be devastated? The huge reserve fleet tied up manpower and dockside space. It was not popular with young seamen who had joined to see the world – not some creek or dockside in Essex or south Wales. It even became the object of satire. A popular film, *Up the Creek*, had Peter Sellers as a corrupt chief petty officer running a reserve ship and fuelling the local economy with pilfered naval stores. The Navy was fighting a rearguard action against cuts, and Lord Louis Mountbatten, First Lord of the Admiralty from 1955, was no fan of the reserve fleet. Battleships, cruisers and destroyers were sent to breaker's yards, soon followed by frigates. Most of the *Rivers* had gone by 1957, and by 1959 there were only half the number in reserve or under refit. There was no movement for preservation, and the British-built *Rivers* were eliminated; only the *Balinderry* survived until 1961. The Australian-built *Diamantina* was put in a dry dock in Brisbane in 1981 and is still on display there.

The Progress of Frigate Design and Anti-Submarine Weapons

Though the concept of the frigate was established by the end of World War II, the nature of anti-submarine warfare was rapidly changing. The Germans adopted the snorkel at the end of the war, allowing the U-boats to use their diesel engines underwater. They were already working on the design of 25-knot submarines, which could outrun a River-class ship even without surfacing. This was only the beginning of a revolution, for within ten years of the war the nuclear-powered submarine had taken to the water, with its ability to remain submerged for months at a time. Moreover, air power would have an increasingly complex effect on all forms of naval warfare, and would be adopted by frigates themselves as a standard part of their armament.

Though the concept of the frigate was established by the *Rivers*, its definition remained flexible. When officially adopted in 1943, it was taken to mean an economic ocean-going anti-submarine vessel, contrasting it with destroyers which were not economic and had not been designed specifically for anti-submarine work; with corvettes which were anti-submarine but had not been designed with the ocean in mind; and destroyer escorts which were not so economical. The ocean-going role was always part of the frigate's specification, but the other two would be questioned over the next sixty years. Like all classes of ship, frigates were fitted with more equipment and became ever more expensive as time went on. The cheaper option was always attractive, and several types of cut-price ship were produced over the years. The specialist anti-submarine role was undermined as early as 1942, when the Bay-class was conceived as an anti-aircraft frigate. After that, 'frigate' tended to imply a specialist ship, but that could not be maintained in the reduced postwar Navy, and it came to mean a general-purpose ship with a good anti-submarine capability.

Unlike the period between the wars, anti-submarine warfare remained very high in the Navy's priorities after 1945. The Cold War with the Soviet Union began almost immediately, and that country had a fleet of about 200 submarines, compared with

Germany's fifty-seven in September 1939. With very obvious and very rapid technological change under the sea and in the air, there was no question of relying on established technologies for defence.

The immediate problem at the end of the war was to deal with the 25-knot submarine. The Admiralty would have like to rebuild the frigate force to cope with it, but this was out of the question after the war, when limited money was needed elsewhere and a huge frigate force had just been built, and then rendered obsolete. To cope with the problem of speed, a number of war-built destroyers were converted to frigates during the 1950s. Twenty-three were given a full conversion in which they were stripped right down to the upper deck and had a new superstructure fitted. Ten more retained their old superstructures, with new weaponry. Their speed of between 31 and 36 knots was enough to chase the new submarines – in fair weather, at least.

Meanwhile, a new type of frigate had been designed, easily distinguishable by the shape of the bows. It was suspected that an enemy submarine would escape by sailing into the wind and sea, allowing it to operate at its own maximum speed while reducing that of the pursuer. The new frigates, known initially as Type 12, were designed to counteract this. As with the *Rivers*, the shape of the bow was all-important. It, too, was flared outwards, and made as high as possible. However, the constraining factor in the River-class – the need to fire the gun directly ahead – was abandoned. The twin-gun turret was mounted aft of the bow, and the deck was lowered so that the centre of gravity was not too high. This gave the ships a 'broken-nosed' appearance which was characteristic of British frigate design until well into the 1970s. The *Whitby*, the first of the class named after seaside resorts, was launched in 1954. An improved version, the Rothesay-class, kept the building slips occupied in the late 1950s. Their main anti-submarine armament was the limbo, an improved version of the squid as used by the Loch-class, for the hedgehog did not survive the war.

In the meantime, the idea of a cheap escort had been revived. The Type 14 had half the displacement of the *Whitby* and no main guns. The class was designed as the minimum size and specification to carry a pair of limbos with a certain amount of defence against air attack. However, the ships were used in the 'Cod Wars' with Iceland, where their lightly built hulls could not stand up to the weather, not to mention ramming by the tough northern patrol boats. They were called 'second-rate' escorts, which in naval parlance simply meant a smaller and cheaper vessel – but this, of course, did nothing for the public image of the ships. More specialised frigates were also built. The four ships of the Leopard-class had four 4.5-in. guns in twin turrets for anti-aircraft use, and diesel engines for maximum range. The four of the Salisbury-class were fitted with extensive radar for aircraft direction. All these classes retained the flared bows and 'broken nose' introduced by the *Whitby*.

The Tribal-class of the late 1950s was a completely separate design, with twin funnels and a gun turret fore and aft, giving a slightly old-fashioned appearance which some believed was intended to impress the government and peoples in the Middle East where they were based. They were general-purpose ships, and there was some heart-searching about whether to call them frigates, rather than revive the term 'sloop'. They did introduce several new features. They had a Royal Marine detachment for shore duties, and each carried a small helicopter. They were designed for an anti-aircraft guided-missile armament, but few were fitted with it to begin with.

These features were also incorporated in the Leander-class, a further development of the *Whitby*-type ships which took to the water throughout most of the 1960s. Armed with the standard twin 4.5-in. gun, four seacat anti-aircraft missiles, a limbo mortar and a helicopter, they proved to be the most successful postwar British design. Yet in fact they represented the last of an old line. The special bow was no longer necessary as the helicopter could do the chasing. And the gun was rapidly being replaced by the guided missile as an anti-aircraft and anti-ship weapon. Most of the *Leanders* were eventually converted to carry French Exocet anti-ship missiles or Australian Ikara anti-submarine missiles.

HMS *Berwick*, a frigate of 1959. The Limbo mortars can be seen sticking up near the stern. (NMM N23545)

The homing torpedo began to succeed the limbo and the depth charge as the main anti-submarine weapon, even more sophisticated missiles were developed and the cost of electronics soared. In yet another attempt at a cheap escort, the Amazon-class or Type 21 frigate was designed largely by private enterprise. The ships turned out to be handsome and rakish compared with the standard frigate, but proved too fragile in the Falklands War of 1982. The Type 21s retained a single 4.5-in. gun forward, but the Type 22s, designed by the Royal Corps of Naval Constructors in the 1970s, abandoned any type of heavy gun. The two ships of the class that were ready in 1982 proved very successful in the Falklands due to their good radar fit and missile armament, but the gun was missed for use against shore targets, as a last-ditch air defence and for firing a warning shot across the bows of a suspected vessel. The last four ships of the class, launched in the later 1980s, revived the single 4.5-in. gun and adopted the Dutch goalkeeper as a close-range anti-aircraft weapon. They were regarded as highly effective ships. Like all modern British frigates, they used gas turbines as part or all of their main power.

The final British frigate design so far, the Type 23s, began as yet another cost-cutting exercise after the rising costs of the 22s, but the price soon rose as the specification increased. The first ships, launched in the early 1990s, were reduced because their intended computer system was not ready, but they eventually became very efficient ships, the mainstay of the modern British frigate force. Compared with earlier vessels, their main innovation is their 'stealth' design which reduces their radar signature.

How do the modern Type 23 frigates of the Duke-class compare with their distant ancestors, the *Rivers*? Both have handsome, well-curved hulls, but the Type 23's appearance is marred by the very angular funnel which reduces the radar profile. At 3500 tonnes, it is 75 percent bigger than the River-class, though more than a thousand tons smaller than its immediate predecessor, the Type 22. Apart from the gun, there is little in common in armament. The Type 23 would sink its prey by homing torpedo launched from the ship or its helicopter, rather then depth charges or hedgehog. It would detect it by sonar, which is a descendant of the *Rivers*' Asdic, but it would tend to use it passively. Rather than sending out a ping, it would listen for any noise the enemy might make and could detect him tens of miles away. The Type 23 has harpoon missiles to take on enemy surface ships and seawolf missiles to defend itself from attack in the air, but it still has Oerlikon guns: 30mm rather than 20mm as used by the *Rivers*.

Despite all these changes, the *Rivers*' contribution to history is significant. They contributed to the turning point of the Battle of the Atlantic; they reintroduced the word 'frigate' to naval terminology, and it has become almost universal. And they started a line of development which can still be seen in today's warships.

Appendix

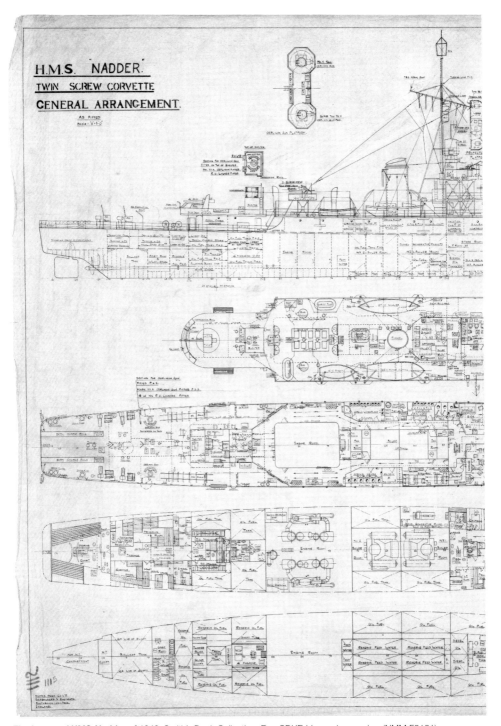

The layout of HMS *Nadder* of 1943. Smith's Dock Collection, Box SDKB44, no plan number (NMM F5151)

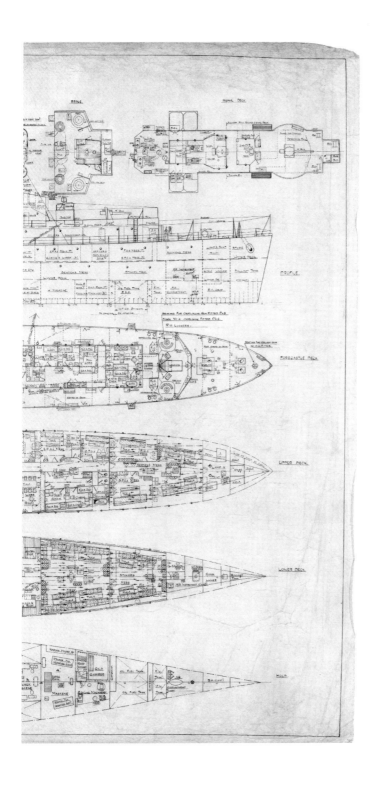

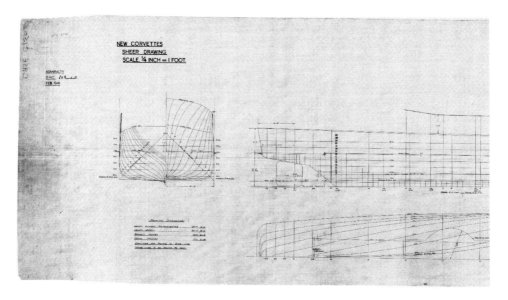

Lines plan of the new corvettes. Admiralty Collection, Box ADRB1475, plan NPRB1475 (NMM F5147)

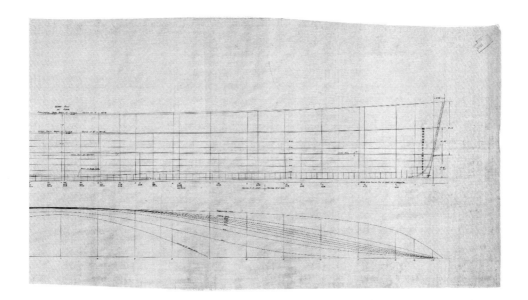

¹ 20mm Oerlikon gun in bows   ⁵ Bridge   ⁹ Topmast
² Hedgehog, under cover   ⁶ Type 277 radar   ¹⁰ High frequency direction finding aerial
³ 4-inch gun   ⁷ Signal flags   ¹¹ Searchlight
⁴ Signal deck   ⁸ Yardarm   ¹² Funnel cap

HMS *Tay*, Photograph by T.R. Dowson & Co Ltd, Tyne Dock, 5 August 1945.

7   6   5   4   3   2   1

17   16   15

¹³ Main mast
¹⁴ 40mm Bofors gun
¹⁵ Anchor
¹⁶ Forecastle

¹⁷ Joins between plates of hull
¹⁸ Bridge wings
¹⁹ Lattice structure
²⁰ Boat davit supports

²¹ Motor boat
²² Whaler

Admiralty 757400a. (By kind permission of Imperial War Museum, London/NMM)

HMS *Tay*, Photograph by T.R. Dowson & Co Ltd, Tyne Dock, 5 August 1945.

[23] 40mm Bofors gun

[24] 20mm Oerlikon

[25] 4-inch gun

[26] Davits for minesweeping gear

[27] Paravane

[28] Ensign staff

[29] Transom stern with pennant number painted on

[30] Boat davits

³¹ Break of forecastle
³² Carley float
³³ Depth charge racks
³⁴ Depth charge throwers

Admiralty 757400b. (By kind permission of Imperial War Museum, London/NMM)

Chapter 1: Origins

The Evolution of the Anti-Submarine Escort   16

1 *Brassey's Naval and Shipping Annual,* 1927, p.419

2 D. K. Brown, *Sir Rowland Baker RCNC in Warship,* 1995, pp.152–53

3 John English, *The Hunts*, World Ship Society, Cumbria, 1987, p.15

4 *British Warship Design*, reprinted London, 1982, p.112

5 John Harland, Catchers and Corvettes, Rotherfield, 1992, p.??? (TBC)

6 NMM Ship Plans and Technical Records Collection, Ship Cover 611c

7 *Ibid*

8 *Ibid*

9 John Fernald, *Destroyer from America*, London, 1942, p.25

10 NMM Ship Plans and Technical Records Collection, Ship Cover 611c

11 D. K. Brown, *Sir Stanley Goodall*, in Warship, 1997, p.59

12 NMM, Ship Cover 611c

The Design of the River-Class   21

13 D. K. Brown, *Sir Stanley Goodall*, in *Warship*, 1997, p.59

14 The British Library, Additional Manuscripts 52791

15 NMM Ship Plans and Technical Records Collection, Ship Cover 645

16 *Ibid*

17 British Warship Design, op cit, p.114

18 *Ibid*

19 BL Additional Manuscripts, 52791

20 NMM, Ship Cover 645

The Evolution of the Armament   27

21 NMM, Ship Cover 645

22 NMM Ship Plans and Technical Records Collection, Ship Cover 645

23 *Ibid*

24 *Ibid*

25 *Ibid*

26 Admiralty, Monthly Anti-Submarine Report, Sept–Oct 1940, p.12

27 *Ibid*, Nov 1940, p.15

28 *Ibid*

29 Derek Howse, ed, *Radar at Sea, the Royal Navy in World War 2*, Basingstoke, 1993, p.86

30 *Monthly Anti-Submarine Report*, May 1941, p.8

31 *Ibid*, Nov 1940, p.15

The Builders   33

32 Scottish Record Office, RHP 45236

33 Ian Macdonald and Ian Tabner, *Smith's Dock Shipbuilders*, Teesside, 1986, no pagination

34 W. F. Knight, *His Majesty's Bristol Built Escort Ships, 1939-1946*, Bristol, 1995, pp. 12–13

35 *Smith's Dock, op cit*

36 *Ibid*

37 Ministry of Information, *Build the Ship*, 1944, p.11

38 *Ibid*, p.32

39 *Merchant Ship Construction*, pp. 187–89

40 NMM Ship Plans and Technical Records Collection, Ship Cover 645 part 16, 15 March 1941

41 *Ibid*

Chapter 2: The Ships

The Hull   40

1 H. J. Pursey, *Merchant Ship Construction*, Glasgow, 1942, p.78

2 NMM, River Class Specification, part II, p.1

3 NMM, Lloyds plans, Smith's Dock

4 Peter Gretton, *Convoy Escort Commander*, London, 1964, p.44

5 W. F. Knight, *His Majesty's Bristol Built Escort Ships, 1939-1946*, Bristol, 1995, passim

6 The Scottish Record Office, GD 339/9/2

Fittings   46

7 TNA CAB 86/3

8 NMM Ship Plans and Technical Records Collection, Ship Cover 645b

9 River Class Specification, p.1

10 The Scottish Record Office, GD 339/9/2, 10/2

11 River-class Specification, p.33

12 TNA, ADM 234/59

13 Admiralty, *A Seaman's Pocket Book*, 1943, p.74

14 Admiralty, *Manual of Seamanship*, 1937, vol. 1 p.291

15 TNA, ADM 217/651

16 TNA, ADM 199/466

17 NMM Ship Cover 645e

18 Admiralty, *Manual of Seamanship*, 1937 edition, vol. I, pp. 160-1, BR9, *Manual of the Admiralty Gyro Compass (Sperry Type)*, 1941, pp.89–91

19 TNA, ADM 116/4520

20 *Ibid*, ADM 1/15871

21 TNA, ADM298/5

22 *Ibid*

23 *Ibid* ADM 319/1, 298/5, 1/11127

24 NMM, Ship Cover 655c, 18 January 1941

Engines

25 Admiralty, *Machinery Handbook*, BR 77, 1941, p.5

26 Admiralty, Confidential Admiralty Fleet Order, 958/43, 1943

27 TNA, ADM 199/427

28 *Ibid*, ADM 237/203

29 Gretton, *op cit*, p.85

30 TNA, ADM 237/203

31 *British Warship Design, op cit*, p.120

Entering Service

32 NMM Ship Plans and Technical Records Collection, Ship Cover 645a

33 Hansard vol. 387, 1942–3, col. 580

34 NMM, Ship Books, SB 99

35 NMM, Ship Books, SB 173

36 P G. A. King, *Not All Plain Sailing*, circa 1988, Typescript in the NMM Library, pp.112–4, 119

37 Peter Gretton, *Escort Group Commander, op cit*, p.107

38 NMM, Ship Cover 645

39 Escort Group Commander, op cit, p.107

40 Nicholas Monsarrat, *HM Frigate*, London, 1945, p.17

41 *Ibid*, pp.27–8

42 NMM, Ship Cover 645e

43 D. K. Brown, ed, *The Design and Construction of British Warships*, vol. ii, London, 1995, p.53

44 NMM Ship Covers

45 Imperial War Museum documents, 99/5/1

46 *HM Frigate, op cit*, p.26

47 Imperial War Museum documents, 82/27/1

48 D A Rayner, *Escort*, London, 1955, p.21

49 C R Benstead, *HMS* Rodney *at Sea*, London, 1932, pp.2–3

The Bridge

50 NMM Ship Plans and Technical Records Collection, Ship Cover 645

51 *Ibid*

52 *Ibid*, Ship Cover 611c, *Flower* class

53 NMM, Ship Cover 645c

54 NMM, Ship Cover 645e

55 Monsarrat, *HM Frigate, op cit*, p.18

56 NMM, River-class Specification

57 *HM Frigate, op cit*, p.17

58 Joseph Wellings, ed John Hattendorf, *On His Majesty's Service*, Newport, Rhode Island, p.66

Chapter 3: Weapons

Guns 74

1 Admiralty, *Gunnery Pocket Book*, 1945, p. 143

2 *Ibid*

3 NMM Ship Plans and Technical Records Collection, Ship Cover 645a

4 NMM, River-class *Specification*, vol. 2, p. 19

5 Admiralty, *Gunnery Pocket Book* 1945, p. 162

6 TNA, ADM 239/298

7 *Ibid*, ADM 217/113

8 *Ibid*, ADM 217/118

9 *Ibid*, ADM 199/466

10 *Ibid*, ADM 217/196

11 *Ibid*, ADM 199/169

12 *Ibid*, ADM 1/29952

13 *Ibid*, ADM 199/169

14 Admiralty, *Monthly Anti-Submarine Report*, Nov 1940

Depth Charges 81

15 NMM Ship Plans and Technical Records Collection, Ship Cover 645a

16 *HM Frigate, op cit*, p.17

17 NMM, River-class Specification, vol. 2, p.18

18 TNA, ADM 1/12322

19 *Monthly Anti-Submarine Report*, September 1942 pp. 32–3

20 *Ibid*, January 1944, p.24

21 TNA, ADM 101/653

22 *Monthly Anti-Submarine Report*, April 1942, p.44

Hedgehog 88

23 *Monthly Anti-Submarine Report*, April 1942, p.44

24 Donald Macintyre, *U-Boat Killer*, reprinted London, 1999, pp.93, 109

25 TNA, ADM 116/5256

26 *Ibid*, ADM 116/5001

27 *Ibid*, ADM 239/612

28 *Monthly Anti-Submarine Report*, April 1942, p.30

29 *Ibid*, September 1942, plate 12, p.42

30 *Ibid*, July 1944, p.6

31 Bob Whinney, *The U Boat Peril*, London, 1986, p. 13–14

32 TNA, ADM 86/3

33 *Monthly Anti-Submarine Report*, June 1943 p.27

34 TNA, ADM 327/115

35 *Monthly Anti-Submarine Report*, August 43, p.7

36 TNA, ADM 116/5256

37 NMM Ship Plans and Technical Records Collection, Ship Cover 645

38 TNA, ADM 116/5001

39 *Monthly Anti-Submarine Report*, February 1944, p.14

40 *Ibid*, April 1944 p.26

41 *Ibid*, July 1944, p.6

42 TNA, ADM 1/16700

Minesweeping Equipment 95

43 NMM Specifications, River-class, vol. 2, Fittings

44 John Palmer, *Luck on my Side*, Barnsley, 2002, p. 122

45 NMM Ship Plans and Technical Records Collection, Ship Cover 645a

46 *Ibid*

Chapter 4: Sensors

Asdic 102

1 *Monthly Anti-Submarine Report*, September 1942, p.40

2 TNA, ADM 1/13680

3 *Ibid*, ADM 199/353

4 *Monthly Anti-Submarine Report*, August 1942, p.43

5 *Ibid*, September 1942, p.41

6 A H Cherry, *Yankee RN*, London, 1951, p.143

7 TNA, ADM 259/38 p.2

8 *Monthly Anti-Submarine Report*, March 1941, p.38

9 National Archives, ADM 1/16700

10 *Ibid*, ADM 199/466

11 *Monthly Anti-Submarine Report*, February 1944, pp.4–5

12 *Ibid*, November 1942, p.40

13 *Ibid*, June 1944, pp. 32–3

Radar 110

14 TNA, ADM 220/109

15 *Ibid*, ADM 220/109

16 *Ibid*, ADM 239/307

17 NMM Ship Plans and Technical Records Collection, Ship Cover 645

18 Imperial War Museum Documents, 92/27/1

19 TNA, 220/109

20 *Ibid*

21 *Ibid*

22 Ibid, ADM 239/307

23 *Ibid*

24 Ibid, ADM 199/353

25 Monthly Anti-Submarine Report, April 1942, p.44

26 TNA, ADM 239/307

Signalling 115

27 TNA, ADM 239/344

28 *Ibid*, ADM 199/353

29 Mackintyre, *U-Boat Killer, op cit*, p.25

30 *Ibid*

31 National Archives, ADM 199/241

32 *Ibid*, ADM 217/113

33 *Ibid*, ADM 239/241

34 *Monthly Anti-Submarine Report*, April 42, p.41

35 TNA, ADM 1/13680

36 Peter Gretton, *Crisis Convoy*, London, 1974, pp.55, 57, 62–3

Chapter 5: Officers

Officers 124

1 *Navy List*, January 1944, passim

2 TNA, ADM 231/235

3 Merseyside Mairtime Museum B/PSNC/38/2

4 King, *Not All Plain Sailing, op cit, passim*

5 Monsarrat, *HM Frigate, op cit*, pp. 15–16

6 D.A. Rayner, *Escort*, London, 1955, p.27

7 *HM Frigate, op cit*, p.19

8 TNA, ADM 101/620

9 *Navy List*, October 1943

10 *HM Frigate, op cit*, p.14

11 TNA, ADM 239/248

12 *Ibid*, ADM 239/303

13 *Ibid*, ADM 231/235

14 *Ibid*, ADM 1/17944

15 Admiralty Fleet Order 5127/42, 1942

16 TNA, ADM 1/17685

17 *Ibid*, ADM 1/14035

18 BR 16, Engineering Manual for His Majesty's Fleet, p. 9

19 *Ibid*, p. 10, para 7

20 TNA, ADM 101/665

21 *Ibid*, ADM 101/688

22 *Ibid*, ADM 101/670

23 *Ibid*, ADM 101/632

24 *Ibid*, ADM 101/665

25 *Ibid*, ADM 101/653

26 *Ibid*, ADM 101/632

Petty Officers and Leading Seamen 131

27 Captain J N Pelly, *An Officer's Aide Memoire*, HMS *King Alfred*, 1943, p.15

28 TNA, ADM 1/12133

29 Confidential Admiralty Fleet Order, 173/43, 1943

30 TNA, ADM 101/624

31 Admiralty Fleet Order 5128/43, 1943

32 Nicholas *Three Corvettes*, reprinted London, 2002, pp.187–8

33 TNA, ADM 231/235

34 Joseph H Wellings, *On His Majesty's Service*, ed John Hattendorf, Newport, Rhode Island, 1983, p.65

35 Admiralty, *Manual of Seamanship*, 1937, vol. 2, p.19

36 Pelly, *An Officer's Aide Memoire*, op cit, p. 20

37 TNA, ADM 1/17685

38 *An Officer's Aide Memoire*, op cit, p.15

39 *King's Regulations and Admiralty Instructions*, 1938 edition, p.112

40 NMM BGY/M/3

The Seamen 135

41 TNA, ADM 1/15575

42 *Ibid*, LAB 29/249

43 *Ibid*, ADM 1/16700

44 Monthly Anti-Submarine Report, June 1944 p.30

45 TNA, ADM 1/15871

46 Confidentiality Admiralty Fleet Order, 1815/42

47 Monsarrat, *Three Corvettes*, reprinted London, 2000, p.189

Engineers and Miscellaneous Ratings 141

48 Admiralty, BR 91, 1936, *Training of Artificer Apprentices*, p.17

49 National Archives, LAB 29/249

50 Admiralty, BR 91, 1936, *Training of Artificer Apprentices*, p.17

51 TNA, ADM 1/29375

52 *Ibid*

53 TNA, LAB 29/249

54 *Ibid*, ADM 1/16700

55 Admiralty, BR 77, *Machinery Handbook*, 1941, p. iv 44 National Archives, ADM 101/624

56 John L. Brown, Diary of a Matelot, 1942-45, Worcester, 1991, p.7

57 BR 97, *Manual for Officers Stewards*, 1932, pp.32, 36, 42

58 Monsarrat, *HM Frigate, op cit*, p.16

Chapter 6: Accommodation

Officers' Accommodation 146

1 NMM Ship Plans and Technical Records Collection, Ship Cover 645, Canadian ships

2 Monsarrat, *HM Frigate, op cit*, p.16

3 *Ibid*, p.16

4 TNA, ADM 231/235

5 Admiralty Fleet Order 42/2247

6 Admiralty Fleet Order, 42/2427, 2429, 1942

Messdecks 150

7 Tristan Jones, *Heart of Oak*, reprinted Shrewsbury, 1997, pp. 216–19

8 TNA, ADM 231/235 p.20

9 Ibid, ADM 101/641, 101/65

10 Admiralty Fleet Order 41/3126, 1941

11 TNA, ADM 101/665

12 NMM Ship Plans and Technical Records Collection, Ship Specifications, River Class

13 Mackintyre, *U-Boat Killer, op cit*, p.79

14 NMM, Ship Plans and Technical Records Collection, Ship Cover 645e

15 TNA, ADM 101/624

16 *Ibid*, ADM 101/624

17 *Ibid*, ADM 101/646

18 NMM Ship Cover 645

19 TNA, ADM 101/665

20 *Ibid*, ADM 101/688

21 *Ibid*, ADM 101/623

22 *Ibid*, ADM 101/665

23 *Ibid*, ADM 101/688

24 *Ibid*, ADM 101/637

Other Areas 155

25 Imperial War Museum, p.188

26 TNA, ADM 101/632

27 *Ibid*, ADM 101/632

28 *Ibid*, ADM101/653

29 NMM River-class Specification, p.8

30 Ibid, p.9

31 TNA, ADM 101/624

32 National Archives, ADM 101/637

33 *Ibid*, ADM 101/624

34 *Ibid*, ADM 101/624

35 *Ibid*, ADM 101/620

Chapter 7: The Frigates in Service

The Battle of the Atlantic 160

1 F. Barley, D. W. Water; ed. Eric Grove, *The Defeat of the Enemy Attack on Shipping 1939–1945*, Navy Records Society, 1995, p.xvi

Working Up 162

2 TNA, ADM 1/13255

3 Admiralty, *Monthly Anti-Submarine Reports*, October 1944, p.18

4 Richard Baker, *The Terror of Tobermory*, reprinted Edinburgh 1999, p.ix

5 *Monthly Anti Submarine Reports*, October 1944, p.17

6 *Ibid*, p.111

7 *Ibid*

8 TNA, ADM 199/1729

9 *Ibid*

10 *Monthly Anti-Submarine Reports*, July [sic] 1941, p.27

11 D. A. Rayner, *Escort, op cit*, pp. 158–59

12 NMM MS93/008, letter from Baker-Cresswell to Admiral Sir Peter Gretton, 1981

Escort and Support Groups 168

13 D. W. Waters, *The Defeat of the Enemy Attack on Shipping, 1939-1945*, Navy Records Society, 1997, p.91

14 D. A. Rayner, *Escort, op cit*, p.230

15 Gertton, *Convoy Escort Commander, op cit*, p.220

16 *Ibid*, p.107

17 Monsarrat, *HM Frigate, op cit*, p.15

18 TNA, ADM 237/114

19 W. S. Chalmers, *Max Horton and the Wrestern Approaches*, London, 1954, pp. 287–8

20 TNA, ADM 199/579

Bases 171

21 Macintyre, *U-Boat Killer, op cit*, p.154

22 TNA, LAB 10/71

23 Stephen W Roskill, *The War at Sea*, Vol. I, *The Defensive*, London, 1954, reprinted 1976, pp. 457–9

24 Nicholas Monsarrat, *Life is a Four Letter Word*, Vol. II, *Breaking Out*, London, 1970, pp. 92–3

25 TNA, ADM 1/17805

26 *Ibid*, ADM 1/17229

27 *Ibid*, ADM 116/4645

28 D. A. Rayner, *Escort, op cit*, p.78

29 *U-Boat Killer, op cit*, p.63

30 TNA, ADM 116/4560

31 Gilbert S. Tucker, *The Naval Service of Canada*, vol. II, Ottawa, 1953, p.203

32 TNA, ADM 1/13011

Convoy Escort 178

33 TNA, ADM 199/2372

34 *Ibid*, ADM 239/344-5

35 *Ibid*, ADM 237/115

36 *Ibid*, ADM 217/734

37 *Ibid*, ADM 233/104

38 *Ibid*, ADM 239/344 Article 129

39 *Ibid*, ADM 239/344, Article 129

40 Confidential Admiralty Fleet Order 515/43, 1943

41 TNA, ADM 239/344 Article 129

42 Gretton, *Crisis Convoy, op cit*, p.150

43 *Monthly Anti-Submarine Report*

44 TNA, ADM 239/344, Article 113

45 *Monthly Anti-Submarine Report*, September 1941, p.41

46 TNA, ADM 239/344, Article 129A

47 TNA, ADM 239/344, Article 129

48 TNA, ADM 1/13415

49 Gretton, *Convoy Escort Commander, op cit*, p.159

50 Macintyre, *U-Boat Killer, op cit*, p.113

Anti-Submarine Defence and Attack 187

51 W. S. Churchill, *The Second World War*, vol II, *Their Finest Hour*, London, 1967, p.529

52 TNA, ADM 239/344, Article 120

53 TNA, ADM 239/344

54 *Ibid*, ADM 237/115

55 *Ibid*, ADM 239/344, Article 134

56 *Ibid*, ADM 239/344, Article 122

57 *Ibid*, ADM 237/115

58 Confidential Admiralty Fleet Order, 92/44, 1944

59 TNA, ADM 199/579

60 Confidential Admiralty Fleet Order 406/43, 1943

61 Gretton, *Crisis Convoy, op cit*, pp. 84–5

62 D K Brown and Phillip Pugh, *Ramming*, in *Warship* 1990, pp.18–34

63 TNA, ADM 237/203

64 *Ibid*, ADM 239/298

65 *Monthly Anti-Submarine Report*, February 1944, p.5

Daily Routine 194

66 Monsarrat, *HM Frigate, op cit*, p.19

67 *Ibid*, p.19

68 Admiralty, *Gunnery Pocket Book*, 1945, pp. 177–78

69 Gretton, *Convoy Escort Commander, op cit*, pp. 7–8

70 TNA, 1/12114

71 Noel Wright and AC G. Sweet, *How to Prepare Food; Tips and Wrinkles for Cooks of Messes in Standard Ration*

Ships, Ipswich, 1941

72 Imperial War Museum, P188

73 TNA, ADM 101/653

74 *Ibid*, ADM 101/632, 653

75 Nicholas Monsarrat, *Life is a Four Letter Word*, London, 1970, p.15

First Actions 198

76 TNA, ADM 1/12322

77 Martin Middlebrook, *Convoy*, reprinted London, 2003, pp.121, 126, 196, 211, 234, 261-2, 279–80

78 TNA, ADM 199/353

79 *Ibid*, ADM 217/113

80 As quoted in Gretton, *Convoy Escort Commander*, op cit, p.147

81 *Op cit*, p.159

82 *Monthly Anti-Submarine Report* June 1943, p.19

83 Karl Dönitz, Memoirs, London, 1959, p.341

84 Monthly Anti-Submarine Report, September 1943, pp. 15–21

Chapter 8: Conclusion

After the war 209

1 Ian Buxton and Ben Warlow, *To Sail No More*, Liskeard, 1997

2 Eric Grove, Vanguard *to Trident*, London, 1987, pp. 63–4

Index
River-class Frigates

Page numbers in bold refer to illustrations